The Little iMac Book

second edition

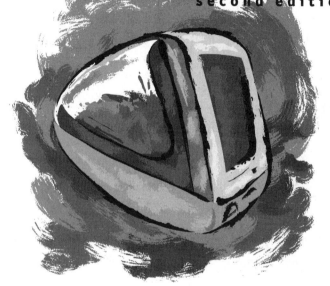

# The Little iMac Book

## second edition

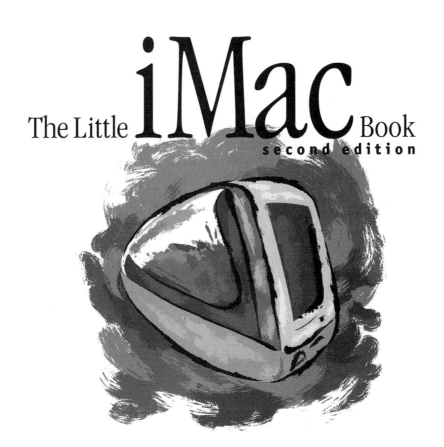

## Robin Williams

 published by Peachpit Press • Berkeley • California

# The Little iMac Book second edition

Robin Williams

## Peachpit Press

1249 Eighth Street
Berkeley, California 94710
800.283.9444
510.524.2178
510.524.2221 fax
Find us on the World Wide Web at **www.peachpit.com**
Peachpit Press is a division of Addison Wesley Longman

## ISBN

0-201-70446-3
10 9 8 7 6 5 4 3 2 1
Printed and bound in the United States of America

The Little iMac Book

second edition

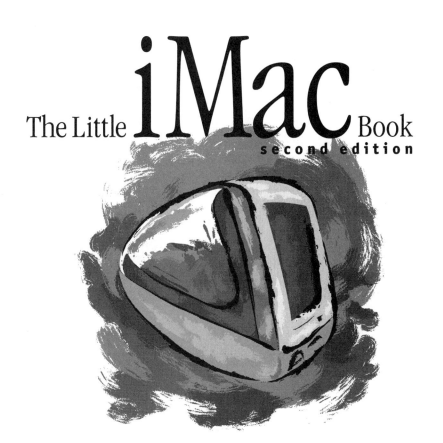

Robin Williams

 published by Peachpit Press • Berkeley • California

# The Little iMac Book second edition

Robin Williams

## Peachpit Press

1249 Eighth Street
Berkeley, California 94710
800.283.9444
510.524.2178
510.524.2221 fax
Find us on the World Wide Web at **www.peachpit.com**
Peachpit Press is a division of Addison Wesley Longman

Cover design by John Tollett
Interior design and production by Robin Williams
Url's Internet Cafe web site by John Tollett
Collection of Macintosh propaganda by Jonas Skardis
Editing by Nancy Davis
Prepress by Kate Reber

## Notice of Rights

## Notice of Liability

## Trademarks

## ISBN

0-201-70446-3
10 9 8 7 6 5 4 3 2 1
Printed and bound in the United States of America

# Contents

# Let's Start at the Very Beginning

# Things to Do with Your iMac

# The Internet and the World Wide Web

# Other Things You Should Know

# Problems and Solutions

# The Stuff at the End

# Introduction

Welcome to the iMac! This book will walk you through just what you need to get up and running on your new machine. There's a lot of stuff I don't tell you in this book because I want you to get started and enjoy yourself without getting bogged down in the details.

When you're ready for details, when you're ready to learn all the little shortcuts, tips, tricks, and troubleshooting, when you're ready for the next level, you should read *The Little Mac Book*. Your iMac operates exactly like any other Macintosh, so *The Little Mac Book* (which is almost 400 pages) will take you the rest of the way.

But today, work your way through this book like a tutorial, and you'll be amazed at how much you can get accomplished on your iMac. In fact, your little iMac is more powerful than the Macintosh I make my living on, and cost one-third as much!

This is not a technical book about the gory details of the iMac—I'm not going to tell you about things like 3Dfx chips, external SCSI devices, PCI cards, or ISDN connectivity. If you want to know things like that, you need a different book.

The one technical thing I will tell you is that this book is written for the Mac OS (operating system, the stuff that runs the computer) called version 9. If you just bought your iMac, your machine uses (is "running") Mac OS 9. But if you bought your iMac a while ago or if someone gave you their older machine, your computer is probably running some version of OS 8, such as 8.1, 8.5, or 8.6, which we lump altogether and call 8.x. If you do have an older operating system, there are a few places in this book where the information on the page won't exactly match what you see on your screen. The differences are minor and I'll mention those when we come across them, so don't worry. Move forward, have fun, and I'll see you on the web!

*OS is pronounced "oh ess."*

Robin

To Jimbo Norrena,
my dear friend,
who first suggested
I should do
this book.
with love
R

# Thanks!

So much thanks to **Jeanne Bahnson,** who helped get the first edition of this book to press on time; **Jonas Skardis,** who collected all the great Mac propaganda; **Nancy Davis,** an incredible editor; **Kate Reber,** prepress wizardess; **John Tollett,** illustrator, cover designer, and sweetheart.

# Let's Start at the Very Beginning

Some of you may have been working on a Macintosh for a while now, or perhaps on another sort of computer, and you feel quite comfortable using a mouse, menus, and windows. If that's so, skip this section. (Or maybe skim through it—you might be surprised at the little tricks you didn't know.)

But if this is your first experience with a computer of any sort, then please just sit down and work along with me. We're going to start from scratch. I'm going to assume you don't know anything about this machine at all. Remember, there are some things I'm not going to tell you yet because you can live a long time without knowing them. But I will tell you exactly what you need to know to start being productive and having fun on your great, new iMac, and I'll tell you where to go for more information when you're ready.

**The iMac has been the best-selling computer for over a year and a half.**

Its own winning streak was broken in January '99 when Apple introduced the new five different colors of the iMac and the market research firms counted each color of the iMac as a separate model. However, for many months after, the newly separated iMac models remained close to the top spot. During that time, the iMac sold more computers than heavyweights such as Dell, IBM, Gateway, and Compaq.

As of January 2000, the iBook has been the best-selling laptop since its introduction six months prior.

**Apple stock has been one of the most profitable stocks of the past three years.**

It has risen over 925 percent of where it started in December of 1997 at 12.75 to a high of 118 in December 1999. During the market drops, Apple's stock stayed stable and even went up. Dell, on the other hand, fell some 20 points in the August '98 downturn.

Since the return of Steve Jobs 2.5 years ago, Apple's market cap has risen from $2 BILLION to over $16 BILLION.

**Apple posted nine straight quarters of profit as of January '00**

$37 million, $56 million, and $100 million respectively in 1998, on up to $183 million in January 2000. Compaq, however, had a loss of $3.6 BILLION in one quarter alone.

**Apple has over $2 billion in the bank,**

according to the Securities and Exchange Commission documents. Apple has plenty for a rainy day. The opinion of renowned stock market analyst Robert Morgan, author of the "Recon for Investors" newsletter, is that Apple is here to stay. Any Mac user could have told him that.

# Mousing, Menus, and More

If you haven't already taken your iMac out of the box and plugged it in, do so now. Follow the directions provided in the box. I know the directions tell you to plug the computer directly into the wall, but you really should get a *surge protector* at the hardware store or office supply store (see the illustration to the right). They only cost about $15. Plug the cable into the surge protector, then plug the surge protector into the wall. This will help protect your computer from the surges of electricity that happen all the time. If you live in an area that has lightning storms (like I do), the only real way to protect your computer is to unplug everything, including any modem and printer cables, right out of the wall.

*This is a typical inexpensive surge protector. Plug your computer into this and plug this into the wall. If you get a surge protector with the phone ports, you should also plug your modem cord into this, then run another cord from this to your jack.*

In this chapter, we're going to turn on the computer and walk through the basics of operating it. If you've never used a Macintosh before, you'll be surprised at how easy it is to be productive (and have fun at the same time).

## Turn it on

To turn on your computer, press one of the **Power buttons:** ⏻ . There's a Power button on the upper-right of the keyboard, and there's one on the bottom right of your monitor. When you're done working on the computer, use the power button on the keyboard to turn it off (on newer iMacs, the button on the monitor puts the iMac to sleep instead of turning it off; see pages 57–58 for details on the difference between the button on the keyboard and the one on the monitor).

### Boot up

It takes a minute or two for your computer to turn itself on. This process is called "booting up" because the iMac is actually going inside of itself and pulling itself up by its own bootstraps, so to speak.

If you watch the screen (also called the monitor) while your computer "boots," you'll see a number of tiny pictures appear and then disappear. Each of these pictures, or icons, represents a separate piece of *software* that your computer is "loading," or getting ready to work for you. When you get to know your iMac better, you'll be able to control which of these pieces of software you want to keep or toss, and eventually you'll probably add new ones. For right now, ignore them all.

### The Mac OS—are you using version 8 or 9?

*This is the Mac OS logo. Darned clever, isn't it?*

The biggest image you'll see when you boot up is the very clever Mac OS logo, the two happy faces, right in the middle of the screen. Just so you know, the phrase "Mac OS" is pronounced "Mac Oh Ess." The OS stands for Operating System. Every computer has some sort of operating system that runs it. The Mac OS, of course, is the best, as evidenced by those who copy it.

There are several versions of the operating system. Notice when your Mac starts up it probably says something like "Mac OS 8.6" or "Mac OS 9." Whatever number it displays is the version of the operating system that your Mac is "running." If your iMac doesn't display any number like that, it's running Mac OS 8 or 8.1. If you haven't notice which version your iMac uses yet, look for it next time you start up. Some of the items in this book will refer to either some version of Mac OS 8 and other features are only found in Mac OS 9, so it's good that you know which operating system you are using.

If you know how to use your mouse and menus already, you can check to see which version of the operating system any Macintosh is running: while you're at the Desktop, go to the Apple menu and choose "About this Computer." A dialog box will appear that tells you loud and clear which OS your particular machine is using. (If those directions don't make sense to you, don't worry about it—come back later and check it out.)

### If this is your first time . . .

If this is the first time you have turned on your iMac, the first message you will see on your screen is the Setup Assistant, as shown below. This will walk you through setting up certain things on your iMac, but you don't have to do it right now. I suggest you put this box away for now (I'll tell you how to do that in a second) and go through the rest of this chapter with me. When we're finished, we'll open this Setup Assistant again and you can finish doing what it wants.

### For right now—

1. See the key on the bottom row of the keyboard with the little apple on it? Hold that key down with a finger on your left hand. Keep holding it down, and with your right hand, tap the letter Q once.

2. You'll get a message asking if you really want to "Quit." Tap the Return key once, and that message will go away.

(If you don't see the Setup Assistant, just move on!)

*This apple is the icon on what is called the "Command" key.*

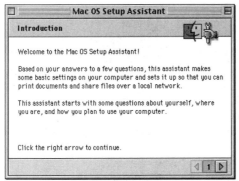

*Depending on which iMac you have, you might see one or the other of these setup screens. It's okay to put this away for now—we'll come back to it in a few minutes.*

### The Desktop

When your computer finishes booting, what you see on the screen is called the **Desktop**—the Desktop is the entire area that fills your monitor (your screen), as shown below and on the opposite page. Now, you might also hear the Desktop referred to as the **Finder.** Specifically, the Finder is actually the software (the programming code) that runs the Desktop, but you can call it by either term you like, and you will hear it called the Finder or the Desktop interchangeably. When you see directions that tell you, "At the Finder . . . ," they mean go back to this Desktop. When they say, "At the Desktop . . . ," they mean at the Finder.

**Below is the Desktop on Mac OS 8, 8.1, 8.5, or 8.6**

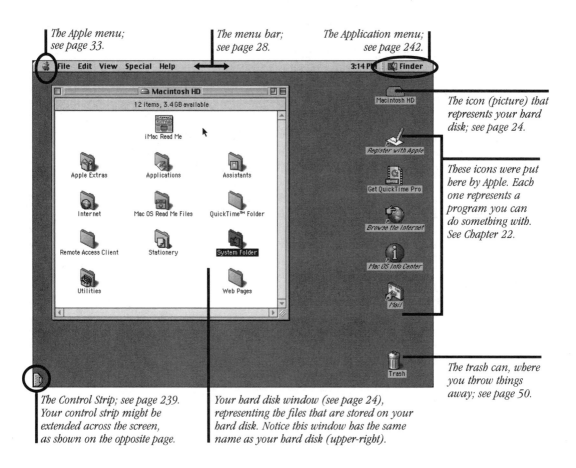

The Apple menu; see page 33.

The menu bar; see page 28.

The Application menu; see page 242.

The icon (picture) that represents your hard disk; see page 24.

These icons were put here by Apple. Each one represents a program you can do something with. See Chapter 22.

The trash can, where you throw things away; see page 50.

The Control Strip; see page 239. Your control strip might be extended across the screen, as shown on the opposite page.

Your hard disk window (see page 24), representing the files that are stored on your hard disk. Notice this window has the same name as your hard disk (upper-right).

Consider the Finder/Desktop as your home base. This is where you will start from and where you will end. It's where you'll store all of your applications (the programs you use to create things with) and all of the documents that you create.

Your Desktop probably looks similar to one of the two shown on these pages. The example on the left is what you see if your iMac is using a version of Mac OS 8; the example below is using Mac OS 9. Everything works the same, no matter which version you have.

In a minute you're going to spend some time poking around the Desktop so you'll feel comfortable with it. But first you need to learn to use the mouse.

**Below is the Desktop on Mac OS 9**

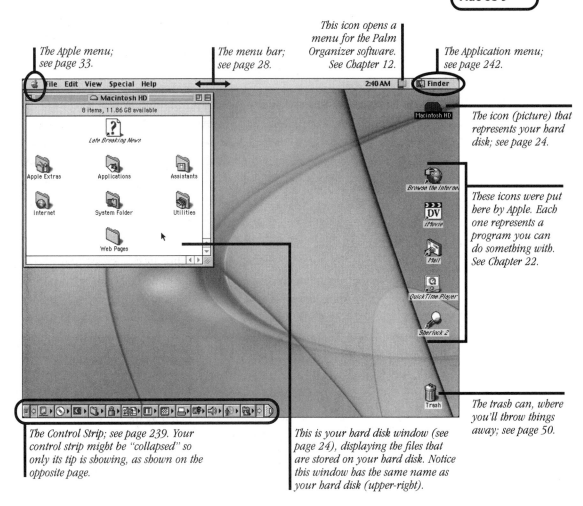

*This icon opens a menu for the Palm Organizer software. See Chapter 12.*

*The Apple menu; see page 33.*

*The menu bar; see page 28.*

*The Application menu; see page 242.*

*The icon (picture) that represents your hard disk; see page 24.*

*These icons were put here by Apple. Each one represents a program you can do something with. See Chapter 22.*

*The trash can, where you'll throw things away; see page 50.*

*The Control Strip; see page 239. Your control strip might be "collapsed" so only its tip is showing, as shown on the opposite page.*

*This is your hard disk window (see page 24), displaying the files that are stored on your hard disk. Notice this window has the same name as your hard disk (upper-right).*

### The mouse

*This is how your hand sits on the iMac mouse:*

The first thing you need to become comfortable with is the **mouse.** You can plug it into either end of the keyboard, depending on whether you're right- or left-handed. It doesn't *have* to sit next to the keyboard—you can put it anywhere you can reach it easily. The mouse sits flat on the tabletop. The tail, I mean the cord, faces away from you. (I have met people who prefer to use the mouse "upside down," with the tail facing toward them. If using the mouse the standard way makes you crazy, try using it upside down. Just make sure the flat part sits flat on the table.)

Position your hand on the mouse so your index finger sits on the "button," the front of the mouse that you can press on. It makes a clicking sound when you press, so we call this "clicking" the mouse.

*This is the **pointer:** You might also hear it referred to as a **cursor.***

**Try it:** Move the mouse around with your hand. Notice the *pointer* on the screen moves as you move the mouse on the desk—if you move the mouse to the right, the pointer moves to the right. Click the mouse button here and there, just don't click on a *picture* of anything yet!

### How to use the mouse

You'll be using the mouse in four ways: single-click, double-click, drag, and something called press-and-drag. Each of these motions accomplishes different things, so it's very important to understand what each one does and when to do it. **Read** the stuff below, **read** the opposite page, **then** turn the page and experiment.

*The very **tip** of the **pointer** is the only part that does anything! Make sure the very **tip** is positioned where you need it before you click or drag.*

### Single-click
Position the pointer, then click the mouse button once.

### Double-click
Position the pointer, then click the mouse button twice very fast. You have to hold the mouse very still—if the mouse moves even a tiny bit between clicks, it won't work. If this happens to you, try again.

### Drag
*Without holding the mouse button down,* just drag the mouse. Usually you click something right before you drag, so it's often called **click-and-drag,** not to be confused with *press*-and-drag (below).

### Press-and-drag
Click and *hold the mouse button down,* then drag the mouse, keeping the button down. When you're done, let go of the button.

### The mouse pad

You might already have a mouse pad, a thin pad of some sort that you place next to your computer and set your mouse upon. You don't *have* to have a mouse pad—there's nothing magical about the pad that makes the mouse work or not work. It's just a piece of plastic or heavy fabric that gives better traction for your mouse than does a typical desktop. I'm sure you've seen millions of mouse pads.

*This is a typical sort of mouse pad.*

### Running out of room on the mouse pad

When you're actually moving your mouse along a pad, you will come to the edge of it regularly. At first you might feel like the pad is much too small. But this is how to deal with it:

> If your finger is holding the mouse button down and you are about to fall off of the pad while dragging, *keep your finger on the button and pick up the mouse.* Keep your finger holding down that button, and just pick up the mouse, put it anywhere you want on the pad, and continue dragging or whatever you were doing.

You will use this technique so much it will start to happen naturally and you won't even notice it.

So now let's go experiment with the mouse!

©2000 John Tollett

### The windows

We're going to experiment with the mouse, using the **windows.** A window, as shown below, is one of the basic features of the Macintosh. (I know, you may have heard the term Windows, with a capital W, in reference to Microsoft and other computers besides Macintosh. Those other computers use technology, um, "inspired" by the Macintosh.)

You'll use windows at the Desktop, and you'll use them in every program you work in, including when you use the Internet, so it's a good idea to get to know them pretty well. You're going to have to resize them, move them, "roll them up," put them away, and get them out again. You can do all of these things with the mouse.

If you just turned on your computer, you probably see this window on the Desktop:

Macintosh HD

*The window to the right is showing you what is on your hard disk. Your hard disk is represented by the tiny picture shown above.*

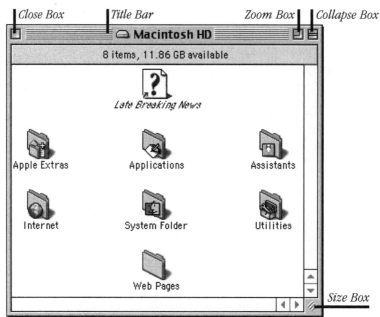

Macintosh HD

*Double-click this icon to open your hard disk window.*

*Above is the window you see when you first turn on your iMac.*
***If you don't see this window,*** *position the tip of your pointer over the little picture (the icon) in the upper-right corner of the Desktop called Macintosh HD.* ***Double-click*** *that icon and you will see this window (or one very similar).*

*All of the icons (pictures) inside of this window represent different files on your computer. We'll talk about them later.*

## Using your mouse, do these things

### Move the window

Position the tip of the pointer anywhere in the Title Bar (except in one of the little boxes). Press the mouse button down *and hold it down; while the button is down,* drag the mouse (this is called **press-and-drag**). The "outline" of the window will move as you drag. Let go of the mouse when you've repositioned the outline, and the window will move to that spot.

**Now try this:** Position the tip of the pointer anywhere along the outside edge of the window, then press-and-drag. This technique will also move any window you'll ever find on the iMac.

If it doesn't work, it's probably because you don't have the very tip of the pointer positioned in the right spot.

### Resize the window

Position the tip of the pointer in the little Size Box in the bottom-right corner of the window. **Press-and-drag**—don't let go! As you drag the mouse around, you see an outline of the window changing size. When you let go, your window will resize and will stay that size until you change it again.

Another way to resize a window very quickly is to position the tip of the pointer in the Zoom Box, in the upper-right of the window (see the illustration). Click once, a **single click,** right in that little box and the window will zoom larger or smaller, depending on whether it's already small or large.

(If you clicked and your window disappeared, it's because you accidentally clicked in the Collapse Box, which is just to the right of the Zoom Box! Click once more in the Collapse Box to show your window again.)

*Remember, the tip*

*is the only part of the pointer that is "hot," or that does anything! The rest of the pointer is just so you can see the darn thing.*

*This is the Size Box.*

*This is the Zoom Box.*

*This one is the Collapse Box.*

### Collapse the window

*This is the Collapse Box.*

Position the tip of the pointer in the little Collapse Box in the upper-right corner of the window. **Click once.** This "rolls up" your window like a window shade. Notice the Title Bar is still visible, and you can move it around. To unroll the window, click in the Collapse Box again.

*Collapse Box*

*This is what your window looks like when it's collapsed!*

### Scroll with the scroll bars

Scroll bars (shown below) are very important features of windows. You see, often there are so many items inside the window that they all can't be displayed at once, so the scroll bars make things "glide" past the window opening. It's sort of like sitting in a train and watching the scenery go by. Read about the scroll bars, below, then follow the steps on the next page to practice using your mouse and learn how to control the scroll bars at the same time.

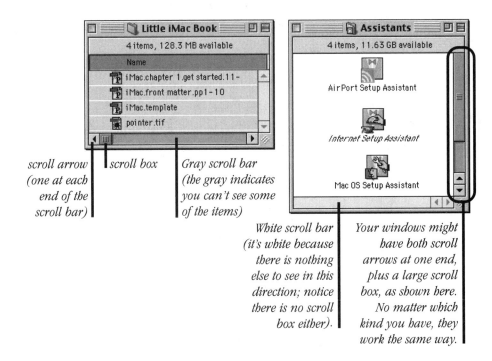

*scroll arrow (one at each end of the scroll bar)*

*scroll box*

*Gray scroll bar (the gray indicates you can't see some of the items)*

*White scroll bar (it's white because there is nothing else to see in this direction; notice there is no scroll box either).*

*Your windows might have both scroll arrows at one end, plus a large scroll box, as shown here. No matter which kind you have, they work the same way.*

### Scroll bar and mouse practice

The scroll bars will be "empty" (white) unless all of the items can't fit inside the window, so for this exercise you have to make sure the window is small enough that you can see the scroll bars, as shown on the opposite page. To **resize** your window so it is fairly small, press on the Size Box in the bottom-right corner, and drag up and to the left.

**Single click** in any gray area of the scroll bar. Notice it pops the items in the window to one side or the other horizontally, or up and down vertically.

Notice where the scroll box is located (see opposite page). **Press** on the little *arrow* on the *opposite* end of the scroll box (if you have a little box) or on the arrow that is pointing in the direction you want the scroll bar to move (don't worry, just press one or the other—you'll see). Watch as the contents of the window slide past. Notice that the scroll box is a visual clue that tells you how close you are to one end or the other of the window.

I know the scroll bars seem like they make things slide in the opposite direction than you think. You'll eventually get used to it and will soon automatically choose the correct arrow to scroll in the direction you need to.

**Press-and-drag** on the scroll box itself to move it somewhere else along the scroll bar. Watch as the contents move.

**Resize** your window big enough so one or both of the scroll bars disappear.

**Pop quiz:** *On first glance, the window below looks empty.*

a. *What are the two visual clues that tell you there actually is something in the window? I haven't explained one of them yet, so don't bother looking in the text. Take a close look at the window and find the clues.*

b. *Exactly how many files (items) are in this window? (That's a clue to the first answer.)*

c. *Name two ways to display the items (I did tell you these).*

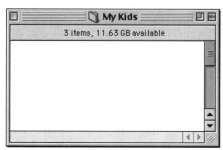

*c. Click in the Zoom Box; drag the scroll box to the opposite ends of the scroll bars.*

*b. The information bar across the top of the window says there are 3 items.*

*a. A scroll bar is gray; the information bar across the top of the window says there are 3 items in this window.*

### The menu bar and menus

Let's use the mouse to see what's in the **menu bar** and how to use **menus.** The menu bar is the strip across the very top of the screen (shown below).

*This is the Desktop menu bar. You'll always see the menu bar, but it displays different items in different applications.*

Each word and icon (picture) in this menu bar has a menu of commands to make the computer do something. A typical menu looks like this:

> **Special**
> Empty Trash
> Eject    ⌘E
> Erase Disk...
> Sleep
> Restart
> Shut Down

*Tip: If you ever use an older Macintosh, you'll notice you cannot just* **click** *to make a menu stay open—you have to* **press** *on the menu* **and drag** *the mouse down the list. That's why they're called "pull-down" menus, because we used to actually "pull" them down.*

**To pull down a menu,** position the tip of the pointer on any word or picture in the menu bar, then **single-click** on it. The menu appears. Go through the menu bar and just take a look at what each menu has to offer. Don't forget to check the Apple menu (under the apple icon on the far left) and the Application menu (under the happy Mac OS icon on the far right).

**To choose an item in the menu,** you will slide the mouse down the menu. As you pass over an item with the pointer, it "highlights," or changes color. That means that item is *selected.* If you **single-click** on a selected menu item, that command is executed. Be careful! There are a number of commands you don't want to execute right now!

*I used the pointer to select the command "Empty Trash."*

> **Special**
> Empty Trash
> Eject    ⌘E
> Erase Disk...
> Sleep
> Restart
> Shut Down

The menu will disappear after a few seconds if you don't click on anything. If you want to **make it go away** instantly, just click anywhere on the Desktop.

You've probably noticed that many **menu items are gray** instead of black, and they don't highlight as you slide your pointer over them. When an item is gray, it means that particular command or item is not available at the moment. For instance, the command "Empty Trash" in *your* Special menu is probably gray, right? (Check to see.) The gray command indicates there is no trash in your trash can to be emptied.

### Select something from a menu

First of all, make sure there is a window open because the command you are going to choose will affect the window. If you have been following along, there should be a window open.

If you don't see an open window:

Macintosh HD

*This is the icon that represents your hard disk.*

> Position the tip of your pointer directly over the icon (tiny picture) of your hard disk, which is in the upper-right corner of the screen, below the menu bar, and is called "Macintosh HD."
>
> Double-click the icon. It will open to a window.

If you still don't see a window, either you moved the mouse between the two clicks and it didn't work (try again), or the window is still collapsed. Do you see a rolled-up window, like this:

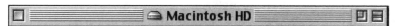

If so, either double-click right there on the name "Macintosh HD," or click in the Collapse Box on the far-right end.

Okay. Whew. We've all got an open window on the screen. Unless you changed things yourself, your window probably looks something like the one shown below, right? Now let's change the way the files are displayed, called the window View (next page).

### List view and Icon view

If you followed the directions on the previous page, you're looking at a window full of icons, which are small pictures that represent the various files stored on your computer. These icons give you clues as to what kinds of files they are (we'll talk about that later). But some people prefer to view the files in a *list* of names, instead of looking at all the pictures. Let's change this window to a **List view,** using the mouse and a menu.

1. **Click once** anywhere on the window, in any blank area. This **selects** the window and makes sure that the command we are about to choose does its business to *this* window.

2. Position the tip of the pointer on the menu called "View," and **click once** right on the word "View." This menu will pop up:

*Notice there is a checkmark next to the choice "as Icons." The checkmark is a visual clue that tells you which view the window is currently displaying.*

3. Do not hold the mouse button down, but slide the pointer down to the choice "as List." The choice will highlight, or turn dark, and when it is dark (which means it's selected), **click once** on it.

So now your window is displaying all of the items as a list, right? It should look similar to the example on the opposite page. This is called a "List view."

Below is an example of a window in the List view. Many people prefer to see their files as a list of names instead of all the icons. It's entirely up to you!

*Click any one of these column headings to organize, or sort, your files by that heading. How can you tell that the files shown below are sorted by "Name"?*

*You can resize the columns. Just position your pointer directly on the dividing line between two column headings; the pointer will turn into a double-headed arrow: ✛. With that arrow, just press-and-drag to the left or right.*

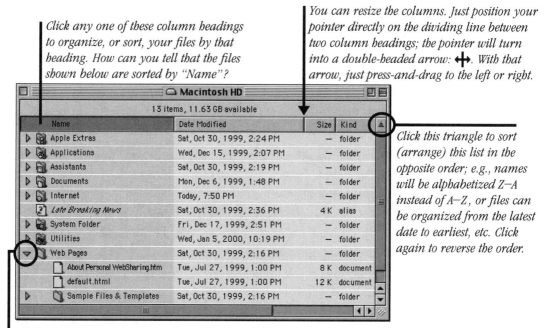

*Click this triangle to sort (arrange) this list in the opposite order; e.g., names will be alphabetized Z–A instead of A–Z, or files can be organized from the latest date to earliest, etc. Click again to reverse the order.*

*Click any tiny triangle to see a list of what is inside that folder. Click again to close it up. Try it.*

*Using that triangle is called "expanding" a folder. (You can also double-click the tiny folder icon to open it up as a window, just as you would if it were a large folder icon in the "as Icons" view.)*

**Tip:** *You can rearrange the columns in any Desktop window. Try this: Press on the "Size" column heading and drag it to the left about an inch. Let go.*

### Click-and-drag vs. press-and-drag

*Unfortunately, in a lot of Macintosh documentation the writers use the term "click-and-drag" when they really mean "press-and-drag." If a click-and-drag instruction doesn't work, try press-and-drag.*

So on the previous two pages you used the mouse movement called **click-and-drag,** where you click once to bring the menu up, then you drag the mouse down the list *without holding the button down,* and click again. You can also use a **press-and-drag** in a menu to do the same thing, where you press, *hold the mouse button down,* then let go on the selected item.

It's a good thing to be conscious of the difference between click-and-drag and press-and-drag, because sometimes you *must* use a press-and-drag because the click-and-drag doesn't work. Also, if you ever work on an older Macintosh, you'll find that the only way to select items from menus is to press-and-drag.

So let's change the window view again using **press-and-drag.** Make sure you are conscious of the difference. It will make everything easier as you learn to use the rest of the iMac features.

1. **Click once** anywhere on the hard disk window, in any blank area. This selects the window and makes sure the command you are about to choose does its business to *this* window.

2. Position the tip of the pointer on the menu called "View," **press** right on the word, *and hold the mouse button down.* The menu will pop up.

3. *Keep holding the mouse button down,* and **drag** the pointer down to the choice "as List" (or "as Icon," whichever one does not have the checkmark next to it). The choice will highlight, or turn dark, and when it is dark, **let go.** Don't try to click! Just let go.

I recommend you switch views several more times and make sure you are conscious of using either the click-and-drag technique or the press-and-drag technique.

Internet

*This is a button. It's just another way of looking at a file icon.*

### Button view and clicking

Notice you can also change the view to **Buttons.** The difference is this: In Icon view and List view, you *double-click* to open files. In Button view, you **single-click.** To drag a button, you must drag the file by its *name*—you can't drag the button itself. To follow the instructions in this book, *don't* choose the Button view. Later, if you decide you want to use buttons, go ahead.

So are you starting to feel more comfortable with the mouse? Let's do one more useful exercise with the mouse, using what's called a Control Panel. Along the way you'll also use the **Apple menu** and take a look at what are called "hierarchical menus."

## Control Panels and the Apple menu

The Macintosh provides many ways for you to customize the computer so it suits the way you work. One way it does this is through small programs called Control Panels. I'm going to show you how a couple of the Control Panels work, and you can open up any others you want and tweak the obvious things. Some of them are very self-explanatory. If you want directions on how to use every one of them, see *The Little Mac Book,* the sixth edition. For right now, let's adjust the "speed" of the mouse you are using.

1. On the far-left end of the menu bar is a tiny icon of the Apple logo. This is actually a menu, called the Apple menu! **Click once** on the Apple to pull down the menu.

2. Find the item called "Control Panels." Notice it has a little triangle pointing to the right. The triangle is a visual clue that indicates if you select that item, another menu will pop out to the right, as shown below. This is called a "hierarchical menu," or "h-menu."   *—continued*

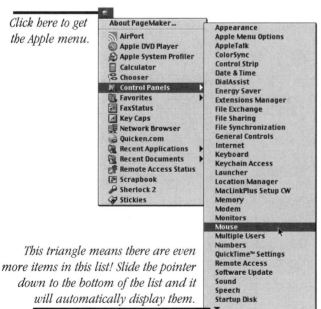

*Click here to get the Apple menu.*

*This triangle means there are even more items in this list! Slide the pointer down to the bottom of the list and it will automatically display them.*

*So this is an h-menu. You'll find them all over your iMac. H-menus can be a little tricky to maneuver in, so don't get upset if they disappear on you now and then. The trick is to follow the highlighted bar horizontally (in this case, across Control Panels), then slide right down the h-menu. In this case, when "Mouse" highlights, click on it (directions continued on the next page).*

*If you're really studious, try using the press-and-drag technique as opposed to the click-and-drag.*

**3.** So point to Control Panels to get the list of items, then slide
down that list and click on "Mouse." The Mouse Control Panel
will appear, as shown on the opposite page.

Remember, if you run out of mouse pad space, just pick up the mouse
and move it. If your finger was holding the mouse button down to get
the menu (pressing), keep it down while you move the mouse.

It can sometimes be a little tricky to grab an item on an h-menu.
If the menu disappears or if a different one pops up, just slide the pointer
back to the item you want (Control Panels, in this case), then slide
directly across the highlighted bar to the right, then down the h-menu.

**Tip for later:** The original Apple menu (the one you have on your iMac, which
looks similar to the one below, left) is a visual mess, in my opinion. I customized
my menu so it is easier to look at and to use (below, right). When you're ready to
do this, see the directions in *The Little Mac Book*.

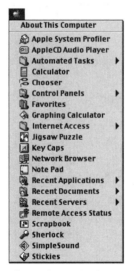

*This is the original
Apple menu in OS 8.5.*

*This is my customized
Apple menu in OS 8.5.*

## Mouse Control Panel

Shown below is the Mouse Control Panel. It has little buttons, called "radio buttons," labeled "Slow" to "Fast." If you click the "Fast" button, it doesn't mean the *mouse* actually moves any *faster*—it means you don't have to move the mouse so far across the mouse pad to make the pointer travel across the screen.

**Try it:** Click the "Slow" button (with the tip of the pointer) and see how far you have to move your hand and the mouse to make the pointer move across the screen. Then click the "Fast" button and see how the pointer moves. I set my tracking speed on "Fast," but many designers and illustrators like to set their speed to "Slow" so they have more control in the painting programs, moving the mouse dot by dot.

You can also change the "Double-Click Speed" of the mouse. I don't recommend setting it to the highest level (on the far right) because then your iMac might sometimes interpret a single click as a double-click. But if you find you can't double-click fast enough, try setting the speed to the lowest level. Then the computer allows you a tiny bit more time between the clicks.

**To put the control panel away,** click in its little Close Box in its upper-left corner (just like you put away windows, right?).

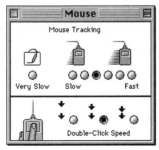

*Experiment with the difference between the mouse tracking speeds—choose a speed, then move the mouse. When you have set the speed you like, close the control panel.*

**Radio buttons** *are round, you can only choose one in the set, and one must be on, just like on a car radio.*

*You will also see* **checkbox buttons;** *with checkboxes, you can choose all, none, or any combination of the options.*

☑ Italic
☑ Bold

## Date & Time Control Panel

Let's go to the "Date & Time" Control Panel for one last exercise in using the mouse, menus, h-menus, and Control Panels.

1. Just as you did before, click on the Apple menu, then slide down to Control Panels, then out and down the list. This time choose "Date & Time" (click once on it).

2. Poke around in this Control Panel. It's quite self-explanatory. The only thing you need to know is that to change the date or time, first **click** right on the number you want to change, then either click the tiny arrows up or down, or type in a new number.

   For instance, to change the month, click once on the month number. Then to the right of that date, the little up and down arrows appear (remember, items are gray until you can use them; in this case, the arrows are gray until you choose which number you want to change). Click an arrow to change the month number. To change the day, click once on the day number, then click the little arrows or type in a new day.

   *Tip: You might find a Control Panel that doesn't have a Close Box! If so, go to the File menu and choose "Quit."*

   To *lock in* the new date, either click on the tiny calendar icon, or just close the Control Panel (click the little Close Box in the upper-left corner).

   Go ahead and click the other buttons and make all the changes you want. You can't hurt anything, and you can always change it again.

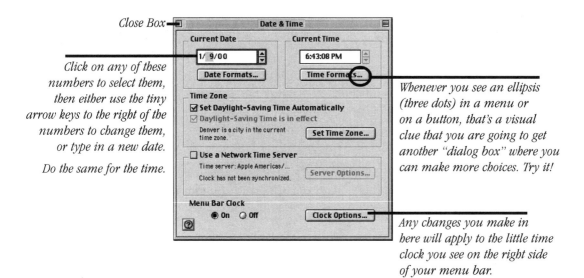

Close Box

*Click on any of these numbers to select them, then either use the tiny arrow keys to the right of the numbers to change them, or type in a new date.*

*Do the same for the time.*

*Whenever you see an ellipsis (three dots) in a menu or on a button, that's a visual clue that you are going to get another "dialog box" where you can make more choices. Try it!*

*Any changes you make in here will apply to the little time clock you see on the right side of your menu bar.*

## Back to the Setup Assistant

If you followed along from the beginning of this book and put the Setup Assistant away as I suggested on page 19, then it's time now to go back and get it. It's very easy to do, especially now that you know how to use the mouse. This will be good practice, and it will customize several features of your Macintosh for you.

First of all, you have to find the icon that represents the Setup Assistant.*

Macintosh HD

**1.** If the hard disk window is not open, open it now (double-click on the hard disk icon in the upper-right of the monitor, the one called Macintosh HD). If the window is already open, go to step **2.**

Assistants

**2.** In the hard disk window, see the folder called "Assistants"? Double-click it to open its window.

*You'll see a few other icons in this folder. Ignore them for now.*

**3.** See the icon called "Mac OS Setup Assistant"? That icon represents the Setup Assistant program. Double-click it.

So now you are where we were to begin with. Let's go through this Setup Assistant. After you do this once, you'll never have to do it again. Most of this process is entirely self-explanatory, so I haven't included pictures of every single thing you'll see. I have provided a few clues for you on the following page to help in confusing spots.

**\*If you are on an iMac that is running Mac OS 9,** you have, in addition to the Setup Assistant described above and on the next several pages, a prettier version you can use instead:

**1.** Double-click the hard drive icon ("Macintosh HD") to open its window.

**2.** Inside the "Macintosh HD" window, find the folder called "Apple Extras." Double-click it.

**3.** Inside the "Apple Extras" window, find the folder called "Setup Assistant." Double-click it.

**4.** Inside the "Setup Assistant" window, find the icon called "Setup Assistant" and double-click it (shown to the right). This opens the program; you'll get to hear fun music and see pretty pictures. It's very self-explanatory. When you get to the part about the Internet, follow it through if you know what you're doing; if you don't, tell the Assistant you'll get on the Internet later, then read the Internet section of this book before you make the connection decisions.

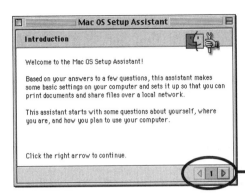

*Click these arrows to move to the previous window or the next window. (If an arrow is gray, that means you can't go any further in that direction.)*

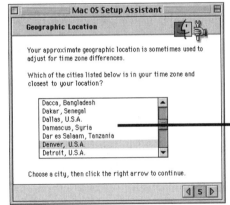

*To select a city name quickly, type the first letter or two of its name. If you live in a small town that's not listed here, select a larger city in your time zone.*

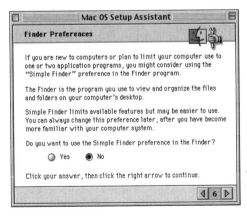

*If you plan to do the exercises in this book, do not choose the Simple Finder.*

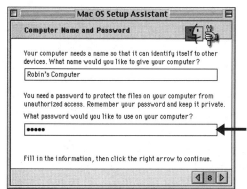

*This doesn't mean you will have to type in a password to use your iMac. If the iMac is at home or in a small office, you may never need the password again, but write it down somewhere anyway!*

*This is called an "edit box," where you type in the information instead of choosing something from a list. Click in the edit box to begin typing.*

*If you are in a large office where all the computers can send messages to each other, you probably want a shared folder.*

*If you are in a small office or home office and you want to be able to send files back and forth between Macs, you probably want a shared folder.*

*If you have no clue what to answer here, choose "No." Even if you don't set up a shared folder now, you can always do it later.*

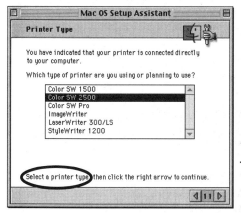

*When the directions tell you to select something, just click on your choice in the list. If you don't have a printer yet, choose any one for now. You can always change it later.*

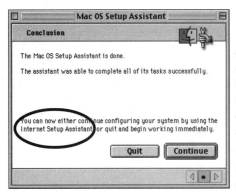

*If you don't have a clue about the Internet yet, you might want to click the "Quit" button now, and come back later to set up your Internet stuff. I'll walk you through it in the Internet section of this book.*

*Or feel free to jump to the information below right now; if it makes sense to you, continue!*

## Using the Internet Setup Assistant

If you want to click the "Continue" button and go ahead with the Internet Setup Assistant, feel free! You have three choices. Read this carefully before you click the "Continue" button. If none of the following makes sense to you, click the "Quit" button and read the Internet section of this book first.

**Note:** *If you have no clue what an ISP is, or America Online, or Earthlink, or how to choose between them, read the Internet section of this book!*

- If you already use or plan to use America Online, *do not* go through the Internet Setup Assistant. America Online (AOL) is your connection to the Internet and when you go through AOL's setup process, it will take care of everything you need. Quit now.

  If you haven't already, open America Online and either set up your existing account on this iMac or start a new account. To find AOL: open the hard disk window; open the "Internet" folder; scroll down the window and open the "Internet Applications" folder; open the "America Online v4.0" folder. Double-click the "America Online" icon. The rest is self-explanatory.

- If you already have a local or national ISP (Internet Service Provider) that you use on other computers (you would know if you do) and you want to use the same ISP on this iMac, make sure you have all of the pertinent information before you go through the Internet Setup Assistant. Call your ISP and ask them if you don't know the answers to any of the items you see in the Internet Setup Assistant.

- If you *don't* have an ISP yet and you *don't* plan to use AOL, you can set up an account with Earthlink through the Internet Setup Assistant. It's quick and easy and inexpensive (unless you live in a place like Hawaii or Alaska or Shakespeare, New Mexico, where you can't get a local number for Earthlink). You'll get an Internet connection and an email account.

*If you go through the whole connection process and try to connect and get a message telling you it didn't work, see page 294.*

# Working at Your Desktop

By now you should feel pretty comfortable using the mouse and menus. In the following section you're going to open an application and write a letter, but first I want you to understand how to work at the Desktop. Lots of computer users know how to open an application and work in it, but don't know how to manage the Desktop. In this chapter we're going to look at the important things the icons are telling you, how to make new folders and put *files* in them, how to use keyboard shortcuts, how to throw away stuff you don't want anymore, how to make copies of things, how to put a disk in and take it out, and how to shut down when you're done for the day.

*file:* This is a generic term for anything on your computer. On the iMac, every file is represented by an icon. Even a folder is actually a file. Applications, documents, control panels — everything you see on your iMac is a file.

## Icons

One of the original features of the Macintosh that made it famous was its use of **icons,** or little pictures, that represent every file in the computer so you can just double-click to open a document, instead of having to dig up the file by typing in awful codes.

Because all the visual stuff on an iMac screen can be so overwhelming, beginners often don't notice that the icons provide very important clues. I'm going to point out the most important clues, and when you're ready you might want to read more about them in *The Little Mac Book.*

The three most important icons you'll work with are these:

### Folders

Novel Research

*This is a folder icon.*

Utilities

*Some special iMac folders have fancy graphics.*

Macintosh folders, whose icons look just like real manila folders, are as important to your organization on the computer as manila folders are to your organization in an office. You must learn how to make new ones, put files inside them, empty them out, rearrange them, throw them away, etc. We'll do all that in a minute. For now, just look on your iMac and find the folders. (Open your hard disk window, if it isn't already.)

When you **double-click** a folder, it opens to a window on your Desktop. (The only other icons that open to *windows* on your Desktop are icons of *disks,* such as your hard disk or a CD.)

### Applications

AppleWorks

Acrobat Reader

SimpleText

*These are application icons.*

Applications are the programs you will be working in to create your own documents. Their icons are typically "fancier" than anything else, and there's no consistent pattern to them. Take a look at the ones to the left.

When you **double-click** an application, the iMac opens the application and usually puts a blank *application* window on the screen for you to work in.

(Some applications, such as AppleWorks, formerly known as ClarisWorks, open up but don't create a new and blank window for you until you first tell it what sort of document you want. After you choose, then you get a new, clean window to work in; as you'll see in the next chapter).

### Documents

When you work in an application and create a document, you *save* it onto your hard disk (see page 87). When you save it, the iMac creates a document file for you and gives it an icon. A document icon always has the upper-right corner turned down (as shown to the right).

Love Letter

My Term Paper

A document icon almost always matches the icon of the application it was created in, also. Take a look at the three icons to the right, and take a look at the three application icons on the bottom-left of the opposite page. Take a second to match each document to its application.

ReadMe.pdf

When you **double-click** a document, the iMac finds the application you used to create the document, then opens that application and puts your document on the screen.

*These are document icons. Notice the upper-right corners.*

## Gray icons

You will see icons that are gray, as shown to the right. Don't worry, there's nothing wrong with them. The gray just means that the file is already open.

If it's a **gray folder icon,** that folder's window is already open. Just go ahead and double-click on the gray icon, and that window will pop to the front. (If you still don't see the window, perhaps it's "collapsed"; see page 26.)

Little iMac Book

If it's a **gray application icon,** that application is already open and running. Go ahead and double-click on the gray icon and that application will come forward and be "active."

Adobe PageMaker

Now, you might not think it's active because you don't see anything, but check the menu bar! It's the menu bar for your application, even though there might not be an active window showing. Check the File menu—you can make a new document or open an existing one. (See page 242 for details on this feature where the application is open, but you still see the Desktop!)

If it's a **gray CD icon,** that CD is already open on your Desktop. Double-click the gray icon and its window will pop forward. (If you double-click a gray CD icon and still don't see the window, the window might be collapsed; see page 26.)

Archie

**Novel Research**

*Get used to working with folders!*

## Folders

Folders are great. Folders are indispensable. Can you imagine having a large filing cabinet in your office and putting all the papers into that filing cabinet without using manila folders? What a mess! Yet that's what people do on their computers. Before we get into organizing things with folders, let's get used to making, moving, and deleting them, as well as putting things inside.

Follow these instructions carefully. I don't want to you move or throw away anything important, so please follow along and don't do anything I don't tell you to do.

### Make a new folder

1. You can put a new folder directly onto the Desktop, into any existing folder, or in your *top level* hard disk window. For right now, let's put one in your top level hard disk window. To do that, we need to make sure your hard disk window is open and is the *active* window, which is always the window on top.

**top level:** *The highest level of storage in your computer. When you double-click on the hard disk icon, that window displays the top level.*

**active window:** *The window that is in use at the moment. You can always tell which window is active because it is the only one with lines in the title bar. Only one window can ever be active at a time, whether you are at the Desktop or in an application.*

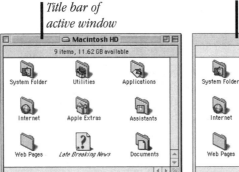

*Title bar of active window*

*Title bar of window that is not active*

*The window on the left is the **active window**. You can tell by the lines in the title bar (shown above, left), and because the non-active window is gray like a ghost (shown above, right).*

***All of the commands at the Desktop and in any application always apply to the active window.***

*That is, if you choose the "Close" command, it will close the active window; if you choose the "New Folder" command, the new folder will appear in the active window.*

2. So open your hard disk window (which is the top level of your entire hard disk) by double-clicking on the hard disk icon. The window probably looks something like the one on the previous page.

3. While this window is *active,* go to the File menu and choose the command "New Folder." Instantly a new folder appears in the *active* window. You should see this:

4. Notice the new folder is named "untitled folder" and has a **border** around its name. This border is a visual clue telling you that you can type and replace the existing name. All you need to do is type. Really. Just put those fingers to the keyboard and rename this folder something like "Toss This Folder" so you know it's practice.

   (If the folder doesn't have a border around the name because you accidentally clicked somewhere else and the border disappeared, don't worry, do this: click directly on the *name* of the folder, not on the *picture* of the folder. Then type.)

5. When you've **finished** renaming the folder, click anywhere outside of the folder; the border will disappear and the name will be set.

   If you decide you want to **rename** it, just click on the name, wait until the border appears, then type.

untitled folder
*If you click anywhere else before you follow the directions in Step 4, you will lose the border around the name! If so, click on the **name** once more to select it again.*

*Here is the folder with its new name. Click anywhere except on the folder itself and the border will disappear.*

### Move the folder

Okay, so now you have a new folder in your hard disk window. Let's **move the folder icon** into a more convenient location. In fact, why don't you rearrange all of those folders in that whole window into an arrangement you prefer. How?

1. Just press-and-drag: position the tip of the pointer on the folder itself, *press and hold the mouse button down,* then *drag* the folder (still holding the button down) to an empty spot.

2. When the folder is positioned where you want it, let go of the mouse button.

*Make sure you don't accidentally drop folders inside of other folders! To prevent that from happening, don't let go of a folder you are dragging when the pointer is positioned over another folder.*

***Tip:** If you accidentally drop one folder inside of another, see page 48, "Take something out of a folder."*

*The folder has a gray look as you drag it. When you let go, the real folder appears in that new position.*

Below is an example of how I prefer to arrange the folders in my hard disk window. I always keep my System Folder in the upper left, my Utilities folder next to that, and then my Applications folder. Practice moving the folders by rearranging them into an order that makes sense to you.

*(Actually, I would throw away a lot of this stuff, or at least hide it all in one folder until I knew what all these things were. See Chapter 22 for an explanation of what all these files are and what to do with them.)*

## Put something into a folder

You will be putting things inside of folders and taking them out constantly. It's easy. But first, I want you to do something to make this process less confusing. We're going to turn off the iMac's feature called "spring-loaded folders." A spring-loaded folder pops open in front of you before you let go of the mouse. When you are feeling confident about your iMac, you can come back and turn that feature back on, if you like. (I leave mine off.)

*Close Box*

*Uncheck the box for "Spring-loaded folders."*

1. Here at the Desktop, go to the Edit menu and choose "Preferences...."

2. Uncheck the box "Spring-loaded folders."

3. Click the Close Box to put the Preferences away.

That was easy. Now let's put something into a folder.

1. First of all, make yourself a new folder so you'll have two of them. Name the new folder something like "Toss Me Too." When you're done, click anywhere else to set the name.

2. Now put one folder (which is a file) inside of the other folder: drag the folder named "Toss This Folder," and drop it directly onto the folder named "Toss Me Too." Remember, the **tip** of the pointer is the hot spot, so the tip of the pointer is what has to be positioned directly over the folder "Toss Me Too." The folder you are putting something into will "highlight," or turn dark, when it is ready to take the item, as shown below.

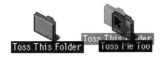

*The folder on the left is highlighted because I pressed my mouse on it. Then, still holding the mouse button down, I dragged that folder over to the other folder, indicated by the shadow. The other folder, "Toss Me Too," is also now highlighted, which means if I let go of the mouse button, the first folder will drop inside. Notice where the tip of the pointer is located— **on the folder.***

**Tip:** You can also drag an item into an open folder (which is, of course, a window). Just drag it and drop it on any blank area in the window.

*If you can't find a blank spot in the window, drop the item right here on the title bar or on the info bar and it will go into the window.*

*The window displays a subtle highlight border around the inside when you drag an item into it. Watch for it.*

3. After you drop the file into the folder, open the folder ("Toss Me Too") and see the file inside.

Toss This Folder copy

*The duplicate file is automatically named the same as the first one, with "copy" added.*

## Duplicate a folder (or any file)

You can make a duplicate of any file on your hard disk. Let's duplicate one of the folders you just made to see how it works.

1. Select the folder named "Toss This Folder" by clicking **once** on it. (You might have to open the folder "Toss Me Too" to find it.) (If you accidentally double-clicked "Toss This Folder" and it opened to its window, close the window.)

2. From the File menu, choose "Duplicate." This will duplicate any selected file. If the selected file is a folder, *it will duplicate the entire contents of the folder.*

3. Drag the new, duplicated folder away from the original (but leave it in the same folder, ready for the next exercise). You'll know which one is the duplicate because it has the word "copy" at the end of its name.

4. Close the "Toss Me Too" window, ready for the next exercise).

## Take something out of a folder

To take things out of a folder, you must first open its window. Use your practice folder for now ("Toss Me Too"); later, follow these directions for any file.

1. Double-click the folder named "Toss Me Too" to open its window.

2. Just drag the item you want *out* of the window. Drop it onto the Desktop, into another window, or on top of another folder to put it inside that other folder.

## COPY a file to another folder (don't just MOVE it)

*You can surprise your Mac-user friends by knowing this trick—they might not know it!*

When you drag a file from one place to another, you *move* the *original* file. But sometimes you don't want to *move* the original file—sometimes you want a *copy* of that same file in another folder. The technique below makes a *copy* of a file as you drag it from one place to another. This is essentially the same as making a duplicate (as described above), but it's a shortcut. You can skip this for now if you want—you'll probably find this tip more useful in a month or two.

1. Select the folder, "Toss This Folder" (click once on it to select it).

2. Hold down the Option key (on the bottom row of the keyboard, to the left). *With the Option key held down,* press-and-drag the selected file from one window to another (or from one window to the Desktop or into another folder). Then let go of the folder and the Option key.

3. You'll notice the new, copied file is named exactly the same as the original one, without "copy" at the end. You can change its name.

## Select more than one item or folder

Often you will want to move, duplicate, or throw away more than one item. You can select more than one at a time, in one window.

1. To select more than one item, hold down the **Shift key.** Each item you select *with the Shift key down* will be added to the selection.

   To **deselect** one of the items in the selected group, hold the **Shift key** down and click on it. You see, the Shift key will do whatever it needs to— it will *add* an item to the group, or it will *remove* an item from the group. Try it.

   This technique is called **Shift-click** because you hold down the Shift key and click. You might run across commands to Option-click or Command-click, which would be similar—hold down that key and click.

2. Make sure you have let go of the Shift key, then press on any one of the selected items, and drag *out* of the window. All of the selected items will come with the one you are dragging. Drop them onto the Desktop, into another window, or on top of another one of your extra folders. Remember, it is the *tip* of the pointer that's the boss—all of the selected items will drop wherever you position the *tip* of the pointer.

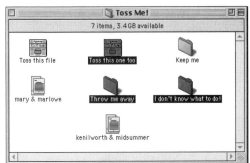

*Whether your window is in List view or Icon view, you can Shift-click to select more than one item. Just make sure before you drag that you **let go** of the Shift key and drag a **highlighted** item.*

*And remember, the files will move to wherever **the tip of the pointer is** when you let go.*

Don't worry—on the next page you're going to throw away these extra folders.

### The trash can and throwing things away

You've surely noticed the trash can sitting in the bottom-right corner of your screen. Looks like the kind of trash can in which you throw things away, doesn't it? It is.

### Throw something in the trash can

*Which trash can is full and needs to be emptied?*

1. Just drag any item you don't want (like one of those practice folders you made) over to the trash.

2. Make sure the *tip of the pointer* highlights the can, then let go and the item will drop into the trash. The icon changes to look like it's overstuffed.

### Empty the trash can

1. What you put in the trash will stay there, even if you turn off your iMac, until you go to the Special menu and choose "Empty Trash."

2. When you choose "Empty Trash," you will get a message asking if you really want to throw it away. If you do, click "OK."

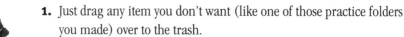

*You must empty the trash before stuff will really go away.*

### Take something out of the trash can

1. Double-click the trash can; it opens to display a window.

2. Drag the item out of the Trash window to your hard disk window. **Or** click once on the item in the trash, then press Command Y (which is the shortcut to the File menu command "Put Away," which will put the item back where it was before you trashed it).

### Use a keyboard shortcut to trash an item

1. Click **once** on the item you want to eliminate.

2. Hold down the Command key and hit Delete.

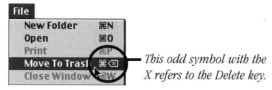

*This odd symbol with the X refers to the Delete key.*

## Create a folder for saving your documents

The Mac has a feature that makes it easy for you to save the documents you create into a special folder where you can always find them. I recommend you follow the instructions here to turn on that feature. If you don't do this, I guarantee you will create documents and then you won't be able to find them again later.

Until you know how to "navigate" through all the hierarchies and folders, let the iMac automatically store your saved documents into the Documents folder (which you will create in these steps). When you are ready for the next step, read *The Little Mac Book* and learn how to save your documents into the folders you make.

*navigate:* The process of opening and getting into folders from anyplace on your computer. You do this to save documents into specific folders, to open files that are within specific folders, etc.

1. Click on the Apple in the menu to display the Apple menu.

2. Slide down to "Control Panels," then out to the right and down to "General Controls." Click once on "General Controls."

3. On the bottom-right of the control panel, in the "Documents" section, click the radio button for "Documents folder." The section looks like this:

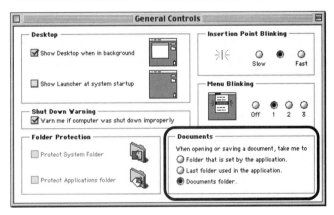

4. Close "General Controls" by clicking in its Close Box (upper-left corner).

Now you will see a new, fancy folder on your Desktop called "Documents" (shown to the left). From now on when you create a document (such as a letter) and save it, it will be stored in this folder. When you want to open that document again, open this Documents folder and double-click its icon.

Documents

*This folder makes it easy to store and find all your documents.*

## Keyboard shortcuts

The iMac lets you do a lot of things using the keyboard without having to pick up the mouse. These are called **keyboard shortcuts.** Once you get used to using keyboard shortcuts, you'll start looking for them.

### Modifier keys

*Spacebar: The Spacebar is not a modifier key because it does something (it makes spaces between words). The Spacebar is the long, blank key at the very bottom of the keyboard.*

Keyboard shortcuts always use "modifier keys," which are those keys that don't do anything when you press them by themselves. For instance, the Shift key is a modifier key—if you press it, nothing happens. Something only happens when you press the Shift key *in combination with* another key, as you do when you want to make capital letters. Each modifier key is represented in the menu by a symbol, shown to the left of the explanations below. The modifier keys are:

⇧ **Shift key,** labeled "shift" on your keyboard.

⌥ **Option key,** labeled "option" on your keyboard.

⌘ **Command key,** which has the Apple on it, plus the symbol that looks like a freeway interchange. (This is sometimes, not often, and don't you do it, referred to as the "Apple key." To a Mac user, calling the Command key the "Apple key" is like calling San Francisco "Frisco" to a Californian. Gag me.)

⌃ **Control key,** labeled "control." You won't see this very often. Don't get the Control key mixed up with the Command key! Take a look at your keyboard and make sure you know which is which.

F3 **Fkeys** are those keys across the very top of the keyboard, the skinny ones labeled from F1 through F12. You might see them in some keyboard shortcuts. (F1 through F4 actually have permanent jobs: they undo, cut, copy, and paste, in that order.)

esc **Escape key** is at the very top left of your keyboard. You won't use it very often.

See the opposite page for instructions on how to use keyboard shortcuts. Once you start using them, you'll feel good and you'll get things done more efficiently.

### Numeric keypad

*+ add*
*- subtract*
*\* multiply*
*/ divide*

*Use these keys as math operators. Most of the time you can use either the ones on the keypad or the ones on the keyboard.*

You also have a **numeric keypad** at the right end of the keyboard, and you have **numerals** across the top. Sometimes in a keyboard shortcut it makes a difference which ones you use. If the numeric keypad doesn't work, try the keyboard numerals.

### How to use shortcuts

To use a shortcut, you first look in the menu to see what it is. For instance, in the File menu (shown to the left) you see the command "Open." You also see an odd symbol combination next to "Open," which is the shortcut you can use *instead* of using the mouse and going to the File menu. This Open shortcut is ⌘O. This means *hold down* the Command key and *tap* the letter key (O) *once*.

Walk through the following exercises to learn how to use keyboard shortcuts, then look for them in your applications.

### Use a shortcut to open a folder

1. Click **once** on a folder to select it.

2. Press Command O (*hold down* the Command key, then *tap* the O).

3. Can you **close** this window, using a keyboard shortcut? Try it—take a look at the File menu and find the shortcut combination. Click once on the Desktop to make the menu go away, and click once on the window to make sure the window is selected, or active). Now use the keyboard shortcut to close that window.

*A selected folder is highlighted, or dark, like this.*

### Make a new folder

1. Click **once** on the window in which you want the new folder to appear. (You can only create new folders in *open* windows or directly on the Desktop. To select the Desktop, click once on your hard disk icon.)

2. Take a peek at the File menu and see what the keyboard shortcut is to create a new folder. (Notice it's Command N, like N for New.) Then ignore the File menu.

3. Hold down the Command key and tap the N once.

*Reminder: One of the rules on the iMac is to **select first, then do it to it.** That is, if you want a new folder to appear inside of an open window, you must **first select the open window.** If you want to open a folder, you must **first select the folder.***

### Inserting and removing a CD

You will probably use CDs often. All major software you buy, including games, will arrive on a CD. Your iMac came with a number of CDs.

### Insert a CD

Archie     Archie

*Like most icons, a CD icon appears gray when its window is open. If you don't see the window, double-click the gray icon and its window will come forward.*

1. Some iMacs have a CD tray that you have to pop out so you can put the CD in. If you see a small, colored button on the front of your computer, right under the word "iMac," you have a machine with a CD tray. Push on that colored button and the CD tray will pop partway out. Grab it and gently pull it the rest of the way out.

   If you don't have a tray, skip to Step 3.

2. Put the CD in the tray, shiny side down, label up. Press down slightly in the middle to snap it onto the centerpiece.

3. Give the tray a gentle push back inside the computer.

   If you don't have a tray, just slide the CD into that slot right under the word "iMac" on the front of your computer.

4. The icon for the CD will appear on the Desktop (it might take several seconds). If the CD doesn't open by itself to display its window, double-click the CD icon (it isn't always a round icon).

### Remove a CD

*unmount: When a disk is working and the computer knows it is there, the disk is considered "mounted." Some disks must be "unmounted" before you can remove them.*

1. You cannot make the CD pop out until you first "unmount" the disk. To start with, close all the windows that belong to anything on the CD and **quit all applications** that you used from it.

2. Press on the CD and drag it to the trash can. Really. This will never remove any data from the disk. Go ahead—put it in the trash. If you have a tray, this will make the tray pop out so you can get the disk. If you don't have a tray, the CD itself will pop out.

You could also use the "Put Away" command to unmount and eject a CD: Select the CD by clicking once on it, then press Command Y.

## Play a music CD!

You can play any music CD right on your iMac. You can even insert earphones into the plug on the front of the iMac so you won't bother anybody else.

1. Insert a music CD as you would any other CD. It will probably start playing all by itself in less than a minute. Whether it does or doesn't, go on—

2. Double-click the CD icon to open its window. It looks something like this:

*Each icon in the CD window represents a song, or track, on the CD.*

3. Double-click any track icon to get the CD player (shown below). Use this player just like you would the controls on your own CD player. You can close the player and continue working while your music plays.

*Click this button (top) to make the tracks loop instead of stopping at the end of the CD.*

*Click the tiny triangle on the left to drop down this playlist. Type in the names of the songs, if you like.*

*If you decide to type in the song titles, then you can select them from the menu (shown below).*

*Click the "Prog" button to get the tracks and playlist side-by-side. Drag song titles from the left side and drop them in slots on the right side to rearrange the playlist to suit you and to prevent any songs you don't want to hear from playing (don't drag them over).*

**System Folder**

*This is the System Folder. Although you **can** rename it, it's best not to. The happy faces indicate that this folder is "blessed," or healthy.*

**System Folder**

*If your System Folder ever loses its happy faces, that's a clue that something is very, very wrong. If your System Folder goes blank, don't turn your computer off or it won't start again. Call your friend who knows a lot about Macs.*

### The System Folder

The most important folder on your iMac is the **System Folder.** This folder stores the stuff that makes your computer work. You could throw away everything else on your entire computer and it would still start up for you. But if you throw away your System Folder, or certain elements inside of it, your iMac won't work.

Don't ever put things in the System Folder unless you absolutely, positively, know they belong there!! And don't take things out of the System Folder unless you know it is absolutely, positively, okay to take them out.

When you are ready to learn more about your System Folder, see *The Little Mac Book.* For now, trust me that you don't need to poke around in there for a while.

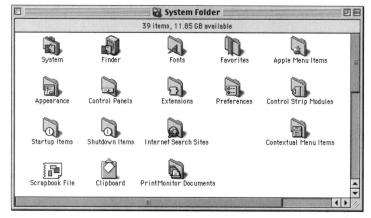

*These are some of the items in your System Folder. Actually, these are the ones that you will probably first start to work with.*

*Remember when you used the Control Panels? They are stored in the Control Panels folder.*

*Remember going to the Apple menu? You can eventually customize that menu by using the Apple Menu Items folder.*

*The typefaces (fonts) you'll use in the Typing chapter are stored here in the Fonts folder.*

## Put your computer to sleep

Your iMac will probably fall asleep if you go away and leave it alone for a while. The screen turns dark and the hard disk "spins down." **To wake it up,** just tap any key at all on the keyboard. It might take a couple of seconds for the computer to wake up—be patient.

You can control how long your iMac waits for you before it goes to sleep by using the Energy Saver control panel:

1. Go to the Apple menu and slide down to "Control Panels." In the menu that pops out to the side, choose "Energy Saver." You'll see this control panel:

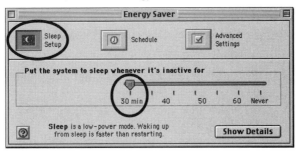

2. Press on the little timer tab (circled, above) and drag it to the right to your desired setting. Feel free to poke all the buttons in here and see what your options are. Put the control panel away by clicking in its little Close Box in the upper-left corner.

### Your monitor Power button might be a Sleep button

On some iMacs (the newest ones) you can put the machine to sleep by pressing the Power button on the monitor (not the one on the keyboard). On the older iMacs, pushing this button will shut down the computer instantly without asking you if you're sure that's what you want to do (it won't hurt anything—if you haven't saved something you were working on, you'll be asked if you want to save your files before it shuts itself off).

How can you tell what *your* machine will do? Well, let it go to sleep at some point. If the green Power button on the monitor pulses and throbs a yellow color, that Power button is actually a Sleep button. You can press it to put your machine to sleep whenever you want, and you can press it while it's pulsing yellow to wake the computer up.

On some iMacs you can use this **keyboard shortcut** to put your machine to sleep: Command Shift 0 (zero, not the letter "O").

## Shut Down

When you have finished working on your computer for the day, you need to shut down. Years ago, people said it was best to leave a computer on all the time, rather than turn it off and back on again, but today it's unnecessary. You will outgrow your computer long before you will turn it on and off too many times.

It's a good habit to quit all of your applications before you shut down (although the iMac will quit them for you if you forget). I explain about opening and quitting applications in Chapter 4, but if you've been following along in this book, you don't have any applications open at the moment.

You can shut down two ways.

1. At the Desktop, go to the Special menu and choose "Shut Down." Your iMac will safely shut down immediately.

2. Or just hit the Power key on your keyboard. You will get this message:

**Restart** will restart your computer without turning the power off.

**Sleep** will put your computer into a "resting" mode. The screen will turn black and the hard disk will stop spinning. **To see the Desktop again,** press any key of your choice on your keyboard.

**Cancel,** of course, will cancel the action of shutting down.

Notice there is a double border around the **Shut Down** button. Whenever you see that double border around a button, it's a visual clue that you can hit the Return or Enter key to activate that button. When you are ready to shut down, try it!

### Power button on the monitor

On the older iMacs you can also Shut Down by pressing the Power button on the monitor. You won't get the reassuring message asking if you're sure you want to shut down, but the iMac will go through its process to close everything up and turn itself off.

On the newer iMacs, the Power button on the monitor does not Shut Down, but puts the iMac to sleep (as explained on the previous page).

# Things to Do with your iMac

Your iMac is loaded with a number of software *applications,* which are programs you use to get work done, like write letters, pay bills, create flyers, and more. This section explains what those applications are and what to do with them. I can't give you a full tutorial on each separate item, but I can tell you what each one does so you can make decisions about which applications you want to ignore, and which ones you want to use and learn more about. And I'll tell you where you can learn more when you're ready.

Many people bought an iMac so they could use the **Internet.** You'll find all the Internet and World Wide Web information in the following section.

**Apple has sold over 2 million iMacs as of December 1999.**

**There are well over 14,000 software applications for the Macintosh.**
Just since May of 1998, over 1,500 **new** applications and peripherals
have been created for the Mac and the iMac.

**It's cheaper for a business to use all Macintoshes.**
The Gartner Group Consulting Service, an independent research firm,
published an extensive study about computers in business. They
concluded that there is no significant extra cost to have both
Macs and PCs in the same business environment, but if a business
used all Macs, their business costs would be lower by 25 percent.

*From Apple's "Why Mac" web site: www.apple.com/whymac/ggstudy*
*Detailed analysis also at MacKiDo web site: www.mackido.com/Myths/Change.html*

**Steve Jobs and Steve Wozniak, inventors of the Apple computer,**
were named the 5th most influential businessmen of this century
in a recent article in the L.A. Times. Oh yeah, Bill Gates was 50th.

**Sure, he makes all his money on Windows, but when it comes to
using it,** it's interesting to note that Microsoft's own annual report
was created on Macintosh computers, and the architectural firm of
Bohlin Cywinski Jackson in Seattle that designed Bill Gate's $50 million
residence used Macintoshes.

# First, an Overview of Applications

Your iMac is filled with all sorts of *programming,* which is the code written by humans that makes the computer work. Different kinds of programming create different kinds of software, such as games, operating systems, utilities, and *applications.* Applications (which are often just called "programs") are written specifically for *you* to create things in, or to work productively in, as opposed to other programs that enable the *computer* to make things happen.

Apple has provided you with several really great applications already installed on your computer. In this chapter you'll read brief explanations of what you have. If any of these applications interest you, read the appropriate chapter for more details about how to get started using it.

**AppleWorks** (it might be called **ClarisWorks** if you have an older iMac) is your main software application. It's called an "integrated software package" because it contains a variety of applications rolled into one package. Each of the next five applications listed on the following pages is actually one module of AppleWorks. Following the brief overview in this chapter is a separate chapter on each module that explains how to open a new document and start creating something in it.

## Word processor

A word processor is the most basic and useful application on any computer—it's a really fancy typewriter. Even the simplest word processor today is more powerful and easier to use than any professional typewriter or typesetting machine in history.

**Use a word processor** to write letters, reports, manuscripts, screenplays, memos, simple newsletters, and anything else you would have used a typewriter for. See pages 76–84 for directions on how to create a word processing document and how to *format* your text.

*format: Make text bold or italic, change typeface or type size, set margins and indents, etc.*

AppleWorks provides you with a number of ready-made files such as letterhead, flyers, résumés, and cover letters, ready for you to customize. See Chapter 4 for an important tutorial on how to use a word processor, including how to save your files.

## Database

A database is like an address book or a recipe box, but you can find and use information much more quickly and powerfully in a computerized database than you can in a paper address book. Let's say you make a contact list in your database that includes checkboxes for whether people are family members, whether you sent them holiday cards, and whether they work at your company or not. In the contact list you also create places (called "fields") where you can type in (called "entering" in computer jargon) birthdates, anniversaries, and the names of their children.

In a paper address book, you would have to flip through all the pages to find the people who have birthdays in October. Using your database, you click a button to find all the people who have birthdays in October. In fact, you can click a button to find all the people who have birthdays in October who also work at your company, live in the neighboring town, and have a child named Ryan.

A database is surprisingly easy to create and work with. **Use a database** to make address books with mailing lists, keep track of business contacts, membership rosters and dues, household or business inventory, or customer information. I guarantee that once you start working with a database you'll find more and more reasons to use it, and you'll be delighted with how easy it is.

*template: A file that is designed and formatted already and is waiting for you to customize it to suit your own needs.*

AppleWorks provides various database *templates* you can customize to keep track of things like collections, family and friends, medical records, and all your music tapes, CDs, and videos, as well as a file to help you plan and keep track of a party or wedding. They are in the AppleWorks Stationery folder inside the AppleWorks (or ClarisWorks) folder. See Chapter 5 for a quick and easy tutorial on putting together a simple database.

## Spreadsheet

A spreadsheet is mostly used for number-crunching and "what-if" scenarios. For instance, you can create a spreadsheet that works out mortgage payments, then change specific data (information) to see what happens if the interest rate goes up or down, if you pay it off in 20 years instead of 30, or if you apply a bigger down payment. You change the *data* and the spreadsheet automatically recalculates everything for you.

*data:* This is simply a computer jargon term that means "information."

You can also enter text in spreadsheets, not just numbers. For instance, you can set up an invoice for your small business that includes your logo, address, contact information, etc., plus an itemized list of the products or services. When you enter the quantity of each item sold, the spreadsheet can calculate the total cost, including the appropriate tax, exactly the way you need it for your particular invoice.

*enter:* Another computer jargon term; this one basically means "type."

You can tell a spreadsheet to look something up; for instance, if you offer a discount on certain quantities, the spreadsheet can look up the correct discount for the number of items you enter, then apply the discount to the total. Of course, the spreadsheet does this "automatically" after *you* have set it up.

You can make all sorts of charts and graphs out of your data. You create the spreadsheet and fill in the data, then click a few buttons and make a variety of visual representations out of all the data or just selected parts of it.

Even if you don't love numbers, there are lots of things you can do with a spreadsheet. In addition to simple and complex invoices, **use a spreadsheet** to create school grading sheets that automatically calculate grades, percentages, and graphs of results; make proposals for clients that display how the variables affect the final estimate; create charts that compare price quotes, etc.

Another great use of a spreadsheet is to make forms, forms of all sorts, even if you never use a number. It's the easiest program in which to make lines, boxes, columns, borders, etc., and you can color in rows, columns, or boxes easily. You can format the text larger, smaller, or use different typefaces.

AppleWorks provides templates to track investments, analyze mortgages, budget events, maintain gradebooks, and more. They are in the AppleWorks Stationery folder in the AppleWorks folder. See Chapter 6 for a short and fun tutorial on how to use a spreadsheet.

## Paint

A paint program lets you "paint" right on the screen. You get to choose from a variety of tools, such as various paintbrushes, pens, a pencil, airbrush, and others. You choose the colors or patterns to paint with and the thickness of the stroke or the style of brush. You can even "pour" paint right from the "can" into a shape, and erase your mistakes. It's too much fun.

Use a paint program to decorate holiday cards, make birthday invitations, entertain your grandchildren, illustrate a story, or anything you would use a paintbrush for in the first place. Don't worry if you don't consider yourself an "artist"—you'll be amazed at what you can do on a computer screen when you have the power to revise on a whim. See Chapter 7 for an unintimidating exercise in using a paint program. Also check out the brief information on Kid Pix on page 74 (not everyone with an iMac has a CD with Kid Pix).

## Draw

A draw program is similar to a paint program in that you are creating artwork of some sort, but a draw program works with hard-edged "objects" instead of with paintbrushes and airbrushes. In a paint program, once you use a brush to paint a color, that's the size and the color it is unless you paint directly over it, just as if you painted it on a wall at home. In a draw program, however, after you draw a shape you can change your mind a million times and replace the color or pattern inside the shape, replace the thickness and color of the border surrounding the shape, and even re-form the shape. You can put shapes in front or in back of each other, and then change the order of the various layers. Rather than painting on a wall, a draw program is more like cutting shapes out of paper and layering them one on top of another.

You can also use text in a draw program and it looks just as good as if you did it in a word processor, plus you can edit (change) it later, just like you can in a word processor. (You can use text in the paint program, but it doesn't look very good when you print it, and the only way to change the text is to erase it and type over.)

See Chapter 8 for a silly exercise in using a draw program.

## Paint vs. draw

So a paint program gives you the flexibility to throw paint around in a very free-form way, and a draw program gives you more flexibility in changing everything, including the size of the finished piece. Walk through the simple tutorials in Chapter 7 (paint) and Chapter 8 (draw) and you'll soon see the difference, and then you can make your own decision about which is the best application to use for a particular project.

## A note about AppleWorks (or ClarisWorks)

All of the applications I've mentioned so far (word processor, database, spreadsheet, paint, and draw) are rolled into the application called AppleWorks on your iMac. However, you can buy an application that is nothing but a very powerful word processor, and you can buy a single application that is nothing but a database, or a spreadsheet, or a paint program. Each individual application, of course, is much more powerful than the one in AppleWorks, but even though the ones you have on your iMac are not quite as powerful as the "dedicated" programs (dedicated to one function), AppleWorks will take you a very long way. When you get to a point where you want more than the applications in AppleWorks can give you, invest in the next level up. You will be able to take all of your data from AppleWorks and put it in the new application. For now, I think you'll probably be happy for quite a while with what you have.

*Tip: When you're ready, go to the Apple web site for lots of tips, techniques, templates, tutorials, free stuff, and other resources for AppleWorks. It's a wonderful gift.*

*www.apple.com/appleworks*

Besides providing so many different applications in one package, AppleWorks makes it so easy to integrate the various elements. For instance, you can write a letter in the word processor that prints out with different names and addresses on each page, the names and addresses coming from your database. You can create a memo for your boss in the word processor with a spreadsheet pie chart directly on the memo. You can create a spreadsheet form and draw your own logo at the top of it using the draw program. Oh, there's so much to do.

*Note: In the Internet folder on your hard disk are the applications you need for online stuff; see the Internet section of this book.*

## Other applications on your iMac (OS 8.x)

The previous pages describe the applications you are most likely to find yourself using regularly. Below is a picture of the Applications folder on iMacs that are running some version of Mac OS 8. In the rest of this chapter are brief descriptions of the purposes of each piece of software; I have provided short, hands-on tutorials for some of the other applications so you can get a good idea of how to use them.

*This player is for playing music CDs on your iMac. See page 55. (The Guide teaches you to use it.)*

*SimpleText is a very basic word processor that can read out loud to you. See page 71.*

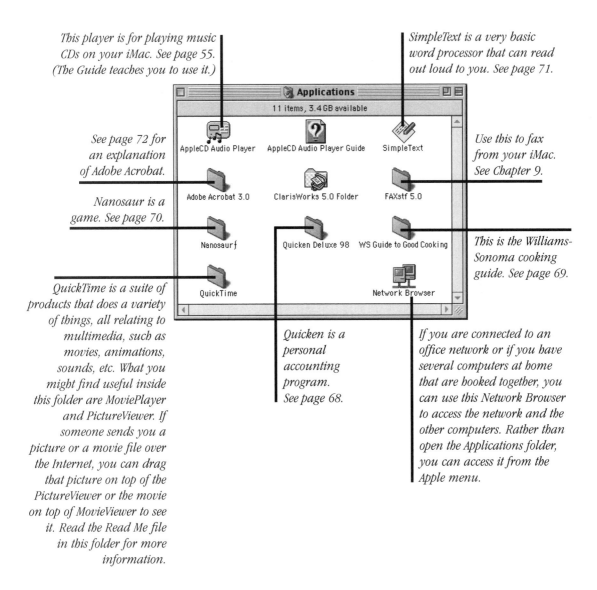

*See page 72 for an explanation of Adobe Acrobat.*

*Nanosaur is a game. See page 70.*

*Use this to fax from your iMac. See Chapter 9.*

*This is the Williams-Sonoma cooking guide. See page 69.*

*QuickTime is a suite of products that does a variety of things, all relating to multimedia, such as movies, animations, sounds, etc. What you might find useful inside this folder are MoviePlayer and PictureViewer. If someone sends you a picture or a movie file over the Internet, you can drag that picture on top of the PictureViewer or the movie on top of MovieViewer to see it. Read the Read Me file in this folder for more information.*

*Quicken is a personal accounting program. See page 68.*

*If you are connected to an office network or if you have several computers at home that are hooked together, you can use this Network Browser to access the network and the other computers. Rather than open the Applications folder, you can access it from the Apple menu.*

## Other applications on your iMac (OS 9)

Below is a picture of the Applications folder on iMacs that are running Mac OS 9. In the rest of this chapter are brief descriptions of the purposes of each piece of software; I have provided short, hands-on tutorials for some of the other applications so you can get a good idea of how to use them.

*Note: In the Internet folder on your hard disk are the applications you need for online stuff; see the Internet section of this book.*

*If you need a graphing calculator, check this out. Double-click this icon to open it, then from the Demo menu choose "Full Demo" to see the amazing things it can do.*

*See Chapter 10 for some tips on viewing DVDs on your iMac.*

*If you are on a fairly large network, this software can make it easier to get around. Check with your human network manager.*

*See page 72 for an explanation of Acrobat.*

*Bugdom is a game. See page 70.*

*iMovie lets you edit your videos. See Chapter 11.*

*SimpleText is a very basic word processor that can read out loud to you. See page 71.*

*This is for playing music CDs on your iMac. See page 55.*

*See Chapter 9 for details on using this software to fax from your iMac.*

*Quicken is a personal accounting program. See page 68.*

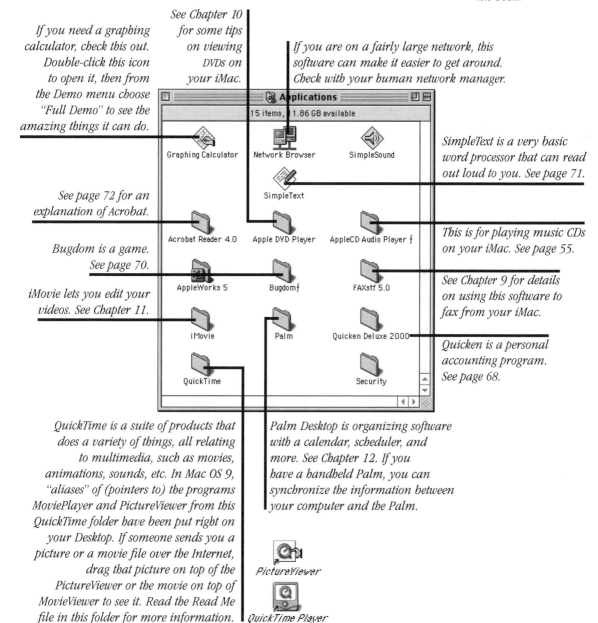

*QuickTime is a suite of products that does a variety of things, all relating to multimedia, such as movies, animations, sounds, etc. In Mac OS 9, "aliases" of (pointers to) the programs MoviePlayer and PictureViewer from this QuickTime folder have been put right on your Desktop. If someone sends you a picture or a movie file over the Internet, drag that picture on top of the PictureViewer or the movie on top of MovieViewer to see it. Read the Read Me file in this folder for more information.*

*Palm Desktop is organizing software with a calendar, scheduler, and more. See Chapter 12. If you have a handheld Palm, you can synchronize the information between your computer and the Palm.*

**Quicken Deluxe 2000**

*Open the Quicken folder. Inside you'll see the icon below.*

**Quicken Deluxe 2000**

*This is the icon for the program. Double-click to open it.*

**Read Me**

*Most applications have a Read Me file in the folder. You should always read it.*

## Quicken

Welcome to the cult of Quicken. This is such an amazing and useful program that there really is practically a cult around it. Quicken is like a very fancy checkbook that knows all about you and fills in the details for you. Actually, it's much more than a checkbook—it's like having your own personal financial manager.

**Use Quicken** to keep track of your bank accounts, cash transactions, assets, liabilities, credit card accounts, portfolios, and mutual funds. You can create one "data file" that holds all the information, yet set up each member of the family with separate accounts within that file so you can keep track of the whole financial picture.

Write your checks in Quicken, and your checkbook is balanced with each check. The account numbers, addresses, and memos can be filled in automatically for recurring bills. Print the checks on your printer, and stuff them into envelopes with windows so the forward and return addresses show through. You can even arrange to have your bills paid electronically, over the Internet, with just the click of a button.

To learn Quicken thoroughly, get the book *Quicken 2000 for Macintosh: Visual QuickStart Guide,* by Tom Negrino, from Peachpit Press.

*The first time you use certain features in Quicken, you get the option to watch these little training movies when you choose various items from the menus. **But** you must first insert the Quicken CD that came with your iMac or you can't watch the movies!*

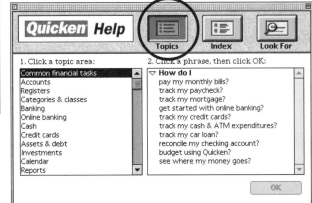

*Quicken has a great "help" file. While Quicken is open, click the Help button at the top of the window. You'll get something like this example. I clicked on the button called "Topics" to get this list of topics. Click the topic of your choice on the left, then find your question on the right. Double-click the question and you'll get an answer. It's great.*

## WS Guide to Good Cooking

This great software is from Williams-Sonoma. It includes a thousand illustrated recipes. You can enter the ingredients you have on hand and find out what recipes can be made with those ingredients, choose how much time you have available to cook, limit the recipes by season, and more.

*The Williams-Sonoma Guide to Good Cooking is an example of "multimedia," meaning it offers a variety of media to enhance the information, such as sound, animation, color, graphics, movies, etc.*

**To use this cooking guide,** you must insert the CD into the iMac *before* you double-click on that WS icon. Once the CD is in, double-click on the "WS Guide" icon, circled below. Once inside the program, click anywhere to make things move along, click to choose items, and use the menu to get to other features. **To quit,** either choose Quit from the little menu at the bottom of the window, or press Command Q (remember, that's a keyboard shortcut—hold the Command key down and tap the letter Q once). **To take the CD out,** make sure you have quit the program, then drag the icon of the CD to the trash. This will pop out the tray slightly (if your iMac has a tray), and you can remove the CD.

WS Guide to Good Cooking
*This folder opens to the window, right.*

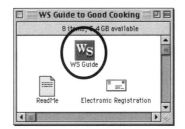

WSGGC
*This is the CD icon.*
**Don't double-click it.**

*After* you insert the CD and you see its icon on the screen (above right), **then** double-click **this** icon in **this** window.

*Click on any of the titles in this picture to go to that section.*

*Just click around and discover things. Use the scroll bars.*

*Click this button to get this menu of options.*

### Bugdom (on newer iMacs)

Bugdomƒ

*The "ƒ" symbol is an old programming clue that means "folder." It's unnecessary now and you can eliminate the symbol wherever you see it.*

Bugdom is a cute little game where Rollie McFly, the last Rollie Pollie in Bugdom, must rescue all the Lady Bugs who are being held prisoner by the evil Fire Ants.

Be sure to read the playing instructions: Double-click "Bugdom Instructions.pdf," which will open the manual in Acrobat (as described on page 72). You can print the manual, if you like. Don't forget to quit Acrobat (press Command Q) when you have finished.

You can speed past the introductory pages by clicking on them. **To quit Bugdom,** press Command Q at any time.

Bugdom™ (OEM)

*This is the game icon. Double-click this one to start the game.*

Bugdom Instructions.pdf

*This is the manual. You need to read it to know how to play the game.*

### Nanosaur (on older iMacs)

Nanosaur is a track-'em-down-and-kill-'em game. Double-click the dinosaur head and the game will start. Once it starts, press the Spacebar to make the images change. Eventually you will get to the game, where a little dinosaur seems to be running from a big dinosaur, and the little dinosaur has a big gun that blows things up. Press the Spacebar to shoot the gun; press the arrow keys to move the dinosaur left, right, and forward. If you want to know more, read the manual (see below), or just bumble your way through it. You can't get hurt.

**To quit,** press Command Q. If you don't think you will ever play this game, feel free to throw the entire Nanosaur folder in the trash. It won't affect anything else on your iMac.

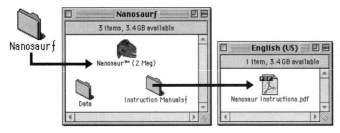

*You'll find an instruction manual in this folder. Double-click the file. You can read it on the screen, or print it up. If you don't want the other manuals in this folder, throw them away. It won't hurt anything.*

## SimpleText

SimpleText is a very small, unsophisticated word processor, but it does some special things. Since you have a full-fledged word processor in AppleWorks (ClarisWorks), you won't really need to use this one to write letters, but you should never throw SimpleText away. Whenever you double-click a file that says "Read Me," that file opens in SimpleText. You can open certain kinds of graphics in it. And a very neat thing it can do is read out loud to you. Try this:

SimpleText

*SimpleText is a sweet little word processor.*

1. Open SimpleText and type some text, or open a Read Me file.

2. Go to the Edit menu and choose "Select All."

3. Go to the Sound menu and choose "Speak Selection." Ha! What a hoot.

4. Now start experimenting with various voices. Go to the Sound menu, slide down to "Voices," and choose another voice from the menu.

5. Go back to the Sound menu and choose "Speak Selection" (make sure the text is selected), or use the keyboard shortcut Command J (if you happen to have accidentally opened an older version of SimpleText, the keyboard shortcut to make the speech is Command H).

Read Me   Read Me First!

*Both of these are SimpleText documents. You should always read the Read Me files.*

Experiment with the story below. Type it into SimpleText exactly as you see it— don't add commas or periods. Go to the Sound menu, slide down to "Voices," and choose "Pipe Organ." Then press Command A to select all, then Command J to hear the story read out loud to you.

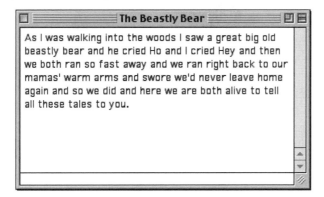

As I was walking into the woods I saw a great big old beastly bear and he cried Ho and I cried Hey and then we both ran so fast away and we ran right back to our mamas' warm arms and swore we'd never leave home again and so we did and here we are both alive to tell all these tales to you.

Adobe Acrobat 3.0

Acrobat Reader 4.0

*This is, of course, the Acrobat folder (you might have version 3 or 4, depending on how new your iMac is).*

Acrobat Reader 3

Acrobat Reader 4

*This is the piece of the Acrobat collection called the Reader. It's free so everyone can read Acrobat files (which are often called "pdf" files, which stands for "portable document format").*

Bugdom Instructions.pdf

*This is an example of a "pdf," an Acrobat file, that you can read with the Acrobat Reader. Just double-click it to open the file in the Reader.*

## Adobe Acrobat

Adobe Acrobat isn't an application that you will be *creating* anything in; it's an application you need to *read* and print documents that someone else wrote. For instance, you probably noticed that you got all these CDs and applications with your iMac, but no printed documentation (no explanations of what to do with it all). But almost every application folder on your iMac includes an "Acrobat" manual, meaning the manual was written, then a copy of it was turned into an "Acrobat" file using the software called Acrobat Distiller. This Acrobat file can be opened and read on any computer (Mac or otherwise), and the pages are fully formatted just as they would look in a printed book. You can choose to read on the screen just the parts of the manual you need, or you can print up the whole thing. It's really great.

You can buy the software Acrobat Exchange and create your own Acrobat files to distribute or put on the web. Get the software at www.adobe.com.

*Click here to turn pages.*

*Click here to print the document.*

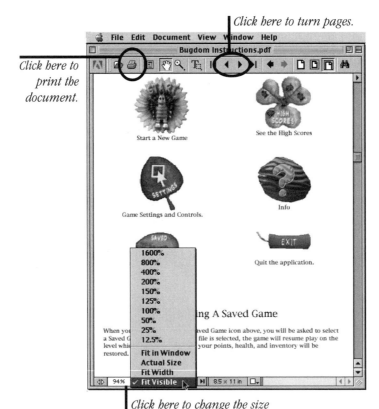

*Click here to change the size of the page on the screen.*

## World Book Encyclopedia

Some iMacs include two CDs for the World Book Encyclopedia. If you have them, they would be in your little packet of CDs that came with your computer.

You have to install part of the encyclopedia software before you can use it, then you must always insert the first CD when you want to find something in it; at times, when you are looking for things, that CD will pop out and you will be asked to insert the other CD. Many articles have links to related material on the World Wide Web; click one of the links and the World Book will connect to the Internet and take you to that page. If your only access to the Internet is America Online, you'll have to open and log on to AOL before you try to read an Internet article by way of World Book.

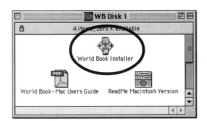

World Book folder

*World Book installs this folder on your hard disk. You can store it wherever you want. To open World Book again, open this folder, then double-click the "World Book" icon.*

*To install World Book, first insert Disk 1 of the World Book Encyclopedia. You'll see this window. Double-click the installer icon (circled, above).*

*After you go through the easy installation process, you'll see this window. Double-click the "World Book" icon to open the program.*

*Experiment with the World Book Encyclopedia. It's very self-explanatory. Hold your mouse over the buttons to see a little tag that tells you what that button is for.*

*Click the Search button.*

*Then type in a topic you want to find in this box.*

*Then click the "Go" button.*

*When you find a topic you like, double-click its name in this list to read the article.*

*This is one of the extra features in the World Book Encyclopedia.*

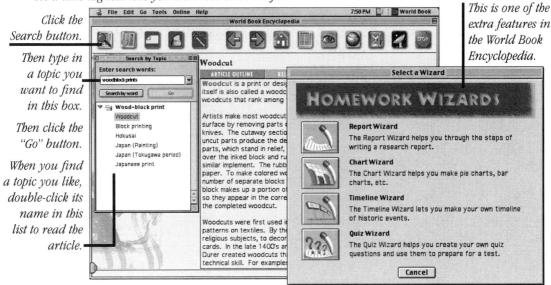

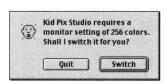

Kid Pix Studio Deluxe

*After you install Kid Pix, you'll have this icon in your hard disk window. Although it looks exactly like the application icon, it's really a folder. (That is not a good example of clear communication.)*

*If you want to make this icon look like a folder so you don't get confused, do this:*

Click once on the icon.

From the File menu, choose "Get Info."

Press Command I.

In the Get Info window that you see, click once on the tiny icon of Kid Pix in the upper-left corner.

From the Edit menu, choose "Clear."

Close the Get Info window (click in its close box).

Now the file looks like the folder it is.

Kid Pix Studio Deluxe

## Kid Pix

Some iMacs include a CD for Kid Pix, a wonderful paint and creativity program for kids (and adults love it, too). If you have it, it would be in your little packet of CDs that came with your computer.

You have to install Kid Pix before you can use it, and for many of the features you have to insert the CD, so you might as well just keep it in while you're working in Kid Pix. Install the application, open it, and experiment. If necessary, have a child show you how it works. If you do the painting tutorial in Chapter 7 before you play with Kid Pix, you'll have a better understanding of how to work with Kid Pix.

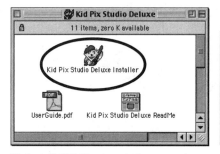

*To install Kid Pix, insert the CD and then double-click the installer icon (circled, above).*

*As soon as the installation is finished, this window will appear. Double-click the application icon (circled, above).*

*When you first open Kid Pix, you'll see this message. It's okay. Kid Pix will switch your monitor settings back to what you had when you quit.*

*There are a number of different modules in Kid Pix, such as Stampimator. While you're in one of the modules, you can use the Application menu (upper-right corner of your menu bar) to go back to the main menu page of Kid Pix. Or press Command Q to quit that particular module.*

*Poke around in the menus! And when all else fails, read the manual! The manual is on the CD—just double-click it. Read it and/or print it.*

UserGuide.pdf

*This is the Kid Pix manual you'll find on the CD.*

# Typing (also called Word Processing) and More*

Typing is one of the basic things you'll be doing on your iMac. In addition to information about typing, this chapter also contains stuff you need to know to work in every application on the iMac. No matter what you plan to use your computer for, you should work through this chapter because all of the things you learn here will apply to everything you'll ever do on the iMac.

If you took a break from the first part of the book and turned off your computer, then of course you must now turn it back on. You're going to open **AppleWorks** (it might be called **ClarisWorks** on an older iMac; they're basically the same program) and make a new word processing document. You'll change the typeface, the type size, the indents, and more. And you'll save the document, close it, and quit the application. It's not an entire tutorial for using a word processor, but it's what you need to get started on your iMac.

### Important note about registering AppleWorks/ClarisWorks

The first time you open AppleWorks, it might ask for your name, business, and the registration number. The registration number is your proof that you own the product, and some software won't even let you install the product until you type in this number. Some AppleWorks messages tell you the registration number is on a card. It's not. You don't have a card. Leave the registration box blank and click the OK button. Later, when it asks when you want to register your product over the modem, click the button "Never." When you register your iMac, that process automatically registers your copy of AppleWorks or ClarisWorks.

*This is the most important chapter in this book! Please read it!

## Open the application AppleWorks (or ClarisWorks)

If you have an older iMac, you might have the application called ClarisWorks instead of the one called AppleWorks 5. If so, just follow any directions for Apple-Works 5. If you have a newer iMac, you might have AppleWorks 6 on your machine. It's the same program as AppleWorks 5, but it's a newer *version;* version 6 looks significantly different from version 5. Follow the directions for AppleWorks 6.

To create a word processing document, you have to open the application AppleWorks because the word processor is one of its components.

*To make it easier to open AppleWorks, you can make an "alias" and put it on your Desktop. See page 237.*

1. Open your hard disk window, if it isn't already open.

2. Double-click the "Applications" folder: see **A,** below.

3. Double-click the "AppleWorks" folder. You'll have either an AppleWorks 5 or AppleWorks 6 folder (on older machines it might be called ClarisWorks): see **B,** below.

4. Find the "AppleWorks" application icon inside that window (**C,** see below). Double-click the application icon.

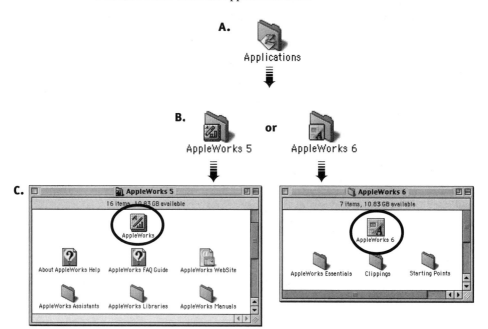

*Circled above are the application icons.*
*Double-click the one you have on your iMac.*

*The manual for AppleWorks is also in the folder.*
*Find it, double-click it, print it, and read it!*

The first thing you see when you "launch" (that is, open) AppleWorks is a dialog box asking which part of the application you want to use because, remember, AppleWorks integrates several applications into one. Depending on whether you have AppleWorks 5 or 6, the "starting points" look different, as shown below. Follow the directions for the version you have to open a new word processing document.

**AppleWorks 5**

Double-click "Word Processing."

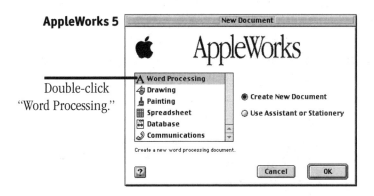

**AppleWorks 6**

Single-click "Word Processing."

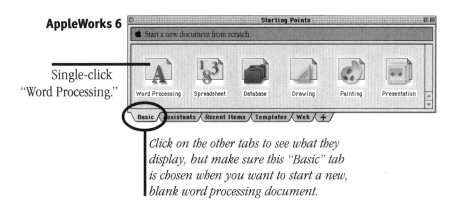

*Click on the other tabs to see what they display, but make sure this "Basic" tab is chosen when you want to start a new, blank word processing document.*

### Create a new page

**Open:** *When you choose the command* **"Open,"** *it means you want to open a document that has already been created! That is very different from creating a **new**, untitled, clean page, as we're doing now.*

So here you are at a blank page! Whenever you create a "new" document on the Macintosh, you will get a clean, blank page, just waiting for you to do something creative to it.

Notice there is a little flashing bar at the top of the page (circled below). That's called the **insertion point,** and you will see it everywhere on the iMac. The insertion point is your visual clue that you are in typing mode. When you touch the keys on the keyboard, *the text will appear wherever that insertion point is flashing.* That's a very important guideline to remember because you'll see the insertion point in every application and in many other places on the iMac.

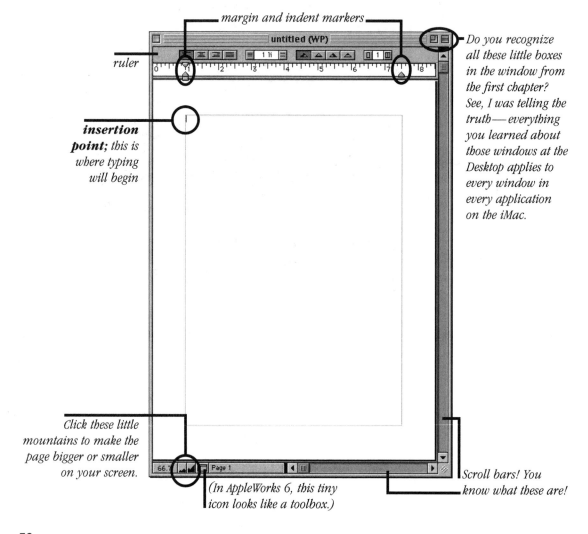

*margin and indent markers*

*ruler*

***insertion point;** this is where typing will begin*

*Do you recognize all these little boxes in the window from the first chapter? See, I was telling the truth—everything you learned about those windows at the Desktop applies to every window in every application on the iMac.*

*Click these little mountains to make the page bigger or smaller on your screen.*

*(In AppleWorks 6, this tiny icon looks like a toolbox.)*

*Scroll bars! You know what these are!*

### Type some text!

Just go ahead and type. When you get to the end of the line, ***do not hit the Return key!*** Just let the type bump into the right edge; it will "wrap" itself onto the next line all by itself. (That's called "word wrap.")

After you have typed a paragraph, go ahead and hit the Return key. In fact, you can hit it twice if you want more space between the paragraphs (later, though, you should read the AppleWorks user's guide [you'll find it in the AppleWorks folder] to learn how to put extra space between the lines without hitting two Returns).

**To fix typos along the way:** If you made a typo just a character or so ago, hit the "Delete" key, found in the upper right of the main section of keys (where the Backspace key is found on typewriters). This will move the insertion point to the left and ***backspace*** over the characters, ***deleting*** them. Make the change and continue typing.

**To fix typos somewhere else on the page:** If the typo is farther back in the line or in another paragraph, of course you don't have to delete all of the characters up to that point! That would be really boring. This is what you do:

1. Put your hand on the mouse and move around on the page (don't click the button!). You'll see that the pointer turns into what's called an **I-beam** while it's positioned over text: ⌶ .

   If you drag the mouse so this I-beam "cursor" is outside of the text area, it turns into a pointer again. Inside the text, it's an I-beam.

2. Okay. So position that I-beam directly to the *right* of the character you want to delete, right between it and the next character, like this:

   seremⅠdipity

3. **Click** the mouse button right there. *This moves the insertion point from wherever it was and positions it where you click.* You can't see the insertion point, though, until you move the I-beam out of the way. So go ahead and push the mouse to the side (don't hold the button down) so the I-beam floats around somewhere else. What you need is that **insertion point.** It should look like this:

   serem|dipity

   *—continued*

*Type one space after periods. This is professional-level type you are creating, not typewriter-level. Read* The Mac is not a typewriter. *By me, of course.*

***Tip:*** *If you want to delete everything on the page and start over, go to the Edit menu and choose "Select All." Then hit the Delete key.*

***cursor:*** *A general term for the moving thing, whether it appears as a pointer, I-beam, insertion point, or anything else.*

**4.** Now that the insertion point is in position, hit the Delete key to remove the wrong character (the one to the *left* of the insertion point), and type the correct character.

serendipity

**5.** To put your insertion point back at the end of your document so you can continue typing (or to put it somewhere else to correct another typo):

- Use the **mouse** to position the I-beam where you want it.
- **Click once.**
- **Move** the I-beam out of the way. *Typing starts at the insertion point, not at the I-beam!*

***Note:*** if you like to keep your hands on the keyboard, you can also use the **arrow keys** on your keyboard to move the insertion point around. Try it.

So type a page. If you want to remove everything you've done so far and start over, go to the Edit menu and choose "Select All," then hit Delete.

**Try this:** Type a headline, then hit two Returns. Type a few paragraphs like the ones shown below. Type a byline at the end ("by" you). Fix your typos. Enjoy yourself. When you've got a few paragraphs, turn the page (of this book) and we'll format the text (change the size, the typeface, indents, etc.).

---

Doll Tearsheet's Answer

Charge me! I scorn you, scurvy companion. What! You poor, base, rascally, cheating, lack-linen mate! Away, you mouldy rogue, away! Away, you cut-purse rascal! You filthy bung, away!

By this swine I'll thrust my knife in your mouldy chaps, an you play the saucy cuttle with me. Away, you bottle-ale rascal! You basket-hilt stale juggler, you!

He, a captain! Hang him, rogue! He lives upon mouldy stewed prunes and dried cakes. A captain! For God's sake, thrust him down stairs; I cannot endure such a fustian rascal.

Doll Tearsheet, from King Henry IV
by William Shakespeare

---

*This is an example of text typed in the word processor of AppleWorks. Yours will look a little different, of course.*

## Formatting in general

Once you understand the basic rule of changing anything on the Macintosh, you can bumble your way through any program. This is the rule:

### Select first. Then do it to it.

That is, the trick is to *select* what you want to change, and *then* go to the menu and make a formatting choice. In a word processor, select text by pressing-and-dragging over the text:

> Position the I-beam at one end of what you want to select,
> then press the mouse button down, hold it down, and drag
> to the other end. **The text will "highlight," like this sentence.**

*Tip: If you miss the last character or two while selecting text, hold down the Shift key, then press-and-drag to select more (or to select less).*

Many changes can be made right from the "ruler," that strip across the top of the page that has all the little icons on it (below), or from the "toolbar" (next page), as well as going to menus and choosing formatting commands.

## Format the text using the ruler

Follow the directions below to use the ruler to change some of the text.

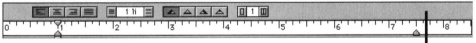

### Center the headline

Select the headline, then click in the tiny icon on the ruler that indicates a centered alignment: ▣ . (Don't ever center a headline by spacing over with the Spacebar—this is not a typewriter!!)

*This whole thing is the **ruler**. Every program that processes text uses a ruler.*

### Justify the rest of the text

Select the rest of the text and click the tiny icon on the ruler that indicates a justified alignment: ▤ (aligned on both the left and right sides).

*Tip: To make any changes to a **paragraph** from the ruler, you don't actually have to select all the characters. Just click once anywhere in the paragraph you want to change.*

### Indent one of the paragraphs

Select a paragraph. In the ruler, position the very tip of the pointer on the tiny rectangle part of the marker on the left of the ruler (shown below). Drag that marker to the *right* to create the indent. Then drag the tiny arrow marker on the right (shown below) to the *left*.

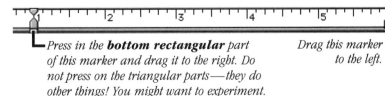

*Press in the **bottom rectangular** part of this marker and drag it to the right. Do not press on the triangular parts—they do other things! You might want to experiment.*

*Drag this marker to the left.*

## Format the text using the toolbar

Of course you've noticed the other bar across the top of the page, full of all kinds of buttons (as shown below). It's rather intimidating, I think, but it will eventually grow useful to you. This is the **toolbar,** and many of the commands from the menus are represented by little buttons so you can click a button instead of having to go to the menu. For instance, which button do you think you could click to make selected text **bold?** As you position your mouse over a button, AppleWorks tells you what that button will do.

The toolbar is customizable (see the user manual). Many of the buttons in it will change when you switch to the different modules in AppleWorks.

**AppleWorks 5**

*This is the **toolbar** in **AppleWorks 5.***

***If your toolbar doesn't look quite like this,*** *perhaps you changed toolbars! Check the toolbar menu (shown to the right) and make sure the "Default" toolbar is selected.*

**AppleWorks 6**

*This is the **toolbar** in **AppleWorks 6.***

### Make text bold or italic

Select the text. Then:

> *In AppleWorks 5,* from the Style menu, choose "Bold" or "Italic."
>
> *In AppleWorks 6,* from the Text menu, choose "Style," then "Bold" or "Italic."

**Or** select the text and use the keyboard shortcut. What is the shortcut for the bold style? For the italic style?

**Or** select the text and use the buttons on the toolbar.

### Change the size of text

Select the text you want to change. In the menu you are about to open, the current size of the text is indicated by the checkmark.

> *In AppleWorks 5,* from the Size menu, choose any size.
> **Or** select the text, then use the Size button on the toolbar. `12 ▼`
>
> *In AppleWorks 6,* from the Text menu, choose "Size," then select a size.

### Change the typeface

Select the text you want to change. In the menu you are about to open, the current font is indicated by the checkmark.

> *In AppleWorks 5,* from the Font menu, choose a typeface (font).
> **Or** select the text, then use the Font button on the toolbar. `Helvetica ▼`
>
> *In AppleWorks 6,* from the Text menu, choose "Font," then choose a typeface (font).

### Color the text

Select the text you want to color. Then:

> *In AppleWorks 5,* click on the tiny color button in the toolbar, as shown below. Slide out to the color of your choice. Just let go when the tip of the pointer is positioned over the color you want.

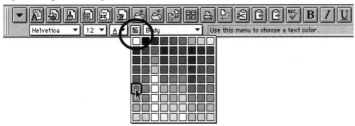

> *In AppleWorks 6,* from the Text menu, choose "Text Color," then choose a color from the palette that appears.

## Unformat the text

To remove bold, italic, or any other formatting, select the text and choose the same formatting again. This is called a *toggle* command, where the same command turns things either on or off.

**Or** choose "Plain Text" to remove all formatting from the selected text. (What is the keyboard shortcut to change selected text to plain text?)

## Example of formatted text

So play around and learn a lot. Below is an example of the same text you saw on page 80, but with simple formatting applied (the headline is red). If you feel comfortable using a word processor, you will feel comfortable anywhere on your iMac.

# Doll Tearsheet's Answer

Charge me! I scorn you, scurvy companion. What! **You poor, base, rascally, cheating, lack-linen mate!** Away, you mouldy rogue, away! Away, you cut-purse rascal! You filthy bung, away!

By this swine I'll thrust my knife in your mouldy chaps, an you play the saucy cuttle with me. Away, you bottle-ale rascal! You basket-hilt stale juggler, you!

He, a captain! Hang him, rogue! He lives upon mouldy stewed prunes and dried cakes. A captain! For God's sake, thrust him down stairs; **I cannot endure such a fustian rascal.**

*Doll Tearsheet, from King Henry IV*
*by William Shakespeare*

## Cut, copy, and paste

One of the most exciting features of working in a word processor is editing. Never again do you have to retype a whole page just to change one paragraph. You can cut (remove) text from one place, put it someplace else, copy a favorite sentence and insert it in the middle of another page, etc. It's too much fun. Makes you want to write books or somethin'.

### Cut

The cut feature **removes** selected text from the page, just as if you took some scissors and cut it out (except there won't be a hole).

### Copy

The copy feature makes a **copy** of the selected text, and leaves the text intact.

### Paste

The paste feature will **insert** onto the page whatever text you *previously* cut or copied. The text will be inserted *wherever the insertion point is flashing*.

## Try it!

So these are the steps to edit your page. Practice on the text you already have on your page, or create a new document (just click on the tiny page icon in the toolbar at the top of the screen).

*Click the button shown below in the toolbar to make a new, blank word processing page.*

*AppleWorks 5, top left on the toolbar.*

### Cut text from one place

1. Select the text by dragging across it (as explained on page 81).
2. From the Edit menu, choose "Cut." Notice the keyboard shortcut is Command X (like Xing or crossing something out).

### Copy text

1. Select the text by dragging across it (as explained on page 81).
2. From the Edit menu, choose "Copy." Notice the keyboard shortcut is Command C (C for copy).

*AppleWorks 6, top right on the toolbar.*

### Paste text somewhere else

1. Click to set the insertion point at the spot where you want to paste the text into.
2. From the Edit menu, choose "Paste." Notice the keyboard shortcut is Command V (like the caret ^ for inserting something).

*Tip: If the Cut, Copy, or Clear commands in the Edit menu are gray, that's because nothing is selected at the moment! Remember, select first, then do it.*

## Clear and Delete

So have you practiced cutting, copying, and pasting? Let me explain what you did. When you cut or copy, the iMac puts the text (or graphic) into an invisible place called the Clipboard. The Clipboard can only hold one item at a time, so as soon as you copy something else, whatever was in the Clipboard disappears. When you paste, you are actually pasting whatever was on the Clipboard. For instance, if you *cut* three different pieces of text and then you *paste,* you will paste the last item that you cut.

You can paste items forever (well, until you turn off the computer). Whatever you cut or copied will stay in the Clipboard even when you change to a different program or come back in several hours. As soon as the power is turned off, though, whatever was in the Clipboard disappears.

*Tip: If you want to see what is currently stored in the Clipboard, go to the Edit menu and choose "Show Clipboard." When you're done, close the Clipboard just like you close any window.*

The **Clear** command from the Edit menu, or the **Delete** key, will get rid of whatever you had *selected,* but it does *not* go to the Clipboard! Think about this for a minute. Let's say you have a photo of your daughter in the Clipboard because you copied it from one document, and you are pasting it into several different letters. If you want to get rid of some text now, you should use the Delete key instead of the Cut command so your daughter's photo stays in the Clipboard, ready to paste again.

## Undo

The Undo command is one of the most important things you can learn. Most of the time you can undo the very last thing you did by going to the Edit menu and choosing "Undo." Let's say you wrote a whole letter and then you selected all the text because you wanted to change the typeface. But before you could choose a new typeface, you leaned on the keyboard and all of the selected text turned into "vnm;id." Before you scream, choose Undo from the Edit menu. Memorize the keyboard shortcut: Command Z. Just undo it.

**Practice using Undo:** Select some text, cut it, then undo it. Paste some text, then undo it.

There are some things you **can't undo** with this command, such as changing a typeface. You just have to change it back to what it was by choosing the first typeface from the menu again. You'll know when an action can't be undone because the Edit menu will tell you.

## Save the document

You have to "save" every document you create on your computer, unless you never want to see it again. Saving it means you store a copy onto the hard disk. After you save a document, you can open it again, make changes, make a copy, add to it, delete from it, etc. You need to save it as soon as you begin, and then you need to save changes every couple of minutes as you work. Why every couple of minutes? Because as you work, all of your changes are being held in "memory," which is a temporary storage space. So temporary, in fact, that if the power in your home or office flickers or goes out, or your computer crashes or freezes up, or the cat chews your power cord, everything that you had not saved will disappear. Nothing can get it back.

Unfortunately, humans seem to learn best through catastrophes. I can almost guarantee that you won't bother saving often until one very late night when you lose the last two hours worth of work on a report that is due first thing in the morning.

*Rule Number One: SOS: Save Often Sweetheart.*

*crash or freeze: When your computer stops working, usually for no reason that you can tell or ever figure out. You will crash. See pages 292–293 to restart your iMac.*

### To save your document

1. From the File menu, choose "Save As…." You will get one of the dialog boxes shown below, depending on your version of AppleWorks.

2. Name your document! Name it something that you will remember and something that gives you a clue as to what this document is about.

3. Click the "Save" button (or hit Return).

4. For right now, your documents will be saved into the folder you made earlier called "Documents" (see page 51).

*Later, when you are more comfortable with your iMac, you need to learn how to save your files into the specific folders you need them in. That's when you should read The Little Mac Book.*

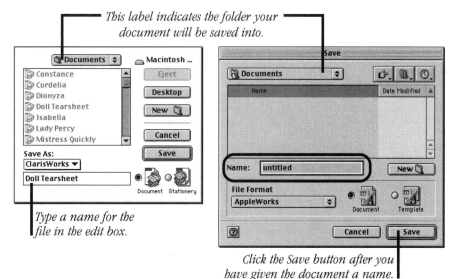

*This label indicates the folder your document will be saved into.*

*Type a name for the file in the edit box.*

*Click the Save button after you have given the document a name.*

## Print the document

You will most likely want to print your documents. First, of course, you must have a printer, and it must be plugged into the iMac and plugged into the wall. (If you don't have a printer yet, see Chapter 21 on "peripherals," which includes printers.)

If you or someone else already hooked up your printer and got your iMac ready to print, then all you have to do to print your document is choose "Print..." from the File menu. You will get a "dialog box," similar to the one shown below, that asks you a few questions. You can ignore everything in that dialog box for now and just click the "Print" button. When you feel like it, go back to this dialog box and poke around, looking at the various options.

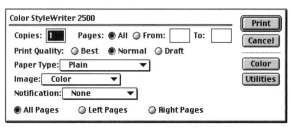

*Your dialog box will probably look different, but it will have many of these same options.*

**Copies:** *If you want more than one copy, type the number in here.*

**Pages:** *If you want to print just a couple of the pages in your document, type the page numbers in these boxes. For instance, you might want to print only pages 5 through 8. If you want to print just page 5, enter 5 in both boxes.*

**Print Quality:** *You might want to experiment with your printer and see what the various qualities look like.*

**Paper Type:** *Some printers print differently to different papers. If you're using transparencies or glossy paper, etc., choose that paper type here.*

**Image:** *You have a choice of printing in black and white, grayscale (still black and white, but with shades of gray), or color (if you have a color printer, of course).*

**Notification:** *In this particular printer's dialog box, notification refers to what sound you want to hear when the printer or computer needs to alert you.*

### Is this your first time?

If this is the very first time you have tried to print, it might not work. Try it. But if it doesn't work, you must quit AppleWorks, do the two steps explained below, and restart the machine. Rather than do that right now, I would suggest you skip the printing part if it doesn't work, finish the rest of this chapter, then come back to this page and setup your iMac for printing.

If no one has prepared your iMac for printing, then you must do two things: **A)** install the "driver" (below) and **B)** choose that driver in the Chooser (next page). After you do this the first time, you (almost) never have to do it again.

### A) Printer drivers

A **printer driver** is a small piece of software that gives your iMac special details about the particular printer you have connected. When you got your printer, you also got a CD with the correct printer driver on it. Follow the directions to install the driver and any related software, or have a knowledgeable friend help you. It's possible that the printer manufacturer wants you to go to the Internet and get the driver. If so, have your friend help you.

The driver must be stored inside a folder called Extensions, which is inside the System Folder. The installation process will put the driver where it belongs. But if you don't see any icon on the CD called "Installer," then you should look for something with the name of your printer. Drag that file from the CD or the Desktop and drop it on top of the closed System Folder. The iMac knows where to put it (inside the Extensions folder) and will put it there for you. You'll get a nice message asking if that's okay. Yes, it is.

SC 740

PSPrinter

LaserWriter 8

Acrobat™ PDFWriter

*These are examples of printer driver icons.*

System Folder

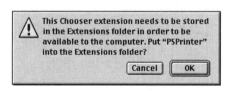

This Chooser extension needs to be stored in the Extensions folder in order to be available to the computer. Put "PSPrinter" into the Extensions folder?

[ Cancel ]  [ OK ]

After installing any software, you should always restart your computer. Go to the Special menu and choose "Restart." After your computer boots all the way up, go to the Chooser (see the next page).

### B) The Chooser

After you install the driver and restart your computer (previous page), you have to go to the **Chooser** and tell your iMac which printer you choose to print to. You only need to do this the very first time you print to a particular printer!

1. Turn on your printer and let it warm up for a minute.

2. From the Apple menu, choose "Chooser."

3. In the left half of the dialog box, click on the icon that represents your printer.

4. If your printer cost less than eight hundred dollars, you'll probably see "USB Port" in the right half of the dialog box, as shown below. Click it.

   If your printer was an expensive PostScript printer (it cost at least a thousand dollars and probably doesn't print in color), click the "Setup" button and click "Auto" (not shown below).

5. You might get a message about AppleTalk because certain printers need it on (active) and other printers need it off (inactive). The iMac will determine whether your printer needs it on or off and will set it to the correct choice.

*All of these icons are various printer drivers. You might see several in your Chooser.*

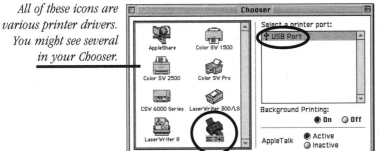

*You must select two items: your driver and the port.*

*If no port appears in this box, the most likely reasons are 1) either the printer is not turned on, or 2) the cable is not attached properly to either the computer or the printer.*

6. To close the Chooser, click in its close box. You will probably see this message:

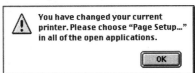

> ⚠ **You have changed your current printer. Please choose "Page Setup…" in all of the open applications.**
>
> [ OK ]

7. Go back to your document. From the File menu, choose "Page Setup…," then just click OK, per the message above.

8. From the File menu, choose "Print…."

## Close the document

When you are finished working on the document, you "close" it, which is like removing the page (the document) from the typewriter (the word processor) and putting the page in a filing cabinet.

1. Click in the little close box, just as you would to close any window.
   **Or** go to the File menu and choose "Close."
   **Or** use the keyboard shortcut, Command W.

2. If you didn't save the document at the last minute, you will get a dialog box asking if you want to save it or not. Of course, you should click "Save."

> ⚠ **Save changes to the document "Queen Gertrude" before closing?**
> [ Don't Save ]  [ Cancel ]  [ Save ]

## Create another document, or open one you already created

1. If you want to **create another** document, just single-click on the word processing icon in the toolbar: 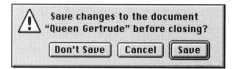 or .

2. If you want to **open a document** you already created, go to the File menu, choose "Open...," and you should see the document's name in the list. Double-click the name.

3. You don't have to close one document before you open another! You can have dozens of documents open at the same time. They will all be listed in the Window menu in AppleWorks.

## If you made a terrible mistake

If you did something terrible to the document, like perhaps you selected everything and accidentally deleted it, do this:

*AppleWorks 5:* Close the document, but *do not* click the "Save" button. Reopen the document and it will appear *just as it was the last time you saved it* (let's hope that wasn't too long ago!).

*AppleWorks 6:* From the File menu, choose "Revert." This will revert the document *back to the way it was the last time you saved it*. That means if you didn't save the document recently, you are out of luck. Save often, sweetie.

## Quit the application

**You don't have to quit right now,** if you want to continue on with the exercises in this section! Or you might want to practice quitting, then you'll just reopen AppleWorks when you are ready to read the next chapter.

AppleWorks 6

*While an application is open, its icon is gray.*

AppleWorks 6

*When you have successfully quit an application, its icon is complete and colorful.*

It's important to understand exactly what happens when you **quit.** You see, when you **close** the document, you are essentially putting that one piece of paper away, but the word processor itself (the typewriter) is still on the desk. Now, it might *look* like you put the word processor away because when you close the document, you see the Desktop, as if nothing is there. But trust me, that typewriter, I mean word processor, is still sitting in the Macintosh memory (desk), taking up space. It does not go away until you **quit.**

### To quit the application

- Go to the File menu and choose "Quit."

  **Or** use the keyboard shortcut, Command Q.

To know whether an application is still open or whether you really did quit, check the **Application menu,** the one on the far-right of the menu bar. If it shows "AppleWorks" (or "ClarisWorks"), then you didn't quit and the word processor is still open. If you see AppleWorks in this menu, select it, then press Command Q again. Check back in this menu to make sure the application has really quit.

*Always check the Application menu to make sure an application has really quit.*

*These three items are applications that are still open (the Finder is always open). The checkmark is next to the one that is "active" at the moment.*

If you like, you can "tear off" that Application menu and leave it sitting on your Desktop so you are always aware of which applications are open and in memory. See page 242 for more information on this important menu.

*Just press-and-drag your mouse down the Application menu (as shown above) and this menu will "tear off" (as shown to the left). When you let go of the mouse, the menu will float right there. Try it.*

*To put this menu away, click its Close Box.*

## On the Desktop, find the document you just created

So you saved and closed the document, and you quit AppleWorks, and now it is the next day and you want to read that letter again or maybe make some changes to it. Where is it? Well, if you did the exercise on page 51 to create a Documents folder on your hard disk, then everything you save automatically goes into that folder. This is a good thing for a while, because you can always go there and find whatever it was you created. Later, when you feel more comfortable working with your iMac, you will want to start creating different folders for different projects and saving your documents directly into the specific folders.

To find your document all you have to do is look inside the Documents folder. Look for it in your hard disk window. If you did not do that exercise to create a Documents folder, then your document was probably automatically stored inside the AppleWorks folder.

Documents

*If you made a Documents folder, this is what it looks like. It's probably on your Desktop.*

*If you can't find your document, see Chapter 19 to use Sherlock to find it for you.*

### Open the Documents folder

1. Open your hard disk window, then double-click on the Documents folder (or go back to the AppleWorks folder). The folder will open to a window, of course, and inside you will probably see icons of every document you've made so far.

2. If you prefer to see a *list* of the documents in this window instead of the icons, as shown in the example below, go to the View menu and choose "by List."

Documents

*This is the Documents folder. Don't rename it or your computer will make you a new one and then you might get confused about where things are stored.*

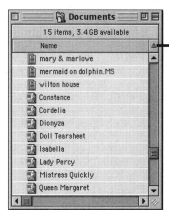

*Click this triangle to alphabetize the files backwards or forwards. Click again to alphabetize them in the other direction.*

*This is an example showing several documents inside the Documents folder.*

### A few guidelines for creating professional-level text

Here are some basic rules for creating type on your iMac. Your iMac is not a typewriter. You have to let go of the rules you either learned from a typing teacher or from someone who grew up on a typewriter—it's different when you are setting type at the professional-level that you are on the Macintosh computers. Trust me. I was trained as a medical secretary and I was trained as a typographer, so I am well aware of the difference between the two.

- One space after periods. Really.

- One space after colons, semicolons, question marks, exclamation points, and all other punctuation.

- Periods and commas always go inside of quotation marks. Always.

- Question marks and exclamation points go inside or outside quotation marks depending on whether they belong to the phrase inside the quotes.

- Professional type does not use the half-inch or five-space indent that we used on typewriters. The correct space is equivalent to about two spaces.

- Use an indent for new paragraphs, **or** space between the paragraphs, but not both.

- Learn to use your software to set about a half-line space between paragraphs, instead of hitting two Returns.

- Read *The Mac is not a typewriter.*

- If you discover you like this typesetting stuff and want to learn much more about how to make your type beautiful and sophisticated, read *The Non-Designer's Type Book,* by me.

# Make a Simple Database

5

A database is like a really fancy recipe card box, like the kind in which you might store recipes, addresses, baseball cards, or dues-paying membership information. But in a database you can do a lot more with the information than you can with the recipe cards.

In this chapter we're going to create a new, blank database to serve as an address book for you. Just follow the steps in this chapter and in a couple of minutes you'll have an address book you can use for years. If you like working in a database, there are several other books that will teach you much more, and you can build directly on the database you create right here. Even without reading anything else, you'll be able to make another database for any other collection of information you happen to have, such as research data, personal possessions, scout troop members, etc.

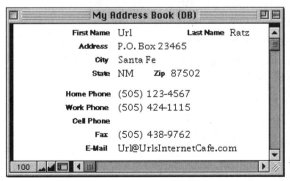

*This is a very simple database that took about five minutes to build. You can add to it, adapt it, change it, rearrange the layout, search it, print labels with it, and much more.*

## Get ready to make a database

Now, you might be in one of four different situations, depending on whether you've been following along or not. Choose the situation you're in and follow the directions:

**A. You just finished the word processing exercise and the letter is still on your screen.**

1. Save this letter once again: press Command S.

2. Click in its little close box in the upper-left corner, or use the keyboard shortcut Command W (W for Window).

**B. You finished the word processing exercise, saved and closed it, and didn't quit AppleWorks. In the far-right corner of the menu bar, it says AppleWorks (or ClarisWorks) with a tiny logo (  ).**

○ You are exactly where you need to be! Don't touch anything. Go to the top of the next page (in this book).

**C. You finished the word processing exercise, saved and closed it, and didn't quit AppleWorks. BUT in the far-right corner of the menu bar, you see a tiny icon of the Macintosh logo ( ).**

1. Click once on that little happy Mac icon to get the Application menu, as shown to the left.

2. If you didn't actually quit AppleWorks, you will see it listed in the Application menu. Select it.

3. After you select AppleWorks, the special toolbar should appear at the top of the screen. Go to the next page (in this book).

*This is the Application menu. The **checkmark** indicates what is active, or open, at the moment.*

**D. You skipped the word processing exercise, or you turned off your computer and came back later, and AppleWorks is not open on your iMac.**

1. Open AppleWorks just like you did the first time: double-click its icon. (Remember, the AppleWorks *application* is inside the AppleWorks *folder!*)

2. *AppleWorks 5:* Double-click the choice "Database."

   *AppleWorks 6:* Single-click the choice "Database."

3. Go to the next page (of this book), but skip the first step because you just started a new document.

AppleWorks 6

AppleWorks 6

*The AppleWorks **application icon** is **inside** the folder!*

## Create a new database document

**1.** If you do not yet have the beginning of a database on your screen (as shown under Step 3), single-click the Database button in the toolbar (circled, below).

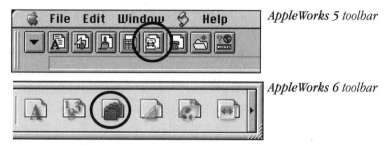

*AppleWorks 5 toolbar*

*AppleWorks 6 toolbar*

**2.** When you start a new database, the first thing you see is the "Define Database Fields" dialog box (shown below).

A database is filled with "fields" that contain information. What you need to do here is *name* the fields that you plan to include in your address book, such as First Name, Last Name, Address, City, State, etc. When you're done, each of these labels will have a space in which to enter the appropriate information.

**3.** So type "First Name" in the edit box, as you see in the example circled below.

*—continued*

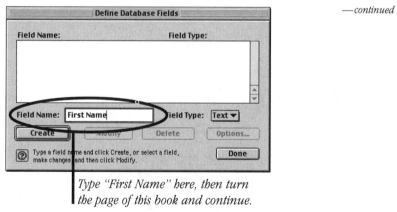

*Type "First Name" here, then turn the page of this book and continue.*

**4.** Click the "Create" button. This puts the field name in the list (shown below), and AppleWorks automatically asks what you want the name of the next field to be. In the next one, type "Last Name," then click "Create."

> **Tip:** You always want to have separate fields for first names and last names because the computer alphabetizes by the *first letter* in the field. If you have both first and last names in one field (such as "Robin Williams"), you'll get an alphabetized list by first names, which isn't useful very often. If you type the last name, comma, first name ("Williams, Robin") then your mailing labels will print exactly that, which is kind of dorky.
>
> So always set up one field for first names and one field for last names.

**5.** Continue adding fields until you have all the ones you need for an address book, until you get to the zip code.

**6.** When you get to the zip code, do an extra step:

Notice to the right of the "Field Name" is "Field Type" (circled, below). A field type will help you automatically format the data that you'll be typing into that field. For instance, if you were to choose the field type "Time," the database would automatically enter the time, and it would be formatted to specifications that you can choose.

So for the zip code field, press on the "Field Type" menu where it says "Text" and you'll get the pop-up menu. Choose "Number," since a zip code is always a number.

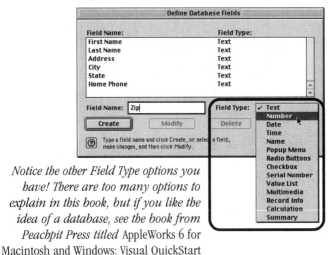

*Notice the other Field Type options you have! There are too many options to explain in this book, but if you like the idea of a database, see the book from Peachpit Press titled* AppleWorks 6 for Macintosh and Windows: Visual QuickStart Guide, *by Nolan Hester, to learn more.*

**7.** Continue to add any other fields you might want in your address book. ***Make sure you change the "Field Type" back to Text (or whatever type you need) for any additions after "zip code."***

**8.** When you have added all the fields you need, click the "Done" button. (You can always add, delete, or modify fields at any time, even after you save the database.)

After you click "Done," you will see the database. It looks something like this:

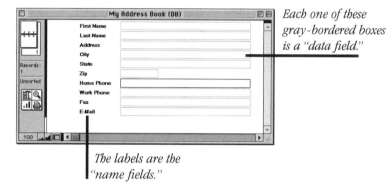

*Each one of these gray-bordered boxes is a "data field."*

*Tip: If you clicked somewhere and everything turned black or another color, click once in the right-hand area where the "data fields" are.*

*The labels are the "name fields."*

**9.** Before you start entering data, save this document! Go to the File menu, choose "Save As…," and name this database.

**10.** Now turn the page of this book and start entering data.

*enter: Computer jargon that simply means to type information.*

### Enter data into the database

Your next task in a database is to "enter data," which means to type in the information. It's so easy.

#### Enter the first address

1. Click in the "First Name" *field*. You should see the insertion point flashing, which is your visual clue that the computer is ready for you to type. So type the first name of the person whose information you want in your database.

*Tip: If you accidentally hit the Tab key too many times, **hold down** the Shift key and hit the Tab key; it will move the insertion point **upward** through the fields.*

2. Now, you *could* pick up the mouse and click in the next field, the one for "Last Name." But the *easier* thing to do is hit the Tab key, which will send the insertion point to the next field.

   So hit the Tab key, type the last name, then hit the Tab key again.

3. Continue through the rest of the fields, typing and tabbing. If you don't have information for one of the fields, just skip it (Tab twice). You can always come back next week and fill it in, or change or delete any information.

   After everything is filled in, your database should look something like this:

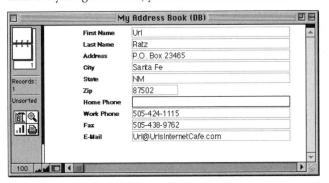

*I didn't know Url's home phone number, so I left it blank. It's okay to leave fields blank.*

## Make more records

This one collection of fields for one person is called a "record." Your database can have hundreds or thousands of records in it. Each individual record is sort of like one recipe card.

### Make another record

1. Go to the Edit menu and choose "New Record," **or** press Command R.
2. The new record will be added directly after the record you are currently in.

## Formatting

You can change the typeface, size, placement, etc., of any field name or of the data in any individual field. This is called "formatting."

### Format the name fields

1. From the Layout menu, choose "Layout."
2. In the record, click on a field *name,* such as "City."
3. To select the rest of the names, hold down the Shift key and click on any of the other name fields that you want to have the same typeface and size. When you've selected all, let go of the Shift key, but don't click anywhere!
4. From the Format menu, slide down to "Font," then out to the side and pick a font (typeface) you like.
5. Click anywhere to deselect the name fields. (To enter more data, go back to the Layout menu and choose "Browse.")

*This is what a name field looks like when you select it.*

### Format the data fields

1. Follow the same directions as above (choose "Layout" from the Layout menu), but this time select the fields themselves: Click on the field *data,* the box where you actually type the text.
2. Hold down the Shift key and click on any of the other data fields that you want to have the same typeface and size. When you have them all selected, let go of the Shift key, but don't click anywhere!
3. Use the Format menu again to format the information.

   *In AppleWorks 5,* try this shortcut: click on the font menu right in the toolbar and choose a font from there: 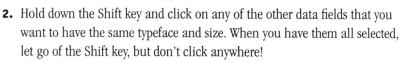 *You can also choose a new type size.*
4. Click anywhere to deselect the data fields.

   To enter more data, go back to the Layout menu and choose "Browse."

*This is what the data field looks like when you select it.*

## Change the layout

You can rearrange the name and data fields, and you can resize them.

1. From the Layout menu, choose "Layout."

2. Press in the *middle* of any field (name or data), and drag it into a **different position.** You can hold the Shift key down and click on more than one field to select a group, then *let go* of the Shift key and move the entire group.

*Press-and-drag in the **middle** of a field to move it.*

3. **Resize any field:** Click once on it, then position the tip of the pointer in one of the tiny, square handles that appears. Press-and-drag any handle to resize the field. Try it.

*Press-and-drag the **handle** of a field to resize it.*

Rearrange your database into a more pleasing and sensible order.

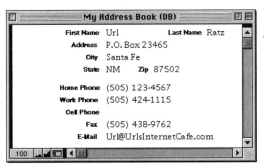

*This is a more logical placement of fields than what automatically appears.*

## Make a list of the records

I find it helpful to view the records as a list. That way I can see a whole collection at a glance. You can enter data while it is in a list view.

1. From the Layout menu, choose "List."

2. **To rearrange the columns,** press-and-drag any column heading.

3. **To resize the width of any column,** position the cursor directly on the dotted line between two column headings (as shown below). The cursor turns into a two-headed arrow. With this cursor, press-and-drag to the left or right to widen or narrow a column.

*Press-and-drag in the **middle** of any column heading to move the column.*

*Press-and-drag **between** columns to resize them.*

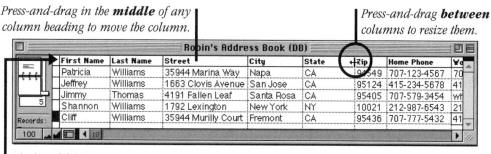

*The list of field names becomes the column headings.*

## Sort the information in your database

*Tip:* *If you don't enter data exactly the same way every time, then your sort won't work very well. For instance, if you enter McCoy (no space) or Mc Coy (with a space), the name with the space will be sorted before the name with no space (in computerized alphabetizing, spaces come before letters).*

*Capital letters are sorted differently from lowercase, also, so Penelope vonSchnitzel would come before Abigail VonSchnitzel if you sort by last names.*

Once your database is set up, you can sort (organize) the information in a number of ways. If you don't have enough records to organize in your file yet, take a moment to add a few more. Then experiment with sorting.

1. From the Layout menu, choose "Browse" or "List."

2. From the Organize menu, choose "Sort Records…."
   You'll get the "Sort Records" dialog box, as shown below.

3. The "Field List" on the left contains every field in your database. Select the field you want to alphabetize by (such as "Last Name"), then click the "Move" button (shown below).

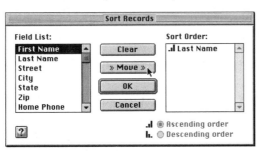

*You can sort by a number of fields. The computer will start with the first field, then sort the next, and so on.*

Maybe you have a lot of people with the same last name. If you move "First Name" over to the "Sort Order" box, under "Last Name," then the iMac will first alphabetize all the last names, and then alphabetize all the first names within that group. So "Gerald Williams" will be in the list before "Patricia Williams."

4. When you have arranged your sort orders, click OK to go back to your list, which is now organized per your request.

So think of it—you can sort by city, then by last name, then by first name. Your database will then display all of your information organized by city, with people's names alphabetized by city. The possibilities are amazing. Enter a whole bunch of records and experiment. Enter your entire music CD collection, then organize them by genre, artist, and recording date from oldest recording to newest.

## Find certain records

Often you will want to select, or find, just certain records. For instance, maybe you want to find the clients who live in a certain city or who owe you money. (Of course, if you want to find the clients who owe you money, you must have set up the database with a field for that information in the first place.)

1. From the Layout menu, choose "Find."

2. You see what looks like a blank record (shown below). Type the data you want to find in the field you want to find. For instance, if you want to find all the people with the last name of Williams, type "Williams" into the "Last Name" field.

   If you want to find all the people named Williams who live in the city of Santa Rosa, type "Williams" in the "Last Name" field, and type "Santa Rosa" in the "City" field.

   (If you want to find all the people who owe you more than $150 and you previously set up a formula field to figure that out, use the "Match" feature, under the Organize menu.)

   You can fill in as many fields as you need to narrow the search down to just what you want to find.

3. On the far left, click "All" if you want to find records within your entire database, or click "Visible" if you did a previous search or match and want to find files within that selection.

4. After you do a search, you probably want all of your records back. From the Organize menu, choose "Show All Records."

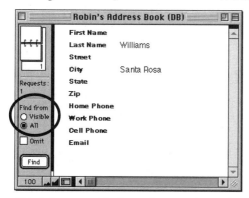

*This is how you "find" a selection of records in your database.*

## Print your database

Of course you can print any of the information in your database. Often you will want to limit the records you print by first finding or matching certain criteria. When you print, only the visible records (the ones you found or matched) will print.

1. If you want to limit the records, find or match the ones to print.

2. From the Layout menu, choose "Browse" if you want to print the data as the record displays it, or "List" if you want to print a list.

3. If you're printing a list, the fields can stretch across several pages. Go to the Window menu and choose "Page Preview" (AppleWorks 5) or "Page View" (AppleWorks 6).

    You will get a preview of how your database will look on the printed page. You might need to enlarge the window as large as possible (drag in the Size Box in the bottom-right corner of the window). Or click the little mountain icon (in the bottom-left corner of the window, as shown on page 78) to reduce the picture on the screen.

    Right in the preview you can make the columns narrower and rearrange them so things fit on the page better (as you did on page 103).

4. From the File menu, choose "Print...." You might have to experiment with various arrangements to get the printed results you want.

# Make a Simple Spreadsheet

A spreadsheet is a very interesting and useful program. It lets you work with numbers and formulas and then play with the possibilities. It can automate just about any sort of scenario you want to create with numbers, such as the various options in a mortgage payment, the variety of discounts and taxable options in an invoice, the ups and downs of your income, and so much more. A spreadsheet is a very versatile program to have on your computer. And it does a lot more than crunch numbers—you can easily make forms, signs, calendars, tables of data, to-do lists, and more.

In this chapter I'll show you the basics of working in a spreadsheet. Once you get the hang of just a couple of key features, you'll have fun creating all kinds of stuff.

## Get ready to create a spreadsheet

Now, you might be in one of four different situations, depending on whether you've been following along or not. Choose the situation you're in and follow the directions:

**A. You just finished the database exercise and that file is still on your screen.**

**1.** Save this file once again: press Command S.

**2.** Click in its little close box in the upper-left corner, or use the keyboard shortcut Command W (W for Window).

**3.** Click the Spreadsheet button in the toolbar:  or  .

**B. You finished the database exercise, saved and closed it, and didn't quit AppleWorks. In the far right corner of the menu bar, you see the word AppleWorks (or ClarisWorks) and a tiny icon ( ).**

○ You are exactly where you need to be! Click the Spreadsheet button in the toolbar: or .

*This is the Application menu. The **checkmark** indicates what is active, or open, at the moment.*

**C. You finished the database exercise, saved and closed it, and did not quit AppleWorks. BUT in the far right corner of the menu bar, you see a tiny icon of the Macintosh logo ( ).**

**1.** Click once on that little happy Mac icon to get the Application menu, as shown to the left.

**2.** If you didn't actually quit AppleWorks, you will see its name listed in the Application menu. Select it.

**3.** After you select AppleWorks, you will see the toolbar across the top. Click the Spreadsheet button: or .

AppleWorks 6

*This icon (or ClarisWorks) is what you double-click to open the application. This icon is **inside** the AppleWorks (ClarisWorks) **folder.***

**D. You skipped the database exercise, or you turned off your computer and came back later, and AppleWorks is not open on your iMac.**

**1.** Open AppleWorks just like you did the first time: double-click the *application* icon (it's *inside* the AppleWorks folder).

**2.** *AppleWorks 5:* Double-click "Spreadsheet."

*AppleWorks 6:* Single-click "Spreadsheet."

## Create a spreadsheet document

Let's make a simple spreadsheet to become familiar with how a spreadsheet functions. It's a little different from other programs you've worked with.

### Columns, rows, and cells

What you see in front of you is basically a huge sheet of grid paper. Across the top you see alphabetic **column headings.** Down the left side you see numeric **row headings.** Each tiny block you see on the screen is a **cell.** Each cell has an **address,** which is the intersection of the column and row. In the example to the right, the selected cell's address is B2 because it is in column B and row 2.

*The selected cell has a darker border around it. This is cell B2.*

### Entering data into the cells

At first, the most odd thing about a spreadsheet is that when you select a cell and try to type something into it, nothing seems to happen—the text does not appear in the cell. The text you type actually appears in the **entry bar,** above the spreadsheet itself, as shown in the example below. Try it: **click in cell B2,** then type *Frogs R Us Web Design.* The text will appear in the entry bar. (If you don't click in cell B2, the rest of this exercise won't work!)

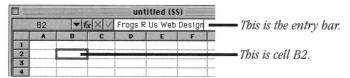

—— *This is the entry bar.*

—— *This is cell B2.*

It doesn't look like the text will fit into that tiny cell, and it won't. But in a spreadsheet, as opposed to a database, the text will just go right through the cell into the next one, as long as the next one is empty. To make the text appear in the cell, you have to **enter** it: hit the Enter key (on the far-right, bottom end of your keyboard). Then it will look like this:

*You still see the text in the entry bar because that cell (B2) is still selected.*

Click in any other cell and that thick selection border will move. Now experiment with this feature of a spreadsheet: Click on the word "Design," which looks like it is in cell C2. Does the text appear in the entry bar? No, because cell C2 is actually empty. Even though the text spills over to C2, it is *entered* into cell B2, and if you want to change the data, you have to *select* cell B2.

**Tip:** *There are a number of ways to enter the data into a cell. Choose the method depending on what you want to do next:*

*The **Return key** enters data and selects the next cell downward.*

*The **Tab key** enters data and selects the next cell to the right.*

*The **Enter key** or clicking the **check mark in the entry bar** enters data and keeps the selected cell selected.*

### Format the spreadsheet text

Go ahead and format that text. Just like in the word processor and the database, you have to select the text first, then choose your formatting, right? In a spreadsheet you select the text by selecting the *cell* in which it is entered. So click once on **B2.**

Now go to the Format menu and choose a font, size, and color. For this example, choose the font Impact and the size 24. Oops, it doesn't fit, does it?

That's okay, let's just open up that row. Position the spreadsheet cursor (✛) **in the row heading** (*not* on the spreadsheet page) directly on the line dividing two rows, as shown below. The cursor will change to a two-headed arrow. While it's the two-headed arrow, press-and-drag the line *downward* until the text fits in nicely. You might want to leave a little extra space at the top so it's not too close to the edge.

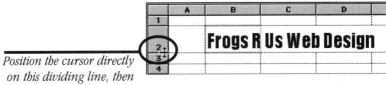

*Position the cursor directly on this dividing line, then drag downward.*

*If you like, also drag the **right side of column heading A** to the left or right, depending on how far away from the left edge you want the title.*

## Add a graphic to the spreadsheet

Let's juice this up a little bit with a graphic. The process is a little different in the two versions of AppleWorks. If you are using AppleWorks 5 or ClarisWorks, follow the directions below. If you are using AppleWorks 6, see the next page.

### Add a graphic in AppleWorks 5 or ClarisWorks

1. From the File menu, slide down to "Library," then from the other menu that pops out (shown below), choose "Animals." You'll get a little floating library "palette" of animal images (also shown below, right).

   This palette acts like any window: scroll to see the list of animals, move it around by dragging the title bar, close it with the Close Box.

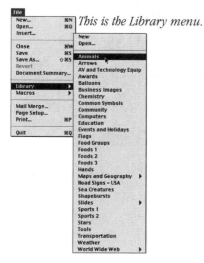
*This is the Library menu.*

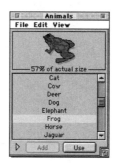
*Once you choose an item from the Library menu, you'll get this floating palette.*

2. Scroll down the list in the Animals palette to find "Frog," click once on "Frog," then click the "Use" button. That cute little frog will land on your spreadsheet, and you'll see "handles" on each corner of the graphic. The handles indicate the graphic is selected.

3. Press in the *middle* of the graphic and drag it into the position shown below.

**Frogs R Us Web Design**

4. You can put the Animals library away now (click in its Close Box).

### Add a graphic in AppleWorks 6

1. From the File menu, choose "Show Clippings." You'll get a floating "palette" with a variety of images, called clippings.

   Click on a tab at the bottom of the palette to see the different categories. Scroll to see the images. Move the palette around by dragging the title bar, and close it with the Close Box.

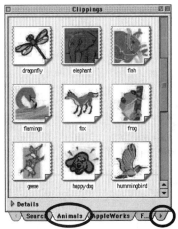

*Click on a tab to display the images in that category.*      *Click the arrow tabs to display more categories.*

2. Click the "Animals" tab. Scroll down the images and find the frog. Press on that frog and drag him to your spreadsheet; let go and he will drop right on the page. You'll see "handles" on each corner of the graphic; the handles indicate the graphic is selected.

3. **Resize the frog:** Hold down the Shift key, then drag a corner handle to make it smaller.

4. **Flip the frog** so it fits into your title: While the frog is still selected (click once on him if it's not), go to the Arrange menu and choose "Flip Horizontally."

5. Press in the *middle* of the graphic and drag it into the position shown below.

6. You can put the Clippings palette away now (click in its Close Box).

## Add names and numbers to the spreadsheet

Now that you've got a fun start, put some numbers in. Let's pretend this is a list of web design clients who owe you money, and you want to see the total of how much money they owe. You need a list of names and amounts.

1. Click in cell **C4.**

2. The entry bar is ready, waiting for you to type. Type the name of someone who owes you money—*but don't hit the Enter key yet!*

3. Instead of using the Enter key, use the **Return key** this time.
   This will enter the data and select the next cell below C4.
   (If you already hit the Enter key, don't worry. Select cell C5 now.)

4. Enter another name, then hit Return. Add three more names this way.
   It should look something like this:

5. Next align those names to the right so they will be next to the numbers you are going to enter. To do that, select all the cells with names in them: press-and-drag from the first name to the last name. The selection will look like the example below. You just selected a "range" of cells.

6. From the Format menu, slide down to Alignment and choose "Right."

*Notice* that when you select a range of cells, the first one has a selection border around it, while the rest are highlighted. That's okay—that's what it does.

Now enter the numbers and format them.

1. Click in cell **D4.**

2. Type the amount this person owes you, *but don't use a dollar sign or commas.* Type just the number (decimal points are okay).

3. Hit the **Return key.** Enter the next amount. Continue down the column. The numbers should look something like you see below.

| | A | B | C | D | E |
|---|---|---|---|---|---|
| 1 | | | | | |
| 2 | | | **Frogs R Us Web Design** | | |
| 3 | | | | | |
| 4 | | | Y. Feaster | 16000 | |
| 5 | | | G. Hackman | 100000 | |
| 6 | | | M. Morgan | 5000 | |
| 7 | | | T. Fisher | 8000 | |
| 8 | | | F. Diaz | 1000 | |
| 9 | | | | | |
| 10 | | | | | |

4. You need to format the numbers into dollars. First you must select them. Try selecting this way:

    Click in the first cell in the number list; *hold the Shift key down;* click in the last cell of that list. With the Shift key down, everything between the two clicks is selected.

*Tip: Double-click on any cell or range of selected cells as a shortcut to bring up this same dialog box.*

5. From the Format menu, choose "Number…." The dialog boxes look different in AppleWorks 5 and AppleWorks 6, but they accomplish the same thing. You're going to choose to format the numbers as "currency," which will automatically apply the dollar sign. And you're going to choose how many numbers you want to appear after the decimal point, which is called "Precision." For instance, if you enter "2" in the Precision edit box, that means any number in the cell will display two places after the decimal point. If you want the dollars in whole numbers (no cents), change the 2 to 0 (zero, not the letter O!). It's up to you. If you choose zero, any cents that may be in the cells will be rounded off.

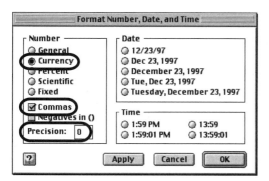

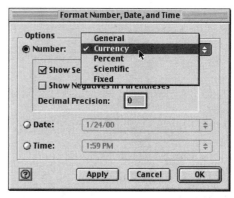

*AppleWorks 5:*

**a.** Click in the "Currency" radio button.

**b.** Check the box for "Commas."

**c.** Enter "0" (zero) in the "Precision" box.

**d.** Click OK.

*AppleWorks 6:*

**a.** Click in the "Number" radio button.

**b.** Press on the menu and choose "Currency."

**c.** Check the box to "Show Separators."

**d.** Enter "0" (zero) in "Decimal Precision."

**e.** Click OK.

**6.** After you click OK, take a look at those numbers!

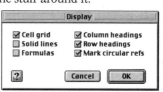

## View the spreadsheet without the grid and headings

Let's take a quick look at how this looks without all the stuff around it.

**1.** From the Options menu, choose "Display...."

**2.** Uncheck "Cell grid," "Column headings," and "Row headings." Click OK.
Your spreadsheet will look something like this:

**3.** To finish this project, turn the cell grid and both headings back on:
Go back to the "Display" dialog box and click those three boxes.

## Add a function

Mathematical formulas and functions (functions are complex formulas) are integral parts of a spreadsheet. They enable you to speculate with the numbers. AppleWorks provides you with a huge number of pre-made functions that you just add the details to. We're going to use a very simple function, called Sum, to total how much these people owe you. (If you want to know more about functions, read the AppleWorks Help file; choose it from the Help menu in AppleWorks.)

*Tip: To enter your own formula, just type an equal sign in the cell. Then type the formula, clicking on the cells whose data you want to add to the formula.*
***Be sure to hit the Enter or Return key as soon as you finish the formula!***

You *could* use a simple formula, such as =D4+D5+D6+D7+D8 for your project, but it's faster and easier to use the function that is already set up.

1.  First, format the cell in preparation for the number you're going to put into it: Double-click on the empty cell **D10** to get the number format dialog box. Choose "Currency," "Commas" or "Show Separators," and the same "Precision" you set in the other cells. Click OK.

2.  Now put the Sum function in the selected cell **D10**:

    *AppleWorks 5:* From the Edit menu, choose "Paste Function…."
    *AppleWorks 6:* From the Edit menu, choose "Insert Function…."

    Type "su" to select the Sum function quickly, or just scroll down the list, admiring all the things you could do if you knew what the heck they were. Select "SUM(number1,number2…)."

*Note: With functions and formulas you can do all kinds of things with numbers.*

*You could have one cell add the numbers, subtract the percentage you owe your agent, and add the tax. Or you could create a "lookup table" where the cell would look up a chart and add a percentage based on the individual amounts owed, or add penalties daily. Don't stop here.*

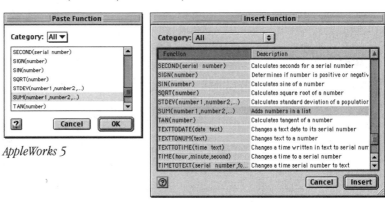

*AppleWorks 5*

*AppleWorks 6*

3.  Click OK. ***Now don't touch anything!***

The reason I yelled "Don't touch anything" on the previous page is because once you put a function in a cell or type an = sign to start a formula, *everything you click on becomes part of the formula.* It can make you crazy. So follow these directions carefully. If weird things happen, like strange stuff starts appearing in your entry bar, click the X in the entry bar and start over, selecting cell D10.

If things are going smoothly, you should see the function you selected in the entry bar. You need to substitute the "arguments" in parentheses (the first number, the second number, etc., that are to be added together) with the actual cell addresses that you want to add together.

**4.** So press-and-drag to select everything between the parentheses, like so:

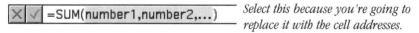 *Select this because you're going to replace it with the cell addresses.*

**5.** While it's selected, *press* (don't click!) in cell D4 and drag to D8, which will enter those cell addresses into the formula. The numbers in those cells will be summed. Before you touch anything else, hit the Enter key (or click the checkmark in the entry bar). Your entry bar should look like this:

And cell D10 should have the sum of the money you are owed.

**6. Change the amount someone owes you,** enter it, and the total amount changes instantly. Try it. If you had made a bar chart or pie chart, the chart would change instantly when you change data.

## Move the data

Perhaps you decided you put all this information in the wrong place. That's easy to fix. Let's move the names and numbers one column to the left.

**1.** Select the cells you want to move: names, numbers, and total.

**2.** Hold down the Command and Option keys, and click in cell **B4.**

Now, click once in cell **D10,** the cell with the formula, and you'll notice that the cell range changed from the original settings of D4..D8 to C4..C8! That's a good thing because there's nothing left in D4..D8. That formula you entered is what's called **relative,** meaning it didn't *really* mean D4..D8 specifically; it meant, "Sum the cells that are 2, 3, 4, 5, and 6 rows above me." So when the formula moved, it still added the correct cells. You can also make **absolute** cells that do not change. See the Help file, under the Help menu in AppleWorks, for details.

*range: A range of cells is any selection of more than one. It is written with two dots between the first and last cell, as you see in your entry bar.*

*All the cells in a range don't have to be in the same row or column. When you move the data in this exercise, you are going to select cells C4..D10.*

## Apply a border

The borders feature is what makes creating forms so very easy. You can apply a border to an individual cell or a range of cells; on any one side or on all sides. For instance, you could select cells B4 through B8 and apply a left border to make a vertical line. Right now, put a border line under the logo.

1. Select all the cells through which the title extends (in my example, that would be B2 through E2), like so:

2. From the Format menu, choose "Borders...."

3. Click "Bottom." Click OK.

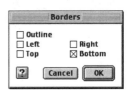

## Change the color of cells

Do one more thing to this spreadsheet: color a cell or two. Colored cells can help the organization and clarity of a large spreadsheet.

*Use the **tool palette** or **Accents palette** to change the color of **cells**.*

*To change the color of the **text** inside the cells, use the color palette in the toolbar across the top of the spreadsheet (Apple-Works 5) or go to the Format menu and choose "Text Color" in AppleWorks 6.*

1. Select the cell with the formula so the total will stand out.

2. If you don't see a tool palette on the left of the screen, click the little tool palette button at the bottom-left of the window, next to the scroll bar:

*AppleWorks 5*                    *AppleWorks 6*

3. *AppleWorks 5:* Click on the tiny color box, as shown below, to get the color palette, then click on the color you want. You can "tear off" this palette (just drag it to the right) and let it float around your spreadsheet; this makes it very easy to change cell colors. See below, left.

   *AppleWorks 6:* From the Windows menu, choose "Show Accents." Click on a color to apply it to the selected cell. See below, center.

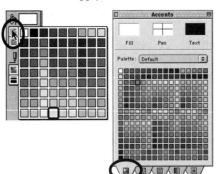

*And this is your finished spreadsheet!*

# Make a Simple Painting 7

Paint programs are too much fun. Don't worry if you think you can't draw or paint — this is a fun exercise to walk through, even if you never plan to use this part of the application. Paint a monster because then no one can say it doesn't look like a monster, whereas if you try to paint a rose, you might not be very happy with your results (unless of course you really are a painter, unlike me).

So don't be intimidated; jump right in and follow the directions. Whether you ever plan to paint things or not, you will learn a lot more about your computer, and you will feel more comfortable and powerful.

If you like painting like this, explore more on your own. I can't tell you *everything* about this program in this short chapter, but AppleWorks has a great Help section: While the program is open, go to the Help menu and choose "AppleWorks Help." Click on the topics you want to learn more about, or type in the name of a topic you are looking for.

## Get ready to paint

Now, you might be in one of four different situations, depending on whether you've been following along or not. Choose the situation you're in and follow the directions:

**A. You just finished the spreadsheet exercise and the spreadsheet is still on your screen.**

**1.** Save this spreadsheet: press Command S.

**2.** Click in its little close box in the upper-left corner, or use the keyboard shortcut Command W (W for Window).

**3.** Go to the next page in this book.

**B. You finished the spreadsheet exercise, saved and closed it, and didn't quit AppleWorks. In the far-right corner of the menu bar, you see "AppleWorks" and a tiny icon of AppleWorks (  ).**

○ You are exactly where you need to be! Go to the next page.

*This is the Application menu. The **checkmark** indicates what is active, or open, at the moment.*

**C. You finished the spreadsheet exercise, saved and closed it, and didn't quit AppleWorks. BUT in the far-right corner of the menu bar, you see a tiny icon of the Macintosh logo ( ).**

**1.** Click once on that little happy Mac icon to get the Application menu, as shown to the left.

**2.** If you didn't actually quit AppleWorks, you will see "AppleWorks" listed in the Application menu. Select it.

**3.** After you select "AppleWorks," you should see the AppleWorks icon on the far-right (where the happy Mac icon was a minute ago) and the toolbar under the menu bar. Go to the next page.

**D. You skipped the spreadsheet exercise, or you turned off your computer and came back later, and AppleWorks is not open on your iMac.**

**1.** Open AppleWorks just like you did the first time: double-click the *application* icon (it's *inside* the AppleWorks folder).

**2.** *AppleWorks 5:* Double-click "Painting."
*AppleWorks 6:* Single-click "Painting."

Go to the next page, but skip the first step, the one that says, "Open a paint document," because you just opened one.

AppleWorks 6

*This is the icon you need to double-click to open the application. This icon is **inside** the AppleWorks **folder.***

## Open a new paint document

- To open a new, blank paint document, use the toolbar: click on the button with the little paintbrush or palette.

*AppleWorks 5*          *AppleWorks 6*
*toolbar button*         *toolbar button*

## Check out the painting tools

Along the left side of the screen you now have special painting tools. Try this:

1. **Click once** on the paintbrush tool (circled, see below).
2. Now move your mouse over to the right, so you are positioned on the page.
3. Press-and-drag the mouse around to draw any sort of shape.
4. If you want to undo the last thing you did, press Command Z for Undo.

  *The paint tool palette in AppleWorks 5.*

  *The paint tool palette in AppleWorks 6.*

Before you make an ugly monster, play with some of these paint tools. They're easy, and they teach you a lot about how other programs work. Follow along on the next several pages to experiment.

### Erase anything or everything you just scribbled

- To erase part of your image, **click once** on the eraser tool. Move the mouse over to the right, and press-and-drag over the area you want to erase.
- To erase everything on the page, **double-click** on the eraser tool.

*The eraser tools*

*The paintbrush tools*

### Dip your paintbrush in a bright color

1. *AppleWorks 5:* In the paint tool palette, you see a four-square box with different colors and patterns in it (shown below). Click in any of those four segments to see the incredible collection of textures, patterns, colors, and gradients you can paint with. Click a color or texture to paint with it.

   These palettes "tear off"—when the palette is showing, drag your mouse to the right and the palette will tear right off. Click on the page and the palette will sit on the page, making it easy to change colors.

   *AppleWorks 6:* From the Window menu, choose "Show Accents" to get the palette shown below, right; click each of the tabs to see the wide variety of textures, patterns, colors, and gradients you can paint with. (The fifth tab is for use with the line tool.) Click a color or texture to paint with it.

2. To move a palette, drag its title bar. To close, click the Close Box.

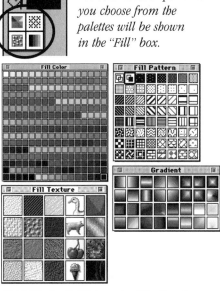

*The color and/or patterns you choose from the palettes will be shown in the "Fill" box.*

*AppleWorks 6: Click on a tab to get another palette. Be sure to check the "Palette" menu, as shown, to see what else is available in each section.*

*AppleWorks 5: Click each of the tiny boxes (circled, above) to get these "paint" palettes for your brush.*

### Get a bigger paintbrush

1. **Double-click** on the paintbrush tool.

2. **Click once** on any of those different "brush shapes," as shown below, then click OK.

3. Paint with that new brush: press-and-drag on the page.

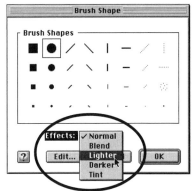

*Click any of these brush shapes to choose it.*

*Choose an "Effect" here, then draw on top of something else. The effect will remain in the paintbrush until you change it back!*

*Click "Edit..." to edit the selected brush shape or make a new one.*

## The trick to painting with your chosen fill and border colors

Experiment with using these colors and patterns! ***The trick is you must choose the color and/or pattern BEFORE you paint something.*** So choose a fancy fill texture and then paint on the page. Then experiment with painting over other items, changing the brush pattern and effect, spray painting, etc.

You can also choose more than one color and pattern. You can choose one of those black-and-white fill patterns, like this: ▧ , then choose a color that you want the pattern to appear in. (You can't change the color of the fancy textures or gradients.)

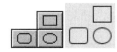

*The shape tools*

*The Fill and Pen
(line) boxes*

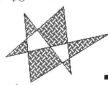

*The irregular
polygon tools.*

*Remember, to stop
the spiderweb tool,
click directly on top
of the first point you
made, or double-
click anywhere.*

### Paint using the shape tools

1. You're not limited to using the paintbrush. Choose one of the three shape tools at the top of the tool palette, as shown to the left.

2. Click on the Fill box and choose a pattern, color, texture, or gradient for the inside of the shape.

3. Click on the Pen box and choose a pattern, color, texture, or gradient for the border of the shape.

   Also choose a width for the border: click on this symbol 🔳 and choose a thickness. (In AppleWorks 5 it's toward the bottom of the toolbar; in Appleworks 6 it's the right-most tab.)

4. On the page, press at one corner with the shape tool and draw diagonally to create a shape. Amazing.

### Try these special tools

- Click on the **irregular polygon tool** shown to the left (I call this the spiderweb tool). On the page, ***don't press-and-drag***—instead, click once, then move the mouse and click somewhere else, then click somewhere else, etc. Cross over the existing lines, if you like. When you have created a shape, click directly on top of the first point you made, or double-click anywhere and the shape will close itself up. It will fill with the pattern or texture you had last chosen.

- Click on the **regular polygon tool:** ◇ or △ . Press and drag— a shape will appear, and it will rotate around as you move your mouse. Let go of the mouse button to put the shape on the page. Try it.

  Double-click on the polygon tool to get a dialog box in which you can choose the number of sides you want in the shape.

### Use the airbrush tool

I'll bet you know what to do: choose the **airbrush tool.** Choose a color and/or pattern, then press-and-drag on the page.

In the tool palette, double-click the airbrush tool to change the spray.

*The airbrush tool*

### Pour paint into a shape with the paint bucket

1. Before you can pour paint, you need a shape to pour it into. So first:

   **a.** Double-click on the **paintbrush tool.** Choose any **solid shape** and the "Normal" effect, and click OK.

   **b.** Then choose a **solid color** from the color palette, and a **solid pattern** from the pattern palette.

   **c.** Paint a shape, like a monster head. It is extremely important that the shape be entirely closed (no holes anywhere) because *if there is the tiniest hole, the paint from the bucket will spill out of the hole and spread all over the entire page.*

2. Now choose the paint bucket tool:  or  .

3. Choose any color, pattern, or texture.

4. Position the bucket inside the shape that you want to fill with paint. The paint pours out of the very tip of the spilling point so make sure the tip is positioned to pour inside the shape.

5. Then just click and the paint will pour into the shape. If you don't like the color, *immediately* press Command Z to undo (or choose Undo from the Edit menu); choose another color or texture, and click again.

*The paintbrush tools*

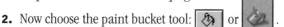

*This little icon removes any pattern and makes the fill a solid color.*

*The paint pours out of the very tip.*

*The selection tools*

*The rectangle selection tool selects the entire rectangular shape.*

*The lasso selects just the object.*

**Tip:** *Try the "Pick Up" command. First paint a shape. Then select it with the lasso tool. Drag it onto some other shape that has a fancy pattern. While the shape is still selected and sitting on that other pattern, choose "Pick Up" from the Transform menu. Then drag the shape out to a clean part of the page. It will have picked up the pattern. You gotta try it to get it.*

### Transform a shape

Here's an important technique to experiment with. Take a look at the Transform menu. All of the commands are probably gray, correct? That's because you must first *select* a shape that you want to transform (remember, select first, then do it to it). You have two selection tools, as shown to the left: a rectangular one and a lasso.

The rectangular tool selects a rectangular shape and picks up any background that it encloses. The lasso tool snaps to the exact shape of the object. To see the difference, draw a heart on the page with the brush. Then:

1. Choose the **rectangular selection tool.** Begin outside of the heart, in the upper-left area, and drag diagonally down to the right.

   Then press the pointer in the center of that selected shape and drag. See, it drags the entire rectangle.

2. Now choose the **lasso tool.** Press-and-drag to draw loosely around the heart. When you let go, the lasso snaps to the heart shape. (You don't even have to draw entirely around the shape—when you let go, the lasso will find the other end of itself and snap to it.)

   To drag that selected shape, make sure you see the pointer—when the lasso tool is positioned on a draggable area of the image, it will turn into the pointer. The tool flips back and forth between lasso and pointer, so make sure you have the pointer before you try to move the object!

3. So that's how you select something. Now draw a shape, any shape.

4. Select that shape with either selection tool.

5. From the Transform menu, experiment with the choices. Choose something like "Perspective." Your selected object will display "handles," as shown below. Position the tip of the pointer tool in any one of those handles, then press-and-drag. Experiment with other options! (You must *re*select the object before you can transform again.)

*Each corner has a handle. Press-and-drag a handle to reshape the object.*

### Type some words and color them

You can also type words onto the page, and you can color those words. But keep in mind that you are painting, not word processing; that is, you won't be able to go back and edit the words or easily change their colors like you can in a word processor. And the text won't print as cleanly as text from a word processor. But it is great fun to do anyway. Follow the directions carefully.

1. Choose the **text tool.**

*The text tools*

2. With the text tool, click on the left side of the painting page so you have room for the text to type out to the right. *As soon as you click, you'll see the menu bar change!* Now, while the insertion point is flashing on the page, you have menu items for text.

3. Before you type anything, choose the typeface, the size, and the color as explained below. Unfortunately, you can't choose any of the patterns, textures, or gradients to type with. But you can choose any solid color.

    *AppleWorks 5:* Go to the Fonts menu and the Size menu and choose the typeface and size that you want. From the Format menu, choose "Text Color." (You must choose the color from the menu or the toolbar only— you can't use the tool palette on the left side for coloring text.)

    *AppleWorks 6:* From the Text menu, choose the font, size, and color.

4. Now type onto the page. Hit the Return key before the type bumps into the right side of the page. If you decide you want a different typeface, size, or color, press-and-drag over the text, then select your new choices. *But don't click outside of the little text box!* The very second you click anywhere outside of that text, the words become paint on the page and you cannot do any sort of editing—if you want to change anything after that point, you'll have to erase it and do it over again. It'll make you a little crazy for a while until you get the hang of it.

5. Once the type is set how you like it, click anywhere outside of the text box. Then you can select it (as described on the previous page) and move it wherever you like, transform it, delete it, etc.

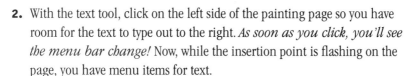

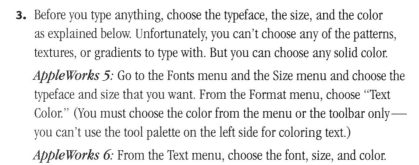

*This is an example of paint text. You can, while typing, choose another typeface, size, and color and whatever you type **next** will be in the new formatting.*

## So now paint an ugly monster

Use shapes or the paintbrush to create your monster. Use the paintbucket to fill in colors or textures. Paint the forest and the castle. Type a poem about your monster. You can't hurt anything, so experiment with all the tools and options—you'll learn a lot. Just remember to choose the tool, then the color/pattern/fill for the inside and the border *before* you paint.

*See, isn't this a stupid-looking monster? So what! Don't be afraid to paint something dorky — enjoy the dorkiness!*

*In paint documents, text is just colored "pixels" (spots) on the screen. You can't edit the text like you can in a word processor. To correct this misspelled name (Gertrude), you would have to erase it with the eraser tool and retype.*

*The "draw" program creates better-looking text and the words are always editable.*

# Make a Simple Drawing

A draw program can be less intimidating than a paint program because you mostly work with lines, boxes, and ovals ("lbo's," affectionately called "elbows"). The things you learn in this exercise will apply to many other programs that have draw tools as part of their features.

It's really a good idea to pair this draw exercise with the preceding paint exercise so you see the difference between a paint program and a draw program. You will not only learn which one to choose for a particular project, but you will feel more comfortable and knowledgeable when you understand the strengths and weaknesses of the two different sorts of applications.

Even if you think you can't draw a thing, go through the exercise and draw a little house. You'll be surprised. Even if your house turns out really silly (it can't be sillier than my drawing), you will have learned a lot.

Remember, if you want to learn more, go to the Help menu in AppleWorks and choose "AppleWorks Help."

## Let's draw!

Now, you might be in one of four different situations, depending on whether you've been following along or not. Choose the situation you're in and follow the directions:

**A. You just finished the paint exercise and the painting is still on your screen.**

    **1.** Save this document: press Command S.

    **2.** Click in its little close box in the upper-left corner, or use the keyboard shortcut Command W (W for Window).

    **3.** Go to the next page in this book.

**B. You finished the paint exercise, saved and closed it, and didn't quit AppleWorks. In the far-right corner of the menu bar, you see "AppleWorks" and a tiny icon of AppleWorks (  ).**

    ✪ You are exactly where you need to be! Go to the next page in this book.

*This is the Application menu. The **checkmark** indicates what is active, or open, at the moment. Choose AppleWorks.*

**C. You finished the paint exercise, saved and closed it, and didn't quit AppleWorks. BUT in the far-right corner of the menu bar, you see a tiny icon of the Macintosh logo ( ).**

    **1.** Click once on that little happy Mac icon to get the Application menu, as shown to the left.

    **2.** If you didn't actually quit AppleWorks, you will see it still listed in the Application menu. Select it.

    **3.** After you select AppleWorks, you should see the AppleWorks icon on the far right (where the happy Mac icon was a minute ago) and the toolbar across the top. Go to the next page of this book.

**D. You skipped the painting exercise (you shouldn't have!), or you turned off your computer and came back later, and AppleWorks is not open.**

    **1.** Open AppleWorks just like you did the first time: double-click the *application* icon (it's *inside* the AppleWorks folder).

    **2.** *AppleWorks 5:* Double-click "Drawing."
       *AppleWorks 6:* Single-click "Drawing."

    Go to the top of the next page, but skip the first step, the one that says, "Open a draw document," because you just opened one.

AppleWorks 6

*This is the icon you need to double-click to open the application. This icon is **inside** the AppleWorks **folder.***

## Open a new draw document

- To open a new, blank draw document, use the toolbar: click on the button with the little paintbrush or palette.

*AppleWorks 5*
*toolbar button*    *AppleWorks 6*
*toolbar button*

## Check out the drawing tools

Along the left side of the screen you now have special drawing tools. If you did the painting exercise, you'll notice you have fewer tools, and there is no paintbrush or spraypaint, nor is there an eraser. Experiment:

*The drawing tool palettes*

### Draw and resize a shape

1. Click once on the **rectangle shape tool** (circled, to the right).

2. Now move the mouse over to the right, so you are positioned on the page.

3. Press-and-drag the mouse to draw a rectangle. If you did the painting exercise, this is no big deal, right? So what's the difference?

4. Did you notice when you draw a rectangle you automatically get "handles" on each corner? (If the handles are gone, click once on a colored part of the object.) If you press the *tip* of the pointer in any one of those handles, you can drag the rectangle into a different rectangular shape. Try it.

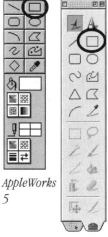

*AppleWorks 5*

*AppleWorks 6*

*This is the original shape. Notice the handles. When an object is **selected**, you see its handles.*

*Press-and-drag on any handle to resize the object.*

*You can resize any object at any time. It is never permanent.*

### Get rid of an object

- You've probably noticed you don't have an eraser in this draw module. That's because each item in this program is seen as a complete object. You must remove an entire object—you cannot remove part of one.
  **To delete:** Select the item (click once on it with the pointer tool), and when you see the handles on the corners, hit the Delete key.

*Tip: If you see a grid pattern in the background, you can choose to turn it off (or on) from the Options menu. Choose "Hide Graphics Grid" to make it go away.*

### Change the fill and border thicknesses and patterns

1. Just like in the paint program, you have palettes from which to choose the fill patterns and colors (shown below). And you have separate palettes from which to choose the border thickness, color, and pattern (also shown below). One difference between the paint program and this draw program is that in paint you must choose the fill and the border *before* you draw the shape; in draw you can change it whenever you feel like it.

*AppleWorks 5: The palettes for both the inside fill and the outside pen border look exactly the same. Make sure you choose the right one!*

*Fill*

*Border/Pen*

*AppleWorks 5: The fill and border quadrants of the tool palette. (Actually, the bottom-right border quadrant, arrows, applies just to straight lines.)*

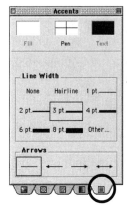

*AppleWorks 6: From the Window menu, choose "Show Accents." The Accents palette looks the same in paint and draw. The last tab is for lines and borders.*

2. At any time—later today, next week, or next year—**click the object to select it** and change the pattern or color of the inside, the thickness and color of the outside line, the size, or the position of the object. Try these actions (select the object first):

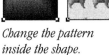

*Change the pattern inside the shape.*

*Change the thickness and pattern of the border.*

*From the Arrange menu, choose "Free Rotate." Then press on any handle, and drag to rotate the object.*

### Use the line tool

1. Choose the **line tool** by clicking once on it.

2. Press-and-drag on the page to draw a line.

3. After the line is drawn, make sure it is selected (you should see handles on both ends; if not, click once on the line), then change the thickness, the color, and add some arrows to one or both ends (use the border/pen tools in the lower quadrant of the tool palette in AppleWorks 5, and on the right-most tab in the Accents palette in AppleWorks 6).

*These are the line tools.*

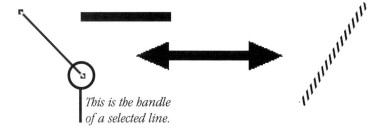

*This is the handle of a selected line.*

### Use the freeform drawing tool

So far you have learned how to draw lines, boxes, and ovals (elbows, remember?). But you can also draw freeform shapes, then reshape them, and of course fill them with different colors or patterns, change the line thicknesses, and rotate and flip them to your heart's content.

You have two freeform tools: the freehand tool and something called the bezigon tool. First try the freehand tool.

*These are the freehand tools.*

1. Choose the **freehand tool** from the tool palette.

2. Press-and-drag as usual, just like you did in the paint program or with any other draw tool.

3. Now this is the interesting thing about a freehand form in the draw program: you can reshape it.

   If the shape doesn't have handles, select it by clicking once on it. Then from the Arrange menu, choose "Reshape."

4. Your cursor changes to a target ( ⊕ ), and the freeform shape gets all these little "points" on it (as shown below).

   Position the center of the target cursor on any of the points, press, and then drag. You have to play with it to get the hang of reshaping.

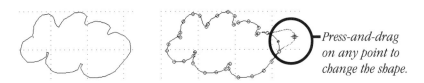

*Press-and-drag on any point to change the shape.*

### Use the bezigon tool

The bezigon tool, which combines something called "bezier curves" with a polygon, is another freehand sort of tool.

*These are the bezigon tools.*

1. Choose the **bezigon tool** from the tool panel.

2. ***Do not press-and-drag!*** Instead, click once on the page, then move the mouse and click once somewhere else. Keep repeating the click-and-move action to create your shape.

3. When you have the basic shape you want, either double-click to finish the shape, or click once directly on top of the first point.

4. While the shape is selected, from the Arrange menu, choose "Reshape." You get the same little points you saw with the freehand tool on the previous page. But if you click on one of those points, you get "control points" with long handles. Position the center of the target cursor on the end of one of those handles, and drag. Watch the shape change. This takes lots of experimenting before you begin to know what to expect when you drag. Try it! If it makes you crazy, don't use it.

*This is the original shape.*

*You can either drag the point itself . . .*

*. . . or drag either end of a point's handles.*

*The outlines display the original shape, plus the new shape, until you let go.*

## Now draw a silly little house

The tools are pretty easy to use, aren't they? Below are a few guidelines to help you use them. The trick to creating something fun in a drawing program (as in life) is to be creative with what you have.

- Keep checking to see which tool is selected. As soon as you draw something, AppleWorks switches back to the pointer tool.

- If you need to select an object and it's not getting handles when you click on it, check to make sure you have the pointer tool.

- No matter what patterns or colors are currently in the borders or the fills of any object, you can always change them.

- Make sure you have the right palette when you try to change a border (line) or a fill.

*These are the text tools.*

- Experiment with the text tool. Choose it, click on the page, and type. Edit the text just like you did in the word processor. The Font, Size, and Style menus (AppleWorks 5) or the Text menu (AppleWorks 6) only appear after you have selected the text tool and clicked on the page!

- ***Select any object and send it behind the other objects, or bring it in front: select the object, then use the Arrange menu.***

*I used the "spiderweb" tool to create the sun's rays, the tree trunk, and the roof.*

*I drew one cat, then used the pointer tool to drag around all of the different objects that make the cat—this selected all the pieces. Then I copied and pasted the cat, and used the arrow keys to move the selected second cat.*

*To create perfect circles and squares, hold the Shift key down while using the oval or rectangle shape tool.*

Our house is a very very fine house.

*After I drew this chimney, using the brick fill pattern and a brown color, I sent it behind the roof.*

*I used the freehand tool to create the cherry tree top and the chimney smoke.*

*Text in the draw program doesn't look any better **on the screen** than it does in paint, but it **prints** beautifully. And you can edit (change) it as often as you like.*

# Fax a Note to Someone

On your iMac you have the software called FAXstf. With this software you can do things like send what's called a "QuickNote," which is just like it sounds—a quick note faxed to someone. Or you can create a letter in any software program of your choice and fax it right from the screen. And you can also receive faxes into your computer (your iMac must be turned on), then print the fax on your own printer (or just read it on the screen and never print it at all). It's great and it's easy. In this chapter I'll walk you through sending a QuickNote fax, a formatted fax page from AppleWorks, and I'll also show you how to set things up so your iMac will receive faxes.

## Warning!

Some models of the iMac have an extra little piece of software that starts up automatically and conflicts with this fax software. I highly recommend you go to page 294 in Chapter 23 and follow the directions to make sure there is no check in the box for an item called "Serial Port Monitor."

### Connect your iMac to a phone line

To fax, you don't have to have an Internet connection or email address or anything like that, but you do have to plug in a phone cable to a phone jack or into an extra port on a telephone. A phone cable came with your iMac. If you've already connected your computer to the Internet through a phone line, you're all set; if you use a cable modem or DSL for your Internet access, you'll need to add the phone cable for faxing. Just plug a phone cable into the little slot on the side of your iMac that is labeled with a tiny picture of a phone handset, and plug the other end into either a wall jack or a phone (the phone must be plugged into the wall jack, of course). You can buy little "doublers" at any office supply store that let you plug two or more cables into one outlet or one phone.

### Options for faxing

You have two basic options for faxing: you can send a short, quick note that has limited formatting and design choices, or you can create and send a nice fax letter with graphics, lovely typefaces, and multiple pages. Instructions for both the **QuickNote** and the **customized fax page** are included in this chapter.

### First, find the fax software

You have to open several folders to get to the fax software, as described below. Once you get there, I recommend making an "alias" of the icon (described on the opposite page) and placing the alias on your Desktop so you won't have to open all those folders whenever you want to send a quick fax note.

1. Open your hard disk window, if it isn't already open.
2. Open the "Applications" folder (double-click the folder icon).
3. Now open the folder labeled "FAXstf 5.0." You'll see the window shown below. Don't double-click anything yet! First make an alias (see opposite page).

*This is the fax software you'll be using.*

### Make an alias of the fax software

An "alias" is a pointer to something. In this case, you're going to make an alias of the fax software so you don't have to open so many folders to send a fax note—you'll just double-click the alias, and the alias will open the fax software for you. It's really easy.

- Hold down the Command and Option keys. With those keys held down, press on the icon labeled "Fax Browser" and drag it to an empty space on the Desktop. Instantly you will have a new icon with an italic label, as shown to the right. That icon is your alias.

*Fax Browser*

*An alias always has an italic label. You can throw away an alias and it won't affect the real program.*

### Open the fax software

You can double-click on either the alias you just made or on the original icon you found in the FAXstf folder (opposite page).

## Register your software

The first time you open the fax software, you will be asked to register it. It's always a good idea to register your software. You can click the button to "Register Later," if you like, but you might as well do it right now.

1. Click "Register." (If you prefer to click "Register Later," then skip to page 143 and send a QuickNote.)

2. One of the first things you'll see is this commercial for the "Pro" version of the software that you can buy. Read it or skip it and click "Done."

*—continued*

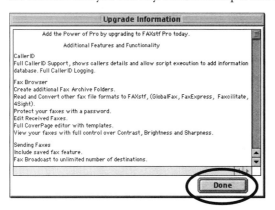

**3.** Now this first step can be confusing: For some unknown reason, the "Fax Browser" window is on top of the window you need for registering. So click on the pale window that is *below* the Fax Browser to bring the actual "Registration" dialog box forward (as shown below).

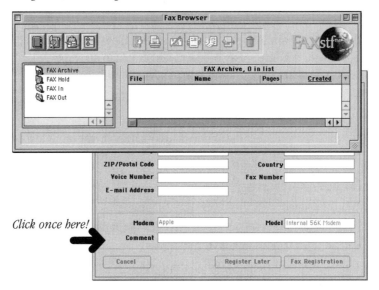

*Click once here!*

**4.** Fill in the information. When you're done, click "Fax Registration."

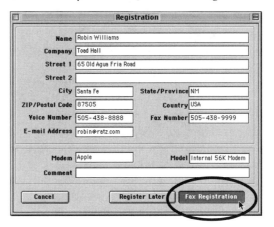

**5.** Hmm. Wouldn't you think that the fax number to send your registration to would be filled in for you already? It isn't. In the dialog box shown on the opposite page, which is what you should see on your screen, press on the label "US Free Registration" that you see in the little box on the left side; drag it to the little box on the right side and drop it, as shown to the right, above.

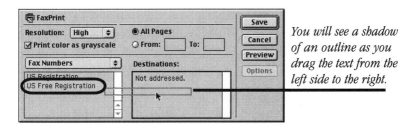

*You will see a shadow of an outline as you drag the text from the left side to the right.*

**6.** Make sure you see "US Free Registration" in the "Destinations" box, as shown below. Then click the "Send" button.

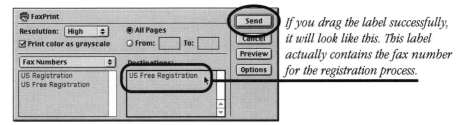

*If you drag the label successfully, it will look like this. This label actually contains the fax number for the registration process.*

**7.** You'll get the unnecessary dialog box shown below. (I suggest *un*checking the box in the bottom left that says, "Ask for options before sending." If you ever want these options in future faxes, just click the "Options" button in the previous dialog box.) Click "OK."

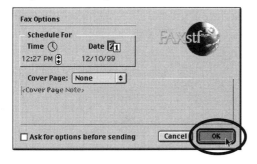

**8.** Your registration is on its way. You will see the "Fax Status" window, and it will display cute little icons in the bottom-right that tell you how it's doing.

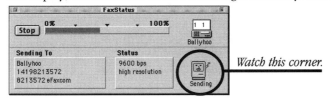

*Watch this corner.*

**9.** Thoughtfully, you'll get a reassuring message that your fax went through.

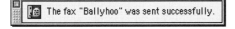

Waiting on Port

***Important note:*** *If you see this little icon in the bottom-right of the Fax Status window, you didn't follow the directions under "Warning" on page 138. Quit FAXstf and go do it.*

141

### Customize the settings before you send your first fax

Take a quick moment to customize a few of the settings before you send a fax. I understand there is actually a federal law that states a fax must be identified, and these settings you're about to customize fulfill that requirement.

1. If you don't have the Fax Browser already on your screen, double-click the Fax Browser icon (see page 138). If you double-click that and still don't see anything, press Command B, or from the Windows menu at the top of the screen, choose "Show Browser." You will see the window shown below.

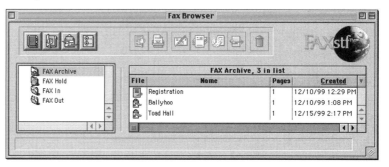

2. See that little row of buttons across the top left? If you position your mouse over each one and wait a second, a label will appear that tells you what that button is for. Right now, click on the far-right button, Settings.

 *This is the Settings button.*

3. The Settings dialog box opens up to the "Cover Page Settings." Type in your information, then click "Done." Now you're ready to send a fax.

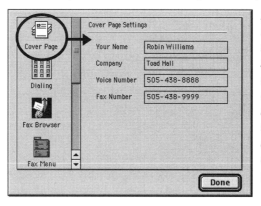

*If you like, click on any of the other icons you see on the left side (scroll down to see more) and you'll find other settings you can customize. Don't change anything if you don't know what it is. For all the gory details, see the manual that came with your software (see page 150).*

## Send a QuickNote fax

Okay, let's finally send a fax to someone. This QuickNote is just what it says—you can send a quick note with about six lines of text (a maximum of 255 characters). To send a longer fax, see the following page.

1. If you don't have the Fax Browser (shown on the opposite page) already on your screen, double-click the Fax Browser icon (see page 138). If you double-click that and still don't see anything, press Command B, or from the Windows menu at the top of the screen, choose "Show Browser."

2. In the row of buttons you see in the upper-left of the Fax Browser window, click on the third one (or from the File menu, choose "QuickNote").

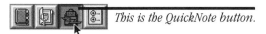 *This is the QuickNote button.*

3. You'll get an "Untitled QuickNote" window, as shown below. Type the information of the person you are sending the fax *to* (remember, you already entered the information about whom the fax is from when you customized the settings, previous page).

   Type the message. If you type too many words, you'll get beeped at and the words just won't show up.

   Click "Send Fax." That's it.

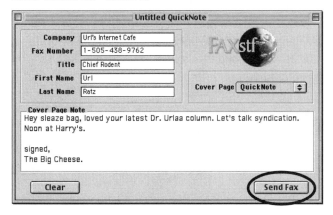

## Send a customized fax

The QuickNote described on the previous page is great for short little faxes. But most of the time you probably want to send something that looks a little more professional, playful, or just plain longer.

1. Create any document on your iMac in any program at all. You might create a letter, spreadsheet, database, or an entire newsletter.

2. When you're ready to fax the document, don't close it! Stay right there. Hold down the Command and Option keys, and while you hold those keys down with one hand, go to the File menu with the mouse in the other hand. You'll notice that the "Print…" command has changed to "Fax One Copy." So slide down and choose "Fax One Copy."

*Note: If for any reason you don't like the fax "hot key" combination of Command and Option, you can change it:*

*Follow the directions on page 142 to get the fax settings.*

*Click the icon on the left labeled "Fax Menu."*

*On the right, choose the key or combination of keys you'd prefer.*

*Close the settings.*

*The File menu typically has a "Print" command.*

*When you hold down the Command and Option keys before you open the File menu, "Print" changes to "Fax One Copy."*

3. When you choose to fax, you'll get the same "FaxPrint" dialog box you saw when you registered your software (if you did that), as shown below. To enter the fax number you want to send it to, press on the menu labeled "Fax Numbers" and choose "Temporary Address…." You'll get a dialog box in which to enter the name and fax number. Enter it and click OK.

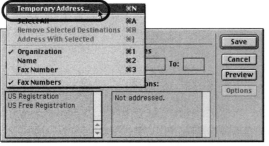

*You can make a "phone book" of fax numbers. Then you just drag a number from the left side of this dialog box over to the right side. See page 148.*

4. You'll see the recipient listed under "Destinations." Click "Send."

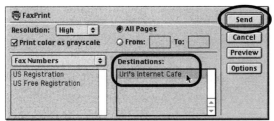

## Receive a fax

Before you can receive a fax, you must first tell the Fax Browser software that you want the software to answer the incoming call and accept the fax:

1. If you don't have the Fax Browser already on your screen, double-click the Fax Browser icon (see page 138). If you double-click that and still don't see anything, press Command B, or from the Windows menu at the top of the screen, choose "Show Browser."

2. In the row of buttons you see in the upper-left of the Fax Browser window, click on the right-most one (or from the Edit menu, choose "Settings....").

3. In the Settings dialog box, as shown below, find the icon in the left part of the window called "Fax Modem." Click once on it.

4. From the "Answer On" menu (circled, below), choose how many times you want the phone to ring before FAXstf picks it up. Click "Done."    —continued

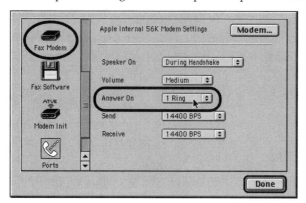

**Warning:** If you use the same phone line for voice calls and for faxing with this software, you will have to open these settings and change the "Answer On" options when you want your iMac to pick up a fax. Otherwise, this will happen:

> Let's say you have one phone line. You tell FAXstf to answer the phone on two rings and receive an incoming fax. If a voice call comes in and you don't answer the phone within two rings, you'll hear the fax squeal when you pick up the phone on the third ring. If you aren't home and a voice call comes in, anyone who calls you will think they got a fax machine instead of your phone. How do you think I know this?

FAXstf cannot tell the difference between an incoming voice call and an incoming fax so if you tell it to answer, FAXstf will answer *every* incoming call.

### Incoming faxes

*If you get a message telling you that the iMac can't change the settings because the port is in use, you have to go turn off the serial port monitor, as explained on page 294.*

*I had to reformat my entire hard disk before the FAXstf software would work properly, especially to receive faxes. See pages 295–298 if you ever decide you want to reformat your hard disk.*

Your iMac must be turned on and the "Fax Modem" options (as shown on the previous page) must be set to answer on at least one ring. You don't have to have the fax software open. Someone sends the fax to the phone number that your line is plugged into. Remember, even if you have an Internet connection through a cable modem or DSL modem, you must have a phone cable connected from your iMac into a phone line to receive faxes—faxes don't go through the Internet.

When a fax comes in, your iMac will let you know you've received it, no matter what you're working on: the apple in the far-left of the menu bar will blink with an icon of the FAXstf logo, 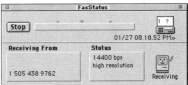, and you should get a status bar as it comes in (shown below). Now, that logo will only flash during the time the fax is being received. If you miss that cue or the status bar because you're away from the computer, you'll just have to check your Fax Browser software, as described below.

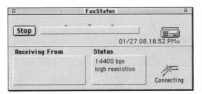

*This is the status bar that will appear as a fax comes in.*
*It changes to tell you what's going on.*

Once you know a fax has come in, or if you want to check to see if something arrived when you weren't looking, open the Fax Browser software.

1. If you don't have the Fax Browser already on your screen, double-click the Fax Browser icon (see page 138). If you double-click that and still don't see anything, press Command B, or from the Windows menu at the top of the screen, choose "Show Browser."

2. Click "FAX in" on the left side; any faxes will appear listed on the right side.

3. Double-click on any fax listed on the right to display and read it.

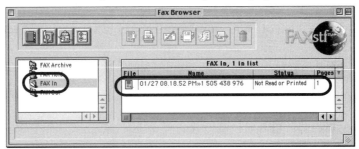

When you double-click on a fax in the list, the message opens up to a window like the one shown below. You get a little toolbox to help you customize the look of the fax onscreen and as it prints. **To print,** go to the File menu and choose "Print."

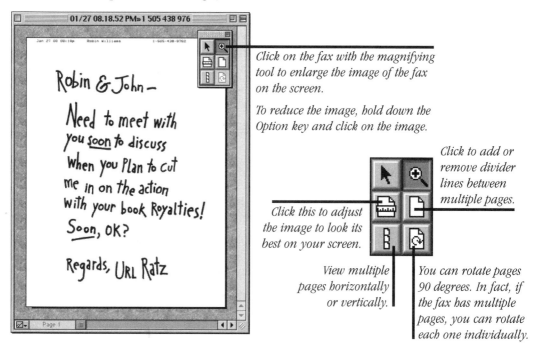

Click on the fax with the magnifying tool to enlarge the image of the fax on the screen.

To reduce the image, hold down the Option key and click on the image.

Click to add or remove divider lines between multiple pages.

Click this to adjust the image to look its best on your screen.

View multiple pages horizontally or vertically.

You can rotate pages 90 degrees. In fact, if the fax has multiple pages, you can rotate each one individually.

### Notify of fax reception

If you use FAXstf regularly, you can set it to notify you when a fax comes in so if you're not sitting at your computer when the status bar displays, you'll know something has arrived. But, as the warning shown below states, your iMac will not go to sleep if FAXstf is constantly checking for incoming faxes. It won't hurt your computer to stay awake, so if you need to be notified, go ahead and check the box.

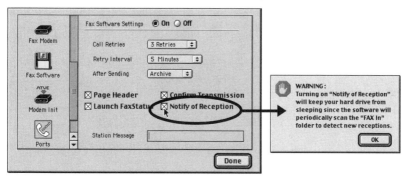

## Make a phonebook of fax numbers

Make a phonebook of fax numbers for all the people you might want to send a fax to. Then when you're ready to send, you can just drag one or more numbers into the "Destinations" box and off they go.

1. If you don't have the Fax Browser already on your screen, double-click the Fax Browser icon (see page 138). If you double-click that and still don't see anything, press Command B, or from the Windows menu at the top of the screen, choose "Show Browser."

2. In that row of buttons in the upper-left of the Fax Browser window, click the "Phonebook" button on the far left.

3. Once you click the Phonebook button, you'll get the "Fax Numbers" window shown below.

   a. The button on the left probably says "Unlock Phonebook." Click it once. (Then the button will change to "Lock Phonebook.")

   b. Click the button labeled "New Contact." This puts a flashing insertion point at the bottom of the window. Just start typing your data (as soon as you start typing, the data will probably jump up to the first line—that's okay). Press the Tab key to get from one column to the next.

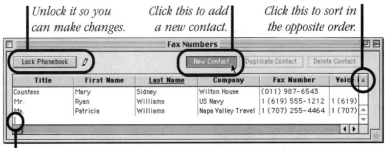

*Unlock it so you can make changes.*     *Click this to add a new contact.*     *Click this to sort in the opposite order.*

*This is the insertion point that appears when you make a new contact.*

**4.** All of the numbers you add to your phonebook will appear in the "FaxPrint" dialog box. Drag a contact name from the left box to the right box, then send.

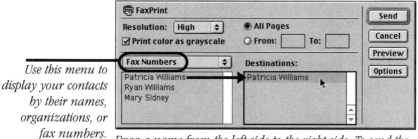

*Use this menu to display your contacts by their names, organizations, or fax numbers.*

*Drag a name from the left side to the right side. To send the same fax to more than one person, drag more than one name.*

### Extra tips

- **To alphabetize, or sort,** by any of the labels (first name, last name, company, etc.), just click on that column heading. The heading with the underline is the one that everything is sorted by.

- **To sort in the opposite order,** click the tiny triangle at the top of the scroll bar.

- **To make more than one contact at the same address,** as in a large company, select the first contact in that company, then click the "Duplicate Contact" button. Make the necessary changes.

- **To delete a contact,** first select it in the list (select it by clicking once on the contact information), then click the "Delete Contact" button.

## Print and read the FAXstf manual

The manual for the FAXstf software is included on your hard disk, right in the application window in which you found FAXstf. It's easy to follow and will provide you with all the details of every aspect of the software. You really should read it.

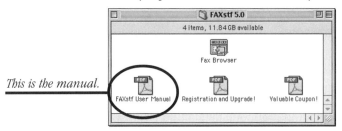

*This is the manual.*

To read and/or print the manual, just double-click on its icon in the folder. This will open the manual in the incredible software application called Acrobat Reader, as shown below. If the page doesn't fit inside the window, go to the View menu and choose "Fit in Window."

*Click the arrows to go forward or backward through the pages.*

*Click this button to print the manual. It's a total of 41 pages, but you don't have to print the first several pages.*

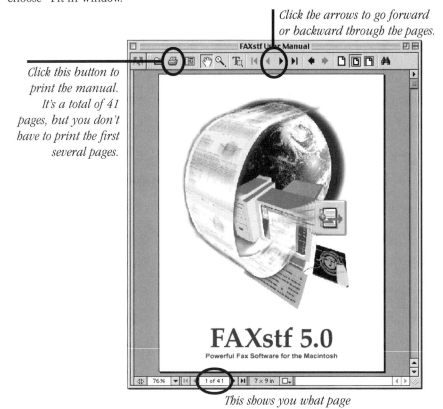

*This shows you what page you are looking at.*

# Play a DVD Movie

You've probably heard a lot about DVD movies. The "DVD" stands for Digital Video Disk, and the disk itself looks just like any other music CD or software CD you might have. An advantage of a DVD movie over a videotape is that you can watch a DVD on a smaller machine without having to hook up a VCR (some DVD players are even handheld). Also, you can choose to see different "chapters" of the movie, easily view just the parts you want, choose subtitles in a different language or hear the audio in a different language, and there are usually extra features like outtakes or interviews or inside information. Different DVD movies offer different features, so if you rent or buy one, check the box to see what "bonus material" it offers.

Not all iMacs can play a DVD, and you can't tell by looking at the computer whether yours will play a DVD or not because the video disk uses the CD player; there isn't an extra piece of equipment for the DVD. Check your Apple menu—if your iMac can play DVDs, you will have an item called "Apple DVD Player" in the menu, as shown to the right.

If you bought an iMac with a DVD player, you probably got the DVD *A Bug's Life* included in your packet of CDs. If you haven't done so already, get it out and put the disk in the CD drive (some iMacs have a tray that must pop out to put the disk in, other iMacs just have a slot in which you insert the disk). Then experiment with the controls. It's pretty easy, but if you need help or want to know the hidden tricks, read this chapter.

*Check for this item in the Apple menu to see if your iMac can play DVDs.*

## Play a DVD

*This is the DVD icon.*

To play a DVD, follow the directions below. Then read on for some tips.

**1.** Insert the DVD into the CD/DVD drive on your iMac.

**2.** Don't bother to double-click the DVD icon that appears! I know that's what you usually do, but that won't play the movie for you. Instead, go to the Apple menu and choose "Apple DVD Player." That opens the viewer and displays the movie on your screen, as shown below.

**3. To start the movie,** tap the Spacebar once.

**To pause the movie,** tap the Spacebar again.

**To quit at any time,** press Command Q
(that is, hold down the Command key and tap the letter Q just once).

*This is the main menu in* A Bug's Life.

## Check out the Controls and Video menus

In the Controls menu, take a couple of seconds to memorize the important keyboard shortcuts for fast forwarding, rewinding, and changing the volume.

In the Video menu, choose "Present Video on Screen" to eliminate everything on your screen except the movie; this is called "presentation mode." The movie will be shown on a black background. Even though you won't see the menu bar in this view, the menu bar will appear as soon as you position the pointer near the top of the screen.

*"Present Video on Screen" makes everything else on the screen disappear except the movie. You can still use the keyboard shortcuts.*

*Notice you can use Command UpArrow and Command DownArrow to turn the volume up or down. Command M will turn the sound off completely.*

*Command RightArrow and Command LeftArrow make the movie fast forward or rewind.*

*And the RightArrow or LeftArrow will each jump you to the next "chapter" of the movie, if the movie you're viewing has chapters (which are like separate scenes in the movie).*

*Use the Window menu to hide and show the Controller.*

## Use the Controller

You can hit the Spacebar and let the movie run to the end, but you can also use the Controller (that big round thing, shown below) to do things with your DVD that you can't do with a VHS tape. If the Controller isn't visible on the screen, go to the Window menu and choose "Show Controller."

*Click here to jump straight to the main menu for the various DVD options.*

*Drag on the Apple to move the Controller around the screen.*

*Click this button to eject the DVD.*

*Click the + or − to raise or lower the volume.*

*These double arrows on both sides of the Controller are the typical rewind and fast forward buttons.*

*Single-click to rewind or fast forward at twice normal speed.*

*Double-click to rewind or fast forward at eight times normal speed.*

*This button toggles between the Play button (as shown on the opposite page) and this Pause button.*

*This is the Stop button.*

*Single-click it, and when you next click the Play button, the movie will start where you left off.*

*Double-click it, and when you next click the Play button, the movie will start at the beginning.*

Besides the obvious things the Controller can do, there are some extra special tricks, as noted below and on the opposite page. Not all DVDs have the same options available, so you'll just have to experiment with each one.

*There might be more than one title on a DVD. For instance, on A Bug's Life, you also get that great animated short about the old guy playing chess (Geri's Game).*

*This readout will display whatever sort of information you choose from the list.*

*Press this little button to get the information options you see here. Choose one of the items in the list of options, and that is what will be displayed in the readout above. (Not all DVDs have "chapters.")*

Click the little "raised dots" above the DVD logo to expose this extra control panel. If the DVD you're watching has features that can be controlled from here, the pointer will become a pointing hand when positioned over a button. If there is no feature for that control, the pointer becomes a hand with the "not" symbol. Try it.

 *This icon means your DVD has that feature and you can use the selected control.*

 *This icon means your DVD does not have that feature and you can't use the selected control.*

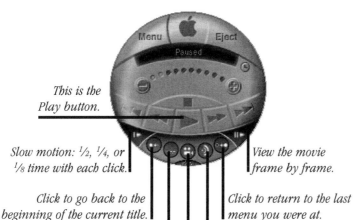

*This is the Play button.*

*Slow motion: ½, ¼, or ⅛ time with each click.*

*View the movie frame by frame.*

*Click to go back to the beginning of the current title.*

*Click to return to the last menu you were at.*

*Subtitles: click to cycle through the options.*

*Soundtracks: there might be alternate languages available, or perhaps director's comments, etc.*

*Angle: some movies have alternate video tracks to choose or let you view scenes from different angles.*

## DVD Preferences

Take a look at the Preferences and see if there's anything you want to change. Get the Preferences from the Edit menu while the Apple DVD Player is open.

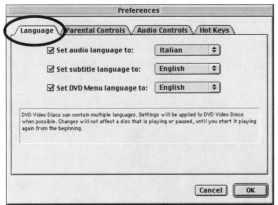

*Different video disks have different options for audio and subtitled languages, as well as the language that appears in the menus in the movie. You must first put a checkmark in the checkbox before you can see which languages appear in the menus.*

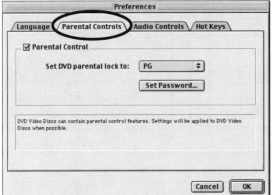

*If you set parental controls and supply a password, your kids (or parents) can't watch any movie with a rating higher than the one you choose unless they know the password.*

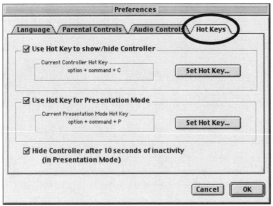

*A "hot key" is a key you press to make something happen. For instance, the default hot key combination to hide or show the Controller is Option Command C. You can change it to something easier like F12—just click the "Set Hot Key…" button, then click the F12 key. "Presentation Mode" is when nothing else is visible on your screen except the movie.*

# Make an iMovie

Some iMacs come with the software iMovie that allows you to view your digital movies on the computer and then edit, cut, rearrange, add sound, make transitions, add titles and credits, and more. It's amazingly easy to do and can actually create professional quality clips. You can save the movie back out to a blank digital tape, then transfer it to other media, if you like. You can also save your creation as something called a QuickTime movie that you can post on a web site or send as an attachment through email. You can even attach QuickTime movies to some word processing or page layout documents, and then others can watch them on their computers.

If you have a collection of non-digital movies, you can buy an adapter (see page 159) and bring them into iMovie to edit.

All of the iMacs that are called the "DV" model have the *FireWire ports* (see Chapter 21) necessary for transferring video to your iMac and have the iMovie software installed. Also, some of the non-DV models also have FireWire ports and the iMovie software. So if you see iMovie on your iMac, check the ports and see if you have one with this icon: . That's FireWire, and that's where you'll plug in your camera or adapter. If you decide you like this digital video editing, you might want to invest in a FireWire hard drive that you can attach to your iMac through the same port; a FireWire drive is big and fast, just what you need for editing movies.

### What's a digital camera?

A digital camera captures images in the same sort of technical format as your computer—in finite, countable chunks. The opposite of digital is analog, which is flowing and infinite. For instance, water is analog; ice cubes are digital; an oil painting is analog, a computer image is digital; a voice is analog, a fax is digital.

A digital camera can send the digital information straight into your computer without having to be changed into another form. iMovie can even control the camcorder, and you can set up your camera to record straight onto the iMac.

At the moment, the digital video cameras listed below can be used with iMovie. For up-to-date information on new devices that are compatible, go to **www.apple. com/imovie**.

| | | |
|---|---|---|
| Sony DCR-PC1 | Sony DCR-TRV8 | Canon XL1 |
| Sony DCR-PC100 | Sony DCR-TRV9 | Canon ZR |
| Sony DCR-TR7000 | Sony DCR-TRV9E | Panasonic AG-EZ20 |
| Sony DCR-TR103 | Sony DCR-TRV900 | Panasonic AG-EZ30 |
| Sony DCR-TRV110 | Sony DCR-TRV900E | Panasonic PV-DV710 |
| Sony DCR-TRV310 | Sony GV-D300 | Panasonic PV-DV910 |
| Sony DCR-TRV310E | Canon Elura | Sharp VL-PD3 |
| Sony DCR-TRV5E | Canon Optura | |
| Sony DCR-TRV510 | Canon Ultura | |
| Sony DCR-TRV7 | Canon Vistura | |

### Is your camera compatible?

If you have a digital movie camera, you can tell if it's compatible with the iMac by looking at the port, or plug, where you connect a cable for input/output. With the right port, you can transfer digital video from your DV (digital video) camcorder to your iMac and start making creative videos with iMovie.

*FireWire symbol*

*i.LINK symbol*

- If you see the FireWire symbol, you're set.

- On some cameras, the FireWire port is called the IEEE 1394 port.

- Sony camcorders have an i.LINK port, which is the same thing as FireWire or IEEE 1394.

## Do you have a FireWire cable?

If your camera did not come with a FireWire cable, look inside the box that came with your iMac—some iMacs ship with a FireWire cable (see below for an idea of what it looks like). You need this to connect your camera to the computer. If there isn't a FireWire cable in the box, go to **www.cameraworld.com** and order one.

*This is the end of the cable that goes into the camera.*

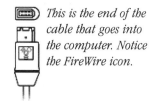

*This is the end of the cable that goes into the computer. Notice the FireWire icon.*

## Don't have digital video?

You can get a special converter box, such as the Sony DVMC-DA1 or DVMC-MS1 AV adapter, that will convert 8mm, Hi8, VHS, or SVHS format to the DV format. This converter box has standard S-video and RCA input/output ports for video and audio from your media, with a FireWire or i.LINK port (mentioned on the opposite page) so you can send the movies in to your iMac and edit them in iMovie. If you use a converter box, though, iMovie will not be able to control the camcorder like it can a digital camera.

Check the Sony web site at **www.sony.com** or a local video electronics store for more information about the converter.

## The iMovie software

Shown below is an example of what the iMovie software looks like. To learn how to use it, the best thing to do is go through the tutorial, as explained on the opposite page. In about twenty minutes you'll know all you need to edit, cut, and rearrange movie clips, add transitions between scenes, add titles and credits to the beginning or the end, add text to any frame, add sound effects or music, and export it all out as a movie in a variety of formats.

*When you open iMovie, you should see something like this, except it will be black where you see the dog's head. Click on any of the clips shown in the upper-right to see that clip in the large frame.*

## Open and use the iMovie tutorial

The tutorial is the fastest and easiest way to learn how to make your own movies.

1. Double-click the "Applications" folder to open it (the "Applications" folder is in the hard disk window).

2. In the "Applications" window, double-click the "iMovie" folder.

3. In the "iMovie" window, double-click the "iMovie Tutorial" folder, as shown below.

4. In the "iMovie Tutorial" window, double-click the icon named "iMovie Tutorial," as shown below. That will open the iMovie software and put the movie clips in position, as shown on the opposite page.

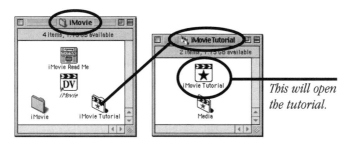

*This will open the tutorial.*

5. Then in iMovie go to the Help menu and choose "iMovie Tutorial," as shown on the opposite page. You'll get the Help file shown to the right. Scroll down through it, and read and follow the directions, clicking on underlined links to get to the next file of information.

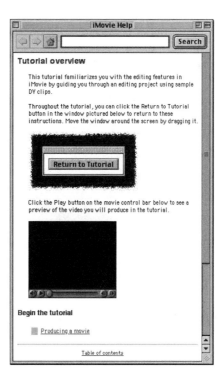

## Open a digital video in iMovie

As you were originally recording the movie on your movie camera, you probably turned the camera on and off, or onto standby, while you were filming, right? Well, when you import that movie into iMovie, iMovie sees each of those parts of the film between on and off as a clip. It puts each individual clip into one of those clip slots on the right side. If you happened to have recorded a very long segment in one shot, you can click the "Import" button as you see the shot roll by (circled, below) and separate the long piece into individual clips. (You can also cut short any of the shorter segments, of course.)

**To connect your camera to the computer** so you can import the movie:

1. First make sure the camera is turned off.
2. Connect the FireWire cable to the camera and the computer (the computer can be turned on).
3. Open the iMovie software. From the File menu, choose "New Project…," which will create a folder in which your movie clips will be saved.
4. Set the camera to **VTR mode;** make sure it is **not** set to "Charge." (You can also set the camera to record and capture live footage into iMovie.)
5. Click the Play button on your camera. You will see your movie playing in the large frame of iMovie. Click the "Import" button (circled, below) to begin making clips, which will automatically appear on the clipping shelf. Click "Import" again at any time to end a scene.
6. Since you finished the tutorial, you know how to edit the movie now!

*Robin's Movie*

*When you save a new project, iMovie creates a folder in which it stores your movie pieces.*

*When you are bringing a movie into your iMac, an Import button appears here. Click it to start and stop clips.*

## Save your movie

You can save individual frames of your movie; you can export the entire thing back out to tape; you can save it as a small movie especially for sending to someone else through email; and you can save it especially for posting on a web site for others to view. Use the File menu to either "Save Frame As…" or "Export Movie…."

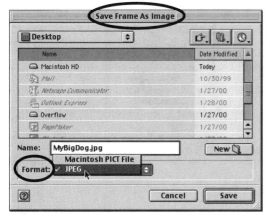

*When you see the frame you want in the large area of iMovie, go to the File menu and choose "Save Frame As…."*

*You have a choice of "Format":*

*Choose "Macintosh PICT file" if you plan to import that frame back into iMovie for later use.*

*Choose "JPEG" if you plan to send it through email or use it on a web page.*

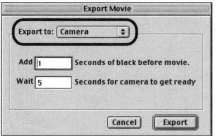

*To export a movie back to a blank digital video tape, from the File menu, choose "Export Movie…."*

*In the "Export to" menu, choose "Camera." Change the values if you like, then click "Export."*

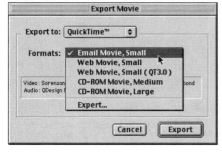

*To export a movie for email, the web, or to burn onto a CD, from the File menu, choose "Export Movie…."*

*In the "Export to" menu, choose "QuickTime™."*

*In the Formats menu, make your choice. For the first two choices, "Email Movie, Small" and "Web Movie, Small," the person who wants to view the movie must have QuickTime version 4.0 or later installed on their machine. If they don't have it, they can download it from* **www.apple.com/quicktime.**

*The choice "Web Movie, Small (QT3.0) is for people who don't have QuickTime 4.0 installed.*

*The "CD-ROM Movie, Large" is better quality, but a much larger file, than "CD-ROM Movie, Medium."*

*QuickTime Player*

*The QuickTime Player will play any QuickTime movie you make in iMovie.*

## Play a QuickTime iMovie

If you've exported a movie as a QuickTime file, as described on the previous page, you'll have a QuickTime icon of it. To play that movie without opening the iMovie application, just double-click the movie icon. Or you can drag the movie icon and drop it onto the "QuickTime Player" alias that is probably sitting on your Desktop.

LoverMan.mov

*Double-click the movie file to open it, or drag the movie icon on top of the QuickTime Player alias.*

*Click the big, round button with the triangle on it to start the movie.*

## Use the iMovie Help files

Everything you need to know about iMovie is on your computer. When the iMovie application is open on your screen, go to the Help menu and choose "iMovie Help." You'll get the help file shown below. Just click the links to go to those topics, or type in a topic of your choice and click the "Search" button.

*There is no manual for iMovie. You need to use this Help file.*

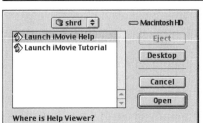

*If by chance your iMac shows you this dialog box and asks where is the Help Viewer, double-click "Launch iMovie Help."*

# Organize Yourself with Palm Desktop

You've probably checked out the menu for the **Palm Desktop Organizer,** the one in the far-right corner, next to the date. This software provides you with a calendar on which you can keep track of appointments, meetings, deadlines, tasks, workshops, vacations, and all those other things we need to keep track of in our lives. You can set up a reminder so a little message appears on your screen telling you what's coming up and what you're supposed to do about it.

*This is the Palm Organizer icon in the menu bar.*

### Synchronize data with your Palm

If you have a nifty handheld Palm Organizer (shown to the right), you can automatically synchronize files between the iMac's Palm Desktop Organizer software and the handheld device; that is, the data from the handheld Palm device can be transferred to the iMac, and the data from the iMac can be transferred to the handheld Palm, all at the same time. If you own a Palm, you'll find all the details about the HotSync operation in your manual (see page 172) and in the online help under the Help menu on your iMac.

*The handheld Palm Organizer from 3Com.*

## Palm Desktop Organizer

The software is already installed on most iMacs. If you don't see the Palm Desktop icon on the far-right of the menu bar, as shown below, you might find a folder called "Palm" in your Applications folder. If so, open the Palm folder and double-click the Installer to install the software.

*This is the original menu in the Palm Desktop software. As you make changes in your organizer, this menu will change.*

The first time you open Palm Desktop, you'll be asked for your name. Any number of people can use the same software and set up individual data files for themselves. These are not private in any way, so don't put items in the calendars or make appointments that you don't want anyone else to know about!

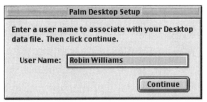

*Enter your name and click the "Continue" button.*

*If you have a handheld Palm Organizer and plan to HotSync, you can set it up now. If you don't know what HotSync is, click "Setup Later" and then read the manual.*

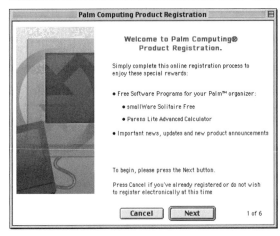

*It's always a good idea to register your software.*

## Open Palm Desktop software

If you just went through the simple setup on the opposite page and now you see a calendar on your screen, skip to the next paragraph. If you set up the program previously and now you want to use it, choose "Open Palm Desktop" from the Palm menu to launch the application.

You should see at least the Palm Desktop toolbar (shown below) on the screen. (If you don't, go to the File menu and choose "Open…" to open the data file you set up earlier.) Read the following pages to learn how to create appointments, tasks, reminders, and more.

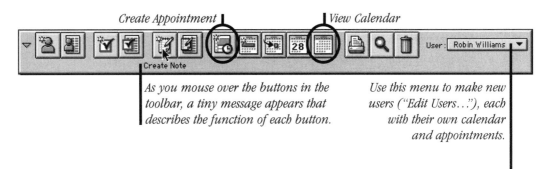

*Create Appointment*  *View Calendar*

*Create Note*

*As you mouse over the buttons in the toolbar, a tiny message appears that describes the function of each button.*

*Use this menu to make new users ("Edit Users…"), each with their own calendar and appointments.*

## Palm Desktop menu

After you have gone through this chapter and created appointments and tasks, etc., the Palm Desktop menu icon will display the list of events, appointments, and tasks that have been entered for the current day.

*This calendar icon will stay in your menu bar so you always have access to the Palm Desktop Organizer.*

## Use the calendar

*This is the toolbar button to "View Calendar."*

To use the calendar, click the "View Calendar" button (shown to the left).

The calendar has three views, Daily, Weekly, and Monthly, labeled on tabs on the right side of the calendar. Click a tab to change the view.

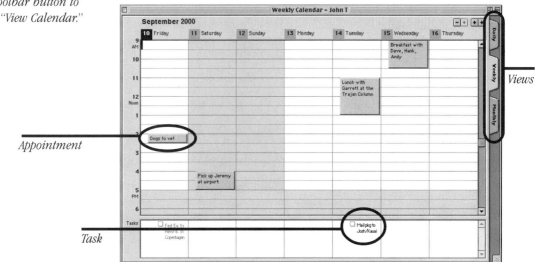

*Views*

*Appointment*

*Task*

## Schedule appointments

*This is the toolbar button to "Create Appointment."*

There are several ways to create appointments.

- Click the "Create Appointment" button in the toolbar to get the Appointment dialog box. Enter the information and click OK.

- **OR** double-click in a cell to bring up the Appointment dialog box.

- **OR** drag across a cell or across several cells. A text field appears in which to type your appointment information.

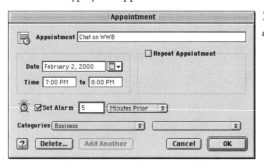

*This is the Appointment dialog box.*

## Set a reminder alarm

Set an alarm to remind you of an appointment. In the Appointment dialog box shown on the opposite page, you see a checkbox labeled "Set Alarm." When you check that box, a field appears in which you can enter how many minutes or hours in advance you'd like to be reminded of the appointment. At that pre-determined time, a reminder dialog box appears on your screen, even if the Palm Desktop Organizer is not open.

*This is a handy little reminder.*

*Check the "Snooze" button if you want the reminder to pop up again later.*

### To edit an appointment in Weekly view

- Click once on an existing appointment. A text box appears with an embossed tab on the left side (shown below). Either type in this text box **or** double-click on the embossed tab to open the Appointment dialog box.

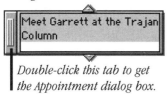

*Double-click this tab to get the Appointment dialog box.*

### To edit an appointment in Daily or Monthly view

- Double-click an appointment to open the Appointment dialog box. Make the edits, then click OK.

- In the Daily view (but not the Monthly), you can use the same technique as described for the Weekly view, above.

**Move an appointment** to another time simply by dragging it to another place on the calendar.

## Schedule tasks

In addition to making appointments, you can schedule Tasks. Open the Task dialog box in one of these two ways:

- Click the "Create Task" icon in the toolbar (circled, below).
- **OR** double-click a Task cell.
  (The Task cells are at the bottom of the calendar in the Weekly view, on the right side of the calendar in the Daily view, and appear as bulleted text on the calendar in the Monthly view; see the example of a weekly Task cell on page 168.)

*Create Task*

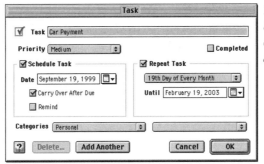

*This is the Task dialog box where you can enter the information and the reminder.*

While in the Task dialog box, you can **set a reminder** of the task deadline by clicking in the "Remind" box. You can **move the task to any other day** by pressing on the tiny calendar icon (next to the "Date" field) and picking a date from the pull-down menu. If you check the "Repeat Task" checkbox, you'll have lots of choices of how often and when to repeat the reminder.

**To move a Task text entry** to another date in any calendar view, just drag it.

## Create event banners

Besides appointments and tasks, you can create event banners that indicate events that span one or more days (up to a year), such as workshops, vacations, or conferences. Click the "Create Event Banner" icon in the toolbar (shown to the right).

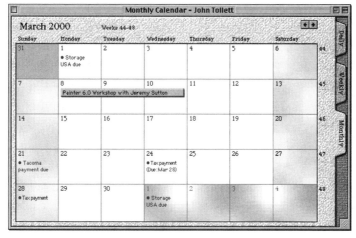

*This calendar displays an event banner. Note also that the appearance of the calendar has been modified from plain gray to linen—see the details below on how to change the appearance.*

## Customize the appearance

You can customize the appearance and behavior of your organizer in the Preferences dialog box. From the Edit menu, choose "Preferences...."

### In the Preferences dialog box you can do things like this (and more)

- Select from fifteen different looks in the "Decor" settings.
- Change fonts to any font on your iMac.
- Choose the time increments to show in the calendar time cells (10, 15, 20, or 30 minute increments).
- Have your iMac dial telephone numbers in your contact list.

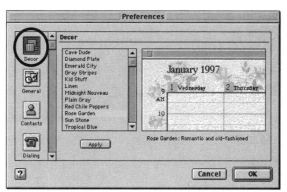

*Modify your calendar's appearance and behavior in the Preferences dialog box. Click one of the icons in the left panel, and the options on the right side will change.*

## For more help

The instructions in this chapter will get you started, but for more complete directions and some great tips and shortcuts, open the Palm Desktop software, then press on the Help menu at the top of the screen. Choose either "Contents...," "Search Index for...," or "Tips...."

You can also print up the manuals that are in the Palm Desktop folder. Look for two files called "Getting Started Guide.pdf" and "Palm Desktop Documentation.pdf." If you don't find these in the Palm folder that's on your iMac, you'll find them on one of the CDs that came with your computer. Do this:

1. Find the CD called "iMac Software Install." Insert it into your iMac.

2. On the CD, find the folder called "Applications" and double-click it to open.

3. Inside that folder, find the folder called "Palm™ Desktop" and double-click it to open.

4. Inside that folder, find the folder called "Documentation" and double-click it to open.

5. Inside that folder (shown below), double-click either of the documentation files (they will open in the Acrobat Reader software, as described on page 72), then print and read.

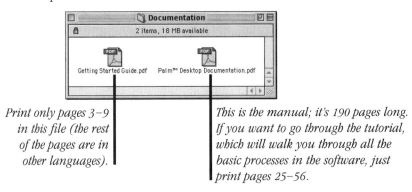

*Print only pages 3–9 in this file (the rest of the pages are in other languages).*

*This is the manual; it's 190 pages long. If you want to go through the tutorial, which will walk you through all the basic processes in the software, just print pages 25–56.*

# The Internet
## and the
# World Wide Web

The "i" in "iMac" stands for Internet. If you are sitting in front of an iMac, you are sitting in front of the easiest and most cost-effective solution to connecting to the Internet. You might have gotten a "cheaper" solution, such as a WebTV box that hooks up to your television, but then you wouldn't be able to do anything else with that machine *except* use the Internet—you wouldn't be able to do your personal accounting, create invoices for your business, or make stationery.

This section discusses what the Internet actually is, what the World Wide Web is, and the sorts of things you can do there. Then you'll walk through getting set up to *log on* and *surf.*

**log on:** *When you use your computer to connect to a communication system such as a phone line to get to the Internet, or a network (system of connected computers) in a large office, the process is called **logging on,** and then you are **online.** Usually to log on you have to enter a password.*

*When you are done, you **log off,** and then you are **offline.***

*The process of logging on and off is similar to calling up a friend and saying hello (logging on), chatting for a while (being online), then saying goodbye (logging off).*

**surf:** *Wander around the World Wide Web.*

**Web pages are predominantly created by people using Macintoshes.** *Even* PC Week *magazine admits this.*

**The Consortium of Liberal Arts Colleges concludes that the Mac is easier.** *The Consortium is a group of fifty colleges; they determined that "the average time to connect a student's Macintosh to a campus network is 10 minutes; the average time to connect a student's IBM-compatible is 45 minutes, with some installations taking more than 10 HOURS."*

Phillip Harriman, Director of Academic Computing, The College of Wooster, quoted in September/October 1998 Mac Today.

**At the Rochester Institute of Technology,** *the oldest, largest, and most prestigious school of photography and printing in the world, 72 percent of the alumni own Macs.*

Contact Sheet, the RIT alumni newsletter

**Desktop video and animation is Macintosh-based.**
*Twice as many Macs than Windows NT PCs are used in video production facilities.\**

*Animation houses use 50 percent more Macs than Windows machines.\**

*CD-ROM and digital video producers are almost twice as likely to use Macs than Windows.\*\**

*These numbers will only grow in the coming months as Final Cut Pro and iMovie become widely adopted. In fact, the most popular digital film editing system in Hollywood is the Avid, which is in essence a souped-up Mac.*

*\*Post Magazine, quoted in March/April 1998 Mac Today.*
*\*\*From a recent study by the independent market research firm Griffin Dix Research Associates, quoted in November/December 1998 Mac Today.*

# What is the Internet?

This Internet thing has been around for over thirty years. In the late '60s the United States military set up a system where computers could send messages to each other through telephone lines. This system of sending messages has grown to include literally millions of computers all around the world, all connected, all capable of sending messages to other computers, sometimes through telephone lines and sometimes through other sorts of specialized lines. And it's this worldwide connection that's now called the Internet.

Think of the Internet as being similar to the electrical wiring in your house. In your house, the wires go into every room, out to the garage, the back porch, the laundry room, and other places. And that wiring allows you to plug in a variety of devices, such as a refrigerator, washing machine, coffee pot, microwave oven, computer, and lamps. The wiring itself doesn't do anything—it is just the system that allows everything else to work.

The Internet works (hypothetically) like your electrical wiring. It potentially connects every home and office on earth, and allows all sorts of things to "plug into it." In this chapter we'll talk about some common uses, such as email, newsgroups, and mailing lists.

In the next chapter we'll talk about the new technology that has changed the world, the **World Wide Web.** The web is not the Internet, just like a lamp in your home is not the electrical system. The web *uses* the Internet to display pages on your computer, just like a lamp uses the electrical system to brighten a room.

## Email

Email stands for "electronic mail," which is a message similar to a letter that is delivered to your mailbox. The difference, of course, is that it is created electronically (in a computer) and is delivered over the Internet straight to another computer. You "open" the electronic mail and read the contents, and you can send an email response instantly. When you receive an email, the phone doesn't ring; your computer doesn't have to be turned on; you can choose to open the email or delete it unopened; you can read it anytime of the day or night; and you can answer it anytime of the day or night.

*modem: The device that translates the information between your computer and the phone lines. Your iMac has a modem built in for a phone line. Even if you have a connection through something like cable or DSL, you need a modem. See page 186.*

No matter where the recipient of your message lives or how long the message, the cost to you is a local phone call because email goes through a *modem* and the phone lines. In fact, on that same local call you can send email to a number of people. It's much quicker and cheaper than using the post office, it's much more fun, and you don't have to get dressed.

Electronic mail can be simply text, or it can include pictures, web pages, or files such as spreadsheets or word processing documents.

When you sign up for Internet access (which I'll walk you through later in this chapter), you will usually be offered an email account; if not, ask for one. You can tell them what you want your email name to be. Your address will look something like this:

### john@something.com   or   john@ratz.com

*See pages 209–211 for details on how to get your email and how to send others email.*

An email address always has the @ symbol, pronounced "at," and the period is always called a "dot." (There is never a space in an email address.) So the address above is pronounced:

*John at Something dot Com*     or     *John at Ratz dot Com*

If you use the EarthLink Total Access software built into your iMac to connect to the Internet, your email address will look something like this:

### yourname@earthlink.net

### Examples of email

Below are several examples of email. Exactly what yours will look like depends on the software you use to receive email, but it will be similar. On the examples below, circle these common items:

| | |
|---|---|
| **To:** | Where you type the address. |
| **Subject:** | Where you type a subject so the receiver knows what this email is about. |
| **Message area:** | Where you type the message. |
| **Attach button:** | Click to find and attach an extra file to send to someone, such as a photograph, newsletter, business report, sound, etc. The file must first be properly prepared to go through the Internet lines. |
| **Send button:** | Click to send the message. |

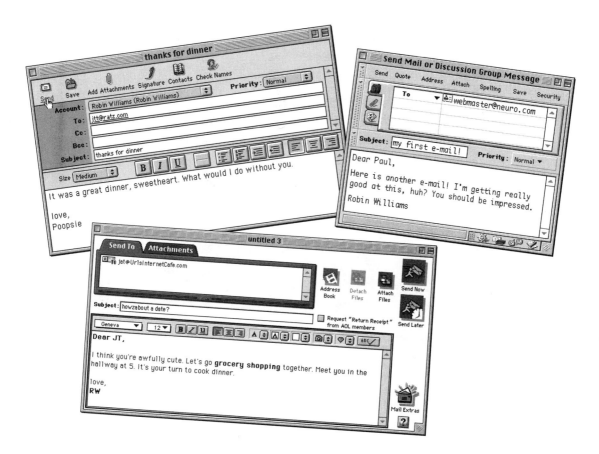

## Newsgroups

One of the popular features of the Internet is **newsgroups,** which are groups of people around the world who have common interests, such as rugby, pet cheetahs, leukemia, pregnancy, hair salons, gay children, Robert Burns, Judaism, various eras of history, collections of all sorts, etc. There are about 30,000 different newsgroups. People in each group "post" their news or questions or comments on the Internet, which is kind of like pinning messages on a bulletin board, and everyone in the group can read them and post their own answers, comments, or questions at any time. It's a wonderful resource.

Some newsgroups are intended for discussion, and some for announcements and queries. Some groups are moderated, where someone reads the postings and perhaps censures messages before posting them.

*protocol:* Set of rules, sometimes spelled out, sometimes expected to be understood.

Newsgroup members often bond together into a tight clique, depending on the newsgroup and its particular members. Thus the one thing you never want to do is bounce into a newsgroup and holler, "Hey! What's goin' on here?" The *protocol* is to "lurk" for a while, just hang around and listen to people, catch the tone, find out what's already been talked about, discover the different personalities, etc. When you do join in, stay on the topic.

*flame:* An irate message or posting, often to new users who didn't read the FAQ. If someone sends you a nasty message, you have been *flamed.* When people start posting nasty messages back and forth to each other, that is a *flame war.*

Also, you must **always** read the "FAQ" (pronounced "fak") which is the list of Frequently Asked Questions. If you dare jump into a newsgroup and ask a dumb question that was covered in the FAQ, you are guaranteed to get pounced upon by some irate member.

NEVER TYPE IN ALL CAPS. Online, all caps is the equivalent of shouting, and people won't hesitate to point it out to you.

### Find a newsgroup

To find a newsgroup that is centered around your particular interest, go to the web site **www.deja.com** (don't worry, I'll tell you how to "go" there in a few minutes, on page 202). The current site is shown below, but it changes all the time. (In addition to newsgroup searches and lists, Deja,which used to be DejaNews, is now a consumer review site.)

### To find people talking about your interest

1. Find the "Power Search" link, and click on it (shown circled, below).

2. In the "Enter Keywords" edit box (circled, below), type in what it is you want to talk with other people about.

3. In the "Results type" menu, choose "Deja Classic" (circled, below). Click the "Search" button.

4. You will get a list of results; click to read any of them. When you read a "posting," you will find a link to add yourself to that newsgroup.

*Tip:* If you use EarthLink as your ISP, then use Microsoft Outlook Express to access every one of the 33,000+ newsgroups. See page 211.

If you use a local ISP, they will provide you with access to the most popular newsgroups. If you find one you want to have regular access to and it's not available at the moment through your local news server, talk to your ISP and they can arrange for you to get it.

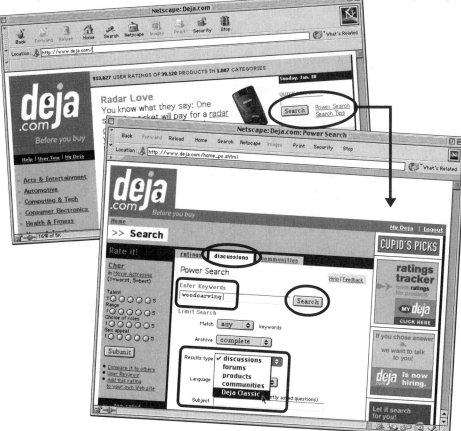

## Mailing lists

Using the Internet you can also join any of 90,000 mailing lists, or listservs, which are similar to newsgroups except instead of posting messages on a bulletin board, you get email delivered to your computer. Once you join a mailing list, any email message sent by anyone on the list automatically goes to everyone else on the whole list. In an active list, this can mean *lots* of mail.

### Find a mailing list

To access the vast list of mailing lists, go to this address when you get connected to the Internet (don't worry, I'll tell you how to get to an address in a minute): **www.liszt.com**.

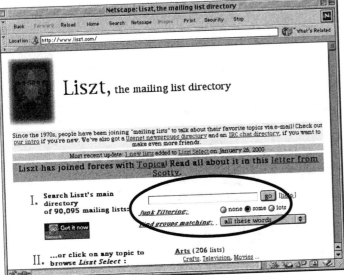

Scroll down the page; click on any topic to get more information, and then if you like you can "subscribe," which is the process of joining the list so you get the mail. Or type in a topic (circled, to the left), click the "Go" button, and see how many mailing lists there are on your favorite topic.

### The most important thing to remember!

One of your first pieces of email from the mailing list will be *instructions on how to get off the list.* **Keep these instructions!** There is only one way to get off the list and stop all the email, and if you don't have the specific directions you will end up accidentally emailing *everybody* on the list telling them you want to get off, and they will all email you back nasty messages, and you will still be on the list.

*This is the Liszt web page where you can find any mailing list.*

An email list is not run by a human; it is run by what's called a "robot," which is actually software, of course. But unless you send the precisely worded message to the right robot, you can't get off the list. So keep those directions in a safe place.

# What is the World Wide Web?

You will definitely be using email, and you might want to join a newsgroup or a mailing list, but the place you'll find most incredibly useful, informative, and downright fun is the World Wide Web.

## What is the World Wide Web?

The part of the Internet we all hear about the most these days is the **World Wide Web.** The Internet itself has been around for thirty years, but it wasn't incredibly popular because you had to be a nerd to know what was there and how to access it. There were no pictures, no sounds —just ugly yellow or green text on a black background and you had to type in weird codes to get what you wanted. Then the Macintosh was invented and changed the way people used computers and changed our expectations of what a computer should do. We grew to expect graphics, sound, and attractive stuff on our monitors.

So several years ago new technology was developed that allows us to send not just text email messages and news postings, but full **pages** through the Internet that include color, sound, graphics, animation, interactivity, and video. And the individual pages have "links" that connect them to each other.

*If you would like to make your own web pages, check out Chapter 17.*

The World Wide Web is actually just millions and millions of individual pages which are very much like the word processing pages you might be used to making. The information and graphics on these pages are sent around the world using the connection called the Internet.

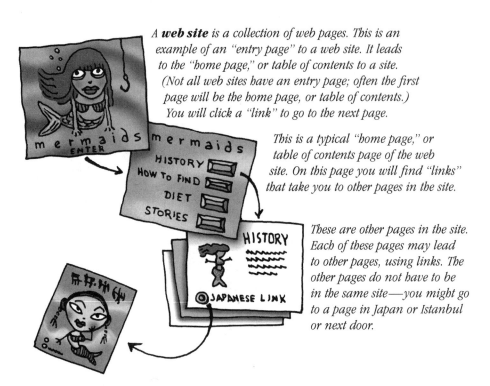

A **web site** is a collection of web pages. This is an example of an "entry page" to a web site. It leads to the "home page," or table of contents to a site. (Not all web sites have an entry page; often the first page will be the home page, or table of contents.) You will click a "link" to go to the next page.

This is a typical "home page," or table of contents page of the web site. On this page you will find "links" that take you to other pages in the site.

These are other pages in the site. Each of these pages may lead to other pages, using links. The other pages do not have to be in the same site—you might go to a page in Japan or Istanbul or next door.

## What's a browser?

Of course, to see web pages, first you have to be connected to the Internet. And you also need special software, called a **browser.**

A browser is just like any other software that has a special purpose. If you want to type a letter, you use the software called a word processor, right? If you want to crunch numbers, you use the software called a spreadsheet. If you want to see World Wide Web pages, you use the software called a browser.

The most popular browser is called **Netscape** (the various versions of Netscape at the moment are called Navigator and Communicator). The other browser is called Microsoft Internet Explorer. Your iMac has both of these browsers already installed. The two browsers are not exactly the same; the same web page will often look slightly different in each of the browsers, and will look slightly different again if you use America Online. I prefer (and everyone I know prefers) Netscape.

As with all software, browsers are constantly being updated and improved. The versions that are installed on your iMac are current as of this writing, and should last you a while.

Netscape Communicator

*This is the icon representing the Netscape Communicator browser. Different versions of Netscape are called different names. You might see Netscape Navigator as well.*

Internet Explorer

*This is the icon representing the Microsoft Internet Explorer browser.*

My name is Browser. I'm a netHound.

©2000 Ballyhoo.llc

## Let's look at a web page

Once you get the computer connected to the Internet (in the next chapter), the rest is easy. Below is a typical web page, displayed on the screen using a browser. One of the most important features on web pages is **links.** You click on a link with your mouse, and the browser "jumps" to another web page with different information. You know an item (either text or a graphic) is a link because your pointer turns into a little pointing hand, like this: 🖑 or 🖑. You can usually tell a *text* link even without the pointing hand because the text is usually <u>underlined</u>.

Another important feature of a web page is its **address.** Every web page has an individual address, just like a house address. The address is also called the **URL** (pronounced "you are ell"). If someone says, "Hey, what's your URL?" they mean, "What's the address to your web site?"

*If you know a web page address, type it in here, then hit Enter or Return. Your browser will find and display that web page.*

*This is called a "navigation bar," a strip of links that take you throughout the web site.*

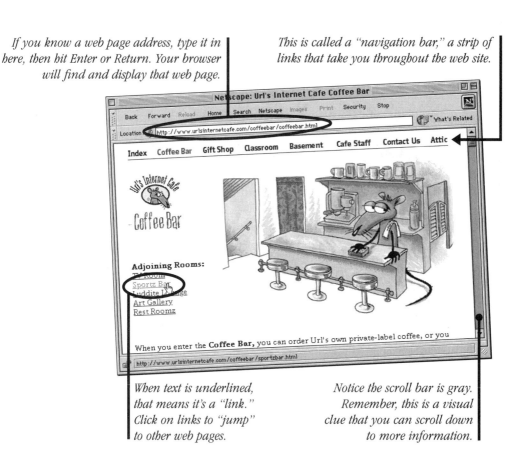

*When text is underlined, that means it's a "link." Click on links to "jump" to other web pages.*

*Notice the scroll bar is gray. Remember, this is a visual clue that you can scroll down to more information.*

### Jump to another page

Do you notice that the web page below has a different address from the previous web page? By clicking the link labeled "Sportz Bar," you jump to this web page that has a variety of fun articles. It's a new page, but it is clearly part of the same web site as the first one.

Besides the underlined text on the web page below, what else do you think might be a link?

*The first part of this address, "UrlsInternetCafe.com" is the same as the address for the web page you see opposite. That means both pages belong to the same web site.*

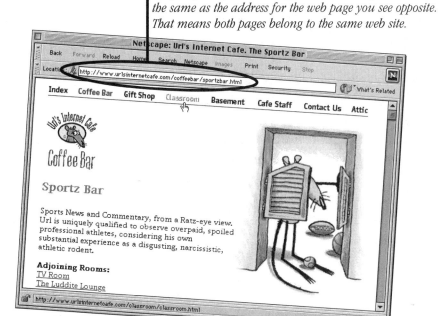

*How many links do you think are on this web page?*

*There are eleven links:*
*Index*
*Coffee Bar*
*Gift Shop*
*Classroom*
*Basement*
*Cafe Staff*
*Contact Us*
*Attic*
*TV Room*
*The Luddite Lounge*
*And "Url's Internet Cafe" logo takes you to the first page of the web site.*

That's basically how easy it is to get around on the World Wide Web. You will learn more bits and pieces as you go along, but for now know that it really is this easy, and that's why it has changed the world.

## And what's a modem, anyway?

It's kind of interesting to understand why you have to use a modem to get online. You see, the computer is **digital,** meaning it can only do things in whole chunks. It can count from 0 to 1; it can understand "on" and "off." It can understand stuff that is counted in whole numbers, like ice cubes.

The phone lines, however, are **analog.** Analog is flowing, infinite, and can be broken down into smaller and smaller pieces. Water is an analog thing.

So to get information from the digital computer to go through the analog phone lines, the modem takes the digital information (ice cubes) and turns it into analog information (water) to send it through the lines. On the other end, another modem takes the analog information (water) and turns it back into the exact same digital information (ice cubes) for the other computer.

How fast a modem can do this is called its "baud rate." The bigger the baud rate number, the more information (ice cubes) it can process. The chart below shows what these numbers mean.

| Speed | Say it | Write it | How fast is it |
|---|---|---|---|
| 2400 | twenty-four hundred | 2400 (2.4) | s l o - o - o - o - w |
| 9600 | ninety-six hundred | 9600 (9.6) | not much better |
| 14,400 | fourteen-four | 14.4 | minimum for the Internet |
| 28,800 | twenty-eight eight | 28.8 | the Internet isn't too bad at 28.8 |
| 33,600 | thirty-three six | 33.6 | pretty good |
| 56,000 | fifty-six k | 56K | pretty fast* |

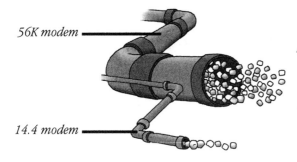

56K modem

14.4 modem

*The faster the modem, the more information it can process at one time.*

*\*You have a 56K modem built into your iMac. However, the baud rate is still dependent on how "clean" your local phone lines are. Rarely will you actually get data at 56K!*

*You might use **cable** or **DSL** to connect to the Internet. Those are very high-speed lines that go through special modems, not your internal iMac modem.*

# Getting Connected

# 15

To get to the Internet, your computer must be connected to a "server," a special computer that has information flowing to and from the Internet 24 hours a day. You probably have one of these situations:

You can connect to the Internet through a **phone line** that is attached to your computer and goes to the phone jack in the wall, or perhaps through another telephone. Typically, your modem will **dial up** your Internet Service Provider. You will most likely only connect for a short time each day, or maybe several times a day. You will log on to the server through your computer, do your Internet and World Wide Web business, then log off.

If you live in a larger town, you might connect to the Internet through something like a television **cable** or **DSL** (digital subscriber line). In that case, you have a special modem supplied by the service you signed up with, and you connect, not with a regular telephone cord, but with a special cord called an Ethernet cable. Your connection is "on" all the time (meaning you never have to "dial up" through the phone line).

Or maybe you work at a business or college that owns their own Internet server, in which case your computer is probably connected to that server 24 hours a day because it is on the company **network.** In that case, you do not "dial up" through a phone line to connect to the Internet—your computer has access all day and night (it's "on" all the time). All you need to do is open your browser or email program.

To get connected to a server, you have to go through a setup process. The process is different depending on what kind of service you choose to be connected through. The first part of this chapter talks about the options you have for connectivity, then explains what the iMac can setup for you automatically, if you so choose. *Read about your options, because you have to make a choice before you start the setup process.*

## What is America Online?

**America Online** is the most popular "online service" in the world. An online service is a self-contained entity that allows you to connect to the electronic world. Within a service you can send and receive email, join clubs, "chat" with people around the world, get answers to questions, "download" new software (which means to copy it from their computer to yours), set up a web site, and much more.

America Online (also called **AOL**) is a nice, friendly place. It's like a safe, contained village. There are guides to help you, "patrol officers" to make sure people are behaving properly, instructions on how to do things and where to go, help for when you get lost, and more. But America Online is not the Internet, nor is it the World Wide Web. When you are on America Online, you are contained within their system of computers that sits right in Virginia, the home of America Online.

If you think of America Online as a village in Virginia, then the Internet is the big, wide world. In the world, there is no one to help you, to point the way, or to keep you safe. You're on your own. America Online, like every other service (such as CompuServe, Genie, or Prodigy), has a back door. You can slip out that back door and go to the World Wide Web, or access anything else on the Internet, such as mailing lists and newsgroups. You can choose from a menu in America Online called "Internet" and "Go to the Web"; when you do that, you leave America Online and head out into the Internet world. You leave the village. However, AOL has been integrating the web into its village and now it is difficult to tell the boundaries. (I'm not sure this is a good thing. It used to be so uncomplicated. Sigh.)

*America Online*

*An alias to America Online is inside the Internet folder on your hard disk. If you decide to use AOL, drag this alias to the Desktop so it's more convenient to connect.*

*There are a few tips about using America Online in the Problems and Solutions section of this book, pages 289–291.*

*This is the clean, safe, friendly village of an online service.*

## What is an ISP?

The acronym ISP stands for **Internet Service Provider.** There are two basic ways to connect to the Internet—one is through an online service, such as America Online (see opposite page). The other way is to find an Internet Service Provider (ISP) who gives you special numbers to dial from your computer at home to connect to their servers, and your iMac has the special software necessary. This software and the numbers connect you to *their* computers (the ISP's), and *their* computers connect *you* to the Internet, as illustrated below.

There are probably several **local providers** in your area. Ask your friends whom they use for Internet access. You will typically pay a set-up fee to the ISP and a monthly fee for your connection. The fees can vary widely, so you might want to ask around about the cost of a local provider.

To make it easy for you, Apple has arranged with a **national provider,** EarthLink, to give you an Internet connection through your iMac; see page 191 for details.

*This is you at your computer.*          *This is an ISP, giving you access to the Internet.*

### Should you use AOL or an ISP?

If you're not yet connected to the Internet, you need to make a choice about how you want to get there—America Online (AOL) or an Internet Service Provider (ISP).

*You have America Online software on your iMac, in the Internet folder. If you want to sign up, just double-click the AOL icon and follow the directions.*

**I used to** suggest that if you are new to the online world, start with an online service such as AOL. Become familiar with email, downloading, chatting, sending and receiving files, etc. Poke around the World Wide Web and the rest of the Internet. When you find you are using your online service only to get to the Internet, it's time to get a direct connection through your local ISP. Many people use both. **But now** the iMac has made it so much simpler to get to the web, use email, and to do everything else that it is just as easy to have a direct Internet connection instead of AOL. I'm afraid you're going to have to make the decision yourself of which one to sign up with.

### If you decide to use America Online

There are several places on your iMac where you can click a button and the computer takes you to your email program or a web page (the "Mail" icon, the "Browse the Internet" icon, searching the web with Sherlock, web site Favorites in the Apple menu, and others). If you have a direct connection through a local or national ISP, the iMac will open the connection, log on, open your browser, and find the web page

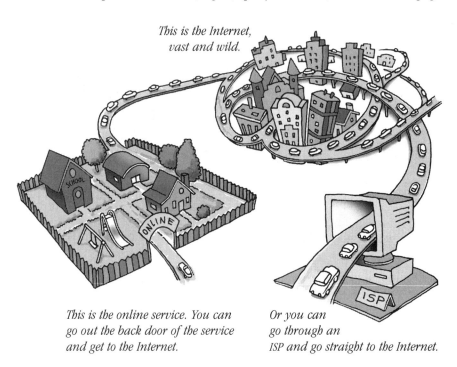

*This is the Internet, vast and wild.*

*This is the online service. You can go out the back door of the service and get to the Internet.*

*Or you can go through an ISP and go straight to the Internet.*

you asked for. **But** if you have an America Online connection, you can set up your iMac so it will *open* AOL for you automatically, you will still have to actually *sign on* yourself; the iMac cannot sign on for you automatically. To set up your iMac so it automatically opens the AOL application, do this:

> **If you're using Mac OS 8.5, 8.6, or 9.0,** go to the Internet Control Panel, click the "Web" tab, and choose "America Online" as your default browser (see details on page 198).

> **If you're using Mac OS 8.1,** the iMac can't establish the connection with America Online automatically. You can, of course, open the AOL program yourself, but the "Mail" or "Browse the Internet" icons, etc., won't do it for you.

*How can you tell which Mac OS you are using? At the Desktop, go to the Apple menu and choose "About This Computer."*

**Note: If you're using an AirPort system** (see Chapter 20) the iMac cannot establish a direct connection with America Online through AirPort. If you use AOL with an ISP, as explained on page 192, the AirPort *can* connect you to AOL.

## EarthLink Total Access

EarthLink is a national ISP (Internet Service Provider), as opposed to a local ISP that would be physically located in your area. The software to connect to EarthLink is already on your iMac. Even though EarthLink is not local to most people, it provides a local access number for most places. If there is no local number available for your area, EarthLink provides an 800 number (although the 800 number costs an *extra* $4.95 an hour). The current cost to connect to EarthLink is something like $19.95 a month, and it will be billed to your credit card automatically. If you choose to connect with EarthLink, you will be given an email address.

If you are in Hawaii or Alaska, be sure to read the fine print for EarthLink service—they apply the foreign rate to those states, which is an *extra* $9 an hour! And check to see just how local the local number is; for instance, in New Mexico there are only two access numbers for the entire state, so most people in New Mexico would have to pay the toll charge for the telephone/modem call on their phone bill in addition to the EarthLink monthly service charge.

You might choose EarthLink for any of these reasons:

1. You don't want to bother trying to find a local ISP and then gathering all the details to fill in the blanks as you go through the setup process— you'd rather take advantage of the arrangement Apple has provided and let the software set up everything for you.
2. There is no local ISP in your area.
3. You travel a lot and you want to have a national ISP that can provide you with local numbers in many areas of the country.

### You need to choose: local or national ISP

Your iMac has an Internet Setup Assistant you will use, starting on the next page. It's going to ask whether you want to use a local ISP or a national one. You must know the answer before you start the setup process.

If you already have a local provider, your decision is already made. If you don't have a local provider, you might want to use EarthLink for now because it's easy and you don't have to think hard to get connected. If you later decide you want to switch, you certainly can.

### America Online and the iMac Internet Setup Assistant

If you already use or plan to use America Online, **do not use the Internet Setup Assistant!** America Online connects you to both their internal service and to the Internet—AOL will be your ISP.

### Using both AOL and an ISP

It is certainly possible to use both AOL and another ISP. In fact, your monthly bill from AOL is less expensive if you are connected to an ISP (although of course the ISP will also bill you monthly). Some people use both because someone in the house wants all the chats, clubs, organization, and structure of the AOL service, but someone else in the house wants the direct, clean connection to the Internet without AOL getting in the way. If this is your plan, go ahead and do both (although there is a slight glitch in something called "AOL link," that you will have to work out; see page 290). If you get to a point where you find you are not using the AOL services very much but are spending most of your time directly on the Internet, then you can cancel AOL at any time.

An advantage to using AOL with an ISP is that the AirPort wireless system, if you decide to use it (see Chapter 20) can connect to AOL *through* your ISP, but cannot connect *directly* to AOL.

## Begin the Internet setup

First decide which of these groups you belong to, then follow the directions.

**If you plan to use only America Online,** *you don't need to read the rest of this section.* Just double-click the AOL icon, found in the Internet folder, and sign up. After you're signed up with AOL, see page 198 and 289–291 for some tips to make sure it works seamlessly on your iMac.

**If you are in a school or large business with a network** (all the computers are connected and can send messages to each other, even without the Internet), you should talk to your network administrator first because you will need to know several technical details to go through the process. See exactly the questions you need to ask in the illustration on page 197.

**If you are at home or a small business** and you either have an existing service with an ISP that you want to get set up on your new iMac or you want to start a new account, use the Internet Setup Assistant as described on these pages. An "existing account" includes an account you have created with an ISP but have never set up on any computer yet. Call the ISP and get the answers to the items you need to fill in, as shown in the illustration on page 196.

*Important note: You do have to have a **credit card** to go through the Internet setup because an Internet connection through an ISP (or America Online) is not free. You will be asked to enter your credit card number on a web page. This is safe. Really. The information is highly encrypted (secret code). It is much easier for someone to get your credit card number in a restaurant, over the telephone, through mail order, from a receipt dropped in the mall parking lot, etc., than it is to get it by hacking into a secure server. And you're usually only liable for $50 if your credit card is used illegally anyway.*

### Step 1: Open the Internet Setup Assistant

Open either the "Assistants" folder or the "Internet" folder, then double-click the icon "Internet Setup Assistant."

 *or*

Assistants    Internet    *Internet Setup Assistant*

**OR** if you want to use the really pretty, new setup assistant in Mac OS 9, open the "Apple Extras" folder, then double-click on this Setup Assistant icon:

Setup Assistant

### Step 2: Follow the directions for a new account

*(If you're **not** creating a **new** account, skip to Step 4.)*

The Internet Setup Assistant will walk you through the process of connecting. It will gather information it needs along the way, and enter that information where it belongs. The process is easy and self-explanatory. You might see any one of the three setup assistants shown below. They all ask for the same information and setup your iMac in the same way. Quit at any time by pressing Command Q.

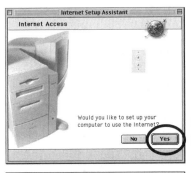

*When you see buttons or arrows, click them to move on.*

Setup Assistant

*This particular icon will open this fancy assistant.*

Get me on the Internet

*If you quit before the process is complete, this icon will appear on your Desktop.*

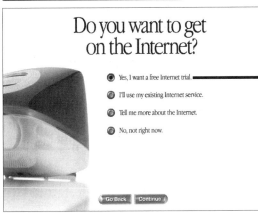

*This choice will set you up with an EarthLink account. The first thirty days, at the moment, are free.*

## Step 3: Finish establishing your new account

The connection process takes you to the Internet and the World Wide Web. The browser that the Setup Assistant uses is Microsoft Internet Explorer. Take a good look at that browser because in a couple of minutes, when this is done, I am going to suggest you switch to the Netscape browser (page 198). Below you see an example of the kind of page you might be presented with (web pages change often, so it might not look exactly like this!). If you got here, you're done. Skip to page 198.

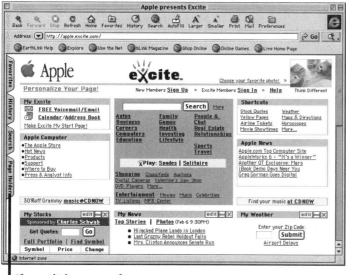

*You'll see a web page like this if you connected through any ISP except EarthLink.*

*If you click on one of these tabs, a big panel pops out, covering half the web page. Click the tab again to send the panel back.*

*You'll see a web page like the one below if you connect through EarthLink.*

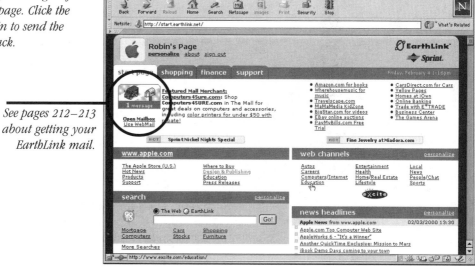

*See pages 212–213 about getting your EarthLink mail.*

### Step 4: Follow the directions for connecting an existing account

The Internet Setup Assistant will walk you through the process of connecting. It will gather information it needs along the way and enter that information where it belongs. Most of the process is very easy, but you must first call your current service provider and get important data from them! I guarantee you can't make this connection without a call to them (unless you have another computer and can take the information from that one and plug it in here, and if you can do that, you're probably not reading this book). You might get either of the setups shown below. When you finish the setup, you're connected and online! Read page 198.

*Your "user name" and "password" as registered with your ISP are not always the same as your email address and password! Ask your ISP what they are!*

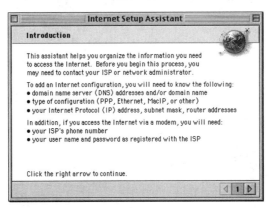

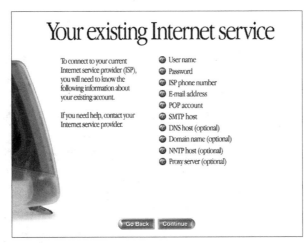

*Before you begin, check this list and make sure you can answer each item. If not, call the ISP and ask them.*

*If you connect through cable, DSL, or a local area network (LAN) in a business or school, also check the next two illustrations for the details you will need for those connections.*

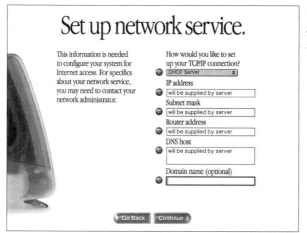

*These are the details you need to know to connect with cable or* DSL, *plus the items listed on the previous page.*

*These are the details you need to know to connect through a local area network (*LAN*) as in a large office building, school system, or even in a small office with lots of computers, like I have.*

*Dang. If you get this message, see page 294 about a known bug in Mac OS 9, and even take a look at pages 295–298 about reformatting your entire hard disk if you find that your machine is constantly having minor problems.*

## Set these defaults

*If you are using or plan to use **America Online,** set both of these options to "America Online." To choose AOL as the default email application, you will have to find it. You'll get a dialog box asking where it is: it's in the Macintosh HD, in the Internet folder, in the America Online folder.*

To make sure things work smoothly for you in the next chapter, take a minute to change these defaults (automatic choices). This will make things happen for you just like they happen in the next chapter. You can always come back and change these defaults at any time; just make sure you are not connected to the Internet and no browser is open while you do it (only because these defaults won't take effect until the next time you connect).

1. Click once on the Apple menu.

2. Slide down to Control Panels, and out to the right; click once on "Internet."

3. Click the tab labeled "E-mail" (circled, below left).

4. At the bottom of this dialog box, press on the menu to the right of "Default E-mail Application." Choose "Outlook Express" or "Netscape Communicator."

5. Now click the tab labeled "Web" (circled, below right).

6. At the bottom of this dialog box, press on the menu to the right of "Default Web Browser." Choose "Netscape Communicator."

7. If you want to learn lots more about this Control Panel, click the Help button in the upper right of the box.

8. To close the Internet Control Panel, click in the little Close Box in the upper-left of the window, in the title bar.

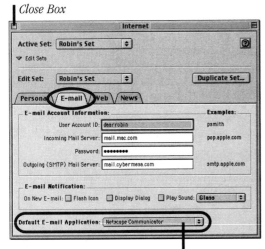

*Close Box*

*Press anywhere in this bar to get the menu of choices. Choose "Select…" to find America Online.*

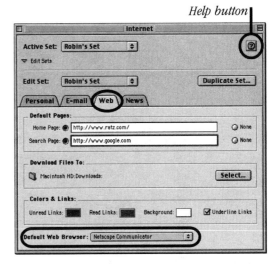

*Help button*

*All of the information you see typed in these boxes was automatically entered when you went through the setup process!*

# Let's Go to the Web!

This chapter walks you through your first adventure on the World Wide Web. I'm assuming you worked through the previous chapter or set up your connection yourself already, and you changed the defaults mentioned on the previous page. If you are using America Online, see page 291 for a few tips about the browser.

## Step 1: Connect to the Internet and open a browser

**a. If you have a permanent connection** such as cable, DSL, a T1 line, or if you're on a network with an Internet connection at the office, then you're already there, connected to the Internet. All you need to do is open your favorite browser by double-clicking its icon.

**b. If you're using America Online,** double-click its icon to open it. If you have a permanent connection as mentioned above, all you have to do is sign on to AOL. If you have a "dial up" connection with a phone line connected from your computer to a phone jack, AOL will connect when you sign on.

**c. If you signed up with a local ISP or with EarthLink** and your modem has to dial a phone number to connect, double-click that icon on the right side of your Desktop called "Browse the Internet." That will open the connection and also open your browser.

If you don't have that icon anymore: Go to the Apple menu, choose "Remote Access Status," and click the "Connect" button; **or** click the telephone pole icon (  ) in the Control Strip and choose "Connect" from the menu. Then double-click the browser icon to open the browser.

*Netscape Communicator*

*America Online*

*You'll find these aliases in the "Internet" folder. Drag them to the Desktop so you can access them easily.*

*Browse the Internet*

*The original of this is in the "Internet Utilities" folder, inside the "Internet" folder.*

*These two icons will flash back and forth when you're connected.*

default: The option
that is automatically
chosen for you.

## Step 2: Check out the default home page

Each browser opens to a "home page," or start page. This is different from the home page in a web site: this home page in your browser will appear every time you open this browser; when you click the little "home" icon at the top, you will go back to this page. If you connected through EarthLink, the illustration on the opposite page displays something similar to what you will see on your screen.

### Change some defaults

Before you go any further, I suggest you make some changes to your browser default so all of your web pages look better. It's easy. (See page 289 for AOL.)

**Important tip:**
*Unless you have cable or DSL, your connection is set up to automatically disconnect if there is no activity for ten minutes. If you get disconnected in the middle of this tutorial, perhaps because you went to get a cup of tea, then do this:*

*Go to the Apple menu.*

*Choose "Remote Access Status."*

*Click Connect.*

*After the squawking stops, go back to your browser and continue.*

*(If you're using AOL, just log on again as usual.)*

1. From the Edit menu, choose "Preferences…."

2. On the left side of the dialog box, click on "Fonts."
   (If "Fonts" isn't showing, click the tiny arrow next to "Appearance.")

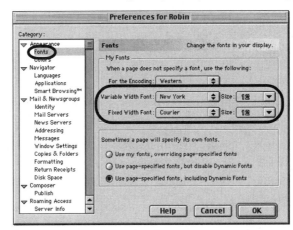

3. Change the "Variable Width Font" to New York. Its size is probably already "12." That's good.

4. Change the "Fixed Width Font" to Monaco, and its size to 12.

5. If you want to make the toolbar across the top smaller than it is right now, click "Appearance" in the left panel. Then click the little button for "Text Only" (not shown above). This will give you more room on the web page.

*If it won't let you do Step 6, click "Identity" in the left panel, then uncheck the box "Use Internet Config." Try Step 6 again.*

6. If you want to change the home page to one of your choice, click "Navigator" in the left panel. Under "Home page location," type the web address, including **http://**, that you want your browser to automatically open to. And when you click the "Home" button, it will go to this page.

7. Click "OK" to keep your preferences and close this box.

## Poke around this web page

This web page is a window just like every window you've used on the iMac! You already know how to use the scroll bars, close the window, resize it, collapse it, move it around the screen, etc.

Everything you see underlined is a **link.** Click once on any link to jump to that page. On this page you also see a lot of **buttons,** such as "shopping," "finance," etc. Click once on any button to jump to that page. Most graphics are also links. Oh, there are so many places to go.

***Click*** *the Back button once to go back to the page you were just at.* ***Press*** *(hold the mouse button down) on the Back button and you will get a menu listing all the pages you have been to; select one. Click the Forward button to go forward after you have backtracked.*

*Click the Home button to come back to this page (or whatever page you have set as your home; see previous page).*

*When a page is "loading," you will see comets flying through this logo. When the comets stop, the page is fully loaded.*

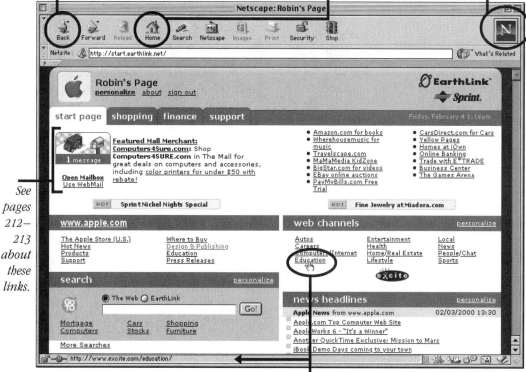

*See pages 212– 213 about these links.*

*Notice when you have your pointer positioned over a* ***link*** *(don't click), the address of the page you will go to is usually displayed here in the* ***status bar.*** *Sometimes this information is handy to have.*

### Step 3: Enter a web address

Enter any web address you may have. If you don't know any specific web addresses, try this one:

## www.UrlsInternetCafe.com

Type the address in the "location box" at the top of the window, as circled below. Then hit the Return or Enter key. The browser will find that page and display it. If you enter **www.UrlsInternetCafe.com,** this is the page that appears:

*Type a web address in here.*
*You don't have to type "http://."*

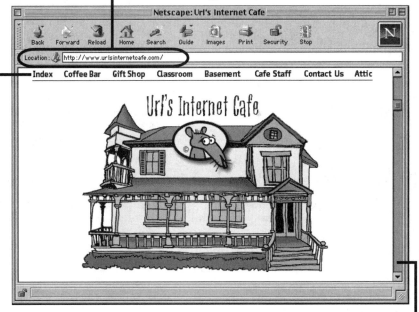

*This is called a "navigation bar" because it has links that help you navigate around a web site. A good site has a clear navigation bar that always tells you where you are within the entire site and lets you get to every other section of the site from every page you happen to be on. Check it out—browse around Url's web site and watch the navigation bar change as you go from room to room.*

*If the scroll bar is gray, that means you can scroll down to see more in the window.*

**Tip:** *In a web address, it doesn't matter if you type capital letters or lowercase **in the first part,** as in www.UrlsInternetCafe.com. But after the first slash (/, which will appear automatically after the .com), **you must type exactly** any capital or lowercase letters or you won't get to the page.*

## Step 4: Find a corporate web site

Just about every major corporation has a web site. You can often find them easily by typing in what seems to be a logical address. For instance, Toyota can probably be found at **www.toyota.com**. The NFL website is probably at **www.nfl.com**. Apple is probably at **www.apple.com**. Try it.

In fact, if the address ends with "**.com**," most of the time you don't even have to type **www.** or **.com**—just type the middle part. For instance, if you want to go to **www.adobe.com**, just type "**adobe**" and hit Return. Try it—try typing **cnn**, **nytimes**, **esprit**, **nfl**, **disney**, **mgm**, or any other favorite.

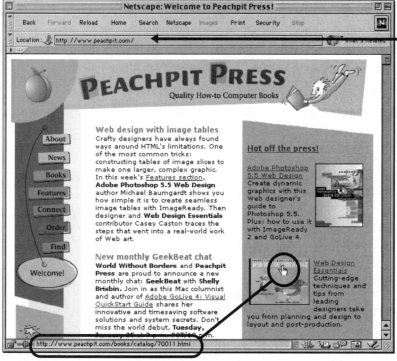

*Type the corporate name in here (make sure you delete everything else first). Then hit Return or Enter. The browser will fill in "www" and ".com." Occasionally this technique doesn't work; if not, type the www and the .com.*

*The trick above only works with .com addresses; if the address ends with .edu, .gov, or any of the other domain extensions, you have to type that extension in.*

***Most graphics on web pages are also links.*** *If your pointer turns into a browser hand when you slide over a graphic (like the one above, on the book), that graphic is a link. Check the status bar at the bottom of the window to see the address of where the graphic link will take you.*

*Do you see Peachpit's navigation bar, down the side? Of course it looks different from Url's. Navigation bars come in lots of different forms.*

## Step 5: Search for something on the web

There are many millions of individual web pages on the Internet. If you don't already know the exact address of the page you want, you need to use a **search tool** (often called a search engine) to find it. Learning how to *really* search the Internet is a valuable skill that takes some time to learn, but everyone needs to know at least a little about how to search.

You don't have to buy the search tools, nor do you have to install them. They are just there on the web. They are just web pages.

The most important thing to realize about search tools is that when you type in something you want to find, such as a particular dog breed, the search tool does not go instantly all over the World Wide Web at that moment and try to find something for you. No, it looks into its own database, or collection, of information to find something. Each search tool chooses what to put into its database, based on varying criteria. Thus you can do the same search with three different search tools and you will get three different lists of results (responses) to your request.

*You can also use the Sherlock feature on your iMac, right at your Desktop, to search for information on the Internet. Get Sherlock from the Apple menu. See Chapter 19.*

Let's do a quick search. "Yahoo" is one of the most popular search tools on the web. Type this into the location box in the browser: **yahoo**. Hit Return. You'll see something like this:

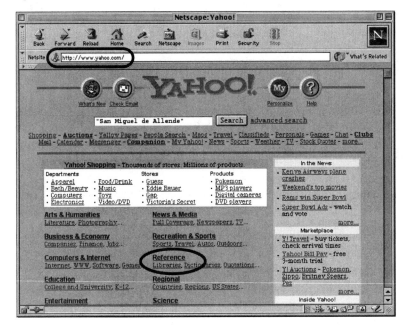

### How to use Yahoo

Yahoo is a search tool that is called a "directory." You see on the Yahoo page a number of categories. These categories have been put together by humans who have decided which web sites belong in the directory and under which category. If you are looking for whole web sites about a particular topic, Yahoo is a good tool to use.

One way to use Yahoo is to "drill down" through the categories. For instance, let's say you are looking for a particular quotation. On the first page of Yahoo, click on the category **Reference** (circled on opposite page). You get a further list of more specific categories. Click on **Quotations** (circled, below). Continue this method of drilling (clicking) down deeper into the categories and you will get to a "results" page, where Yahoo has found very specific sites about all kinds of quotations. Click any of those pages to go to that web site. Use your Back button to go back to the list of Yahoo results.

- **Libraries** *(1855)*
- **Maps@**

*Tip: The number in parentheses after a category tells you how many individual entries are in that category. The @ symbol means that category is subdivided into even more categories.*

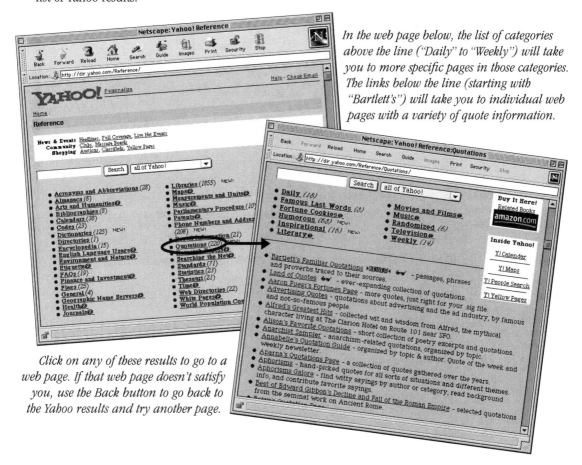

*In the web page below, the list of categories above the line ("Daily" to "Weekly") will take you to more specific pages in those categories. The links below the line (starting with "Bartlett's") will take you to individual web pages with a variety of quote information.*

*Click on any of these results to go to a web page. If that web page doesn't satisfy you, use the Back button to go back to the Yahoo results and try another page.*

### How to use AltaVista

AltaVista is another search tool that collects information for its database in a very different way from Yahoo. AltaVista is a "word search" engine that uses automatic software called "spiders" or "robots." If you are looking for a word or phrase that might not have an entire web site devoted to it, AltaVista is a good place to search. To get to AltaVista, type this address, **www. altavista.com**, in the *location box*, then hit the Return or Enter key. You should see something like the illustration shown opposite.

*Tip: You can also use Yahoo in this same way, by typing in a request and clicking the search button.*

In the *search edit box* (circled, opposite), type the word or phrase you want to find, then click the "Search" button. If you type a phrase or first and last name, put quotation marks before and after the phrase or name, like so:

"Santa Fe Railroad"     "George Washington"     "French sheepdogs"

If you *don't* put quotation marks around something like "Santa Fe Railroad," AltaVista will find every page with the word "Santa" on it, *plus* every page with the word "Fe," *plus* every page with the word "railroad." The quotation marks help to limit the results so you are more likely to find something useful.

All search engines have tips for narrowing the search. Look for the "Tips" or "Help" button and follow the guidelines. One technique you can use in most search engines goes by the scary name of "Boolean operators." All that means is you can use AND, OR, and NOT (some search tools use + instead of AND and − instead of NOT).

For instance, let's say I'm looking for people who breed Briards.

*This is my Briard, Reilly. He's very large. He adores me.*

If I enter **briard breeder** I will get every page with the word "briard" on it, plus every page with the word "breeder" on it.

If I enter **"briard breeder"** with quotation marks I will only get pages that have the words "briard" and "breeder" directly next to each other.

But if I enter **briard AND breeder** I will get pages that have both the word "briard" and the word "breeder," even if they are not next to each other.

And if I enter **briard NOT breeder** I will get pages that have the word "briard" but *not* the word "breeder."

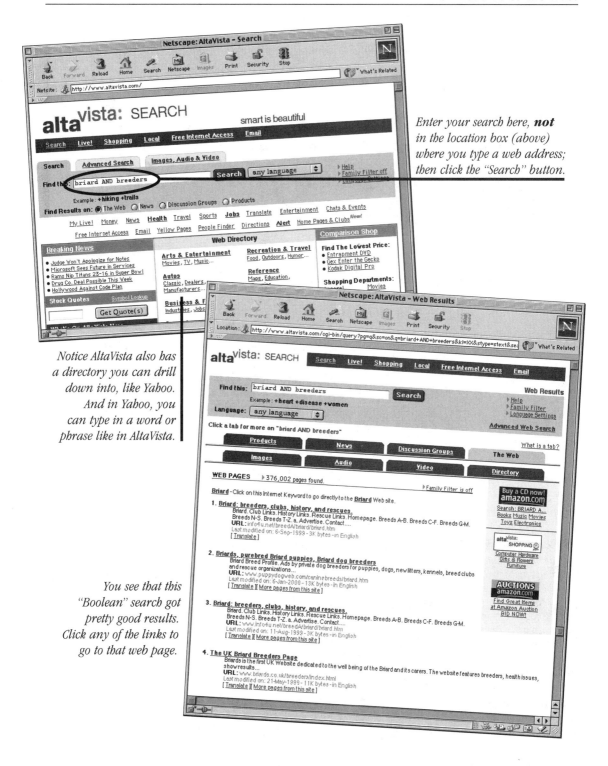

*Enter your search here, **not** in the location box (above) where you type a web address; then click the "Search" button.*

*Notice AltaVista also has a directory you can drill down into, like Yahoo. And in Yahoo, you can type in a word or phrase like in AltaVista.*

*You see that this "Boolean" search got pretty good results. Click any of the links to go to that web page.*

## Other search tools to use

These are the addresses for some of the most popular search tools. The description that follows each address does not mean that is the only thing the tool does—it just indicates one of its strengths. Go to each one and play around. You'll find one or two you like best.

*If you need to really learn how to search, get the book* Search Engines for the World Wide Web: Visual QuickStart Guide, *by Alfred and Emily Glossbrenner. Published by Peachpit Press.*

| | |
|---|---|
| **Yahoo** | **www.yahoo.com** (best used as directory to "drill" down to find whole web sites) |
| **AltaVista** | **www.altavista.com** (word search; searches web and newsgroups) |
| **Go.Com** | **www.go.com** (has a directory like Yahoo and a word search like AltaVista; can search web, FAQs, newsgroups, email addresses, current news, company listings; can also ask questions like, "Where was George Washington born?") |
| **Excite** | **www.excite.com** (great for when you don't know the exact term you need; is conceptual/finds related topics; can ask questions of it) |
| **HotBot** | **www.hotbot.com** (can find sites with specific technology, such as sites that use JavaScript or Shockwave; very popular general search engine as well) |
| **About.Com** | **www.about.com** (hundreds of human guides search the web for you and compile selected results here; try this!) |
| **Deja** | **www.deja.com** (searches newsgroup subjects and postings; lists consumer reports) |
| **Google** | **www.google.com** (great for finding colleges, businesses—use the "I'm feeling lucky" button) |
| **Ask Jeeves** | **www.ask.com** (type in a question, such as "What's the difference between apple juice and apple cider?") |
| **Electric Library** | **www.elibrary.com** (30 days free access, then a fee; search magazines, maps, pictures, over 2,000 books, more than 150 newspapers and newswires, radio, and TV transcripts) |
| **Search.Com** | **www.search.com** (check out their list of over 100 Specialty Searches A–Z) |
| **software** | **www.shareware.com** (shareware and freeware) <br> **www.download.com** (commercial software) |

*shareware: Software that someone has created and that you can download (copy) right off the web. If you decide you like it and want to use it, you send the author a small fee, as explained in the Read Me file that will be with the shareware.*

*freeware: Software that someone has created that you can copy and use for absolutely free.*

**Also try this:** In Netscape, simply type your search phrase directly into the location box, right where you would type a web address. Hit Return or Enter, and Netscape will send your request to a search tool of its choice. The results are often astonishingly good. Try it!

## Step 6: Send email from a web page

Most web sites have email links (circled, below). You click the link, an email form pops up, you type the subject and your message, and click the Send button. The form is automatically return-addressed from you. Try it. (Just don't be upset if you don't get a response when you send someone you don't know unsolicited email.)

If you can't find any other web site with an email address, feel free to go to **UrlsInternetCafe.com,** click "Contact Us" in the navigation bar, and send Url an email. Send *someone* an email message so you can turn the page (of this book) and learn about other email features.

Outlook Express

*If you ever decide you want to use a different email program, you can install it and then change the default in the Internet Control Panel. Outlook Express is the one you already have on your iMac, along with Netscape Mail built into Netscape Communicator. Many people prefer Eudora from Qualcomm, or the program called Claris Emailer.*

*This is an email link. Even if it didn't say so, you can always tell because email addresses always include the @ symbol. Also check the status bar—notice it doesn't display a web address, but the code "mailto." That is another clue that if you click this link, you'll get an email form.*

*The "To" field (box) is already filled in for you, and the return address (Account) is already filled in for you. Just type your message in the message field and click the Send button.*

**Note:** *If you are using the version of Netscape called "Navigator," when you click on an email link on a web page it will open the email program you chose in the Internet control panel (see page 198). In any browser, if you get a message telling you the program is not set up yet for email, go into the Preferences and enter your email information.*

### What about *your* email?

When you signed up with EarthLink (or whomever you signed up with), you got an email address. It looks something like "ohscarlett@earthlink.net." That's the address you give to people. If you have forgotten your email address, you can see it in the Internet Control Panel, in the "Personal" tab. You do have to know your password, though, to get your email. If you've forgotten it, you'll have to call your service provider, prove who you are, and get your password from them.

*Mail*

### Get your mail

Whether your browser is open or not, double-click that icon that's been on your Desktop all this time called "Mail" (shown to the left). This icon will open the email program that you choose in the Internet control panel, as explained on page 198. If you didn't choose one yourself, the Mail icon will automatically open Outlook Express. The Internet Setup Assistant you went through earlier set this up for you already, so if you have any email, your "Inbox" will be bold and it will tell you how many messages you have. You probably have at least one from your service provider, welcoming you. Click once on it to read its message.

*If this alias icon is no longer on your Desktop, you can make a new one: Open the "Internet" folder, then open the "Internet Utilities" folder. Hold down the Command and Option keys, then press on the "Mail" icon and drag it to the Desktop; let go. Your new alias will be on the Desktop and you can close those other folders.*

To see how your email works, you can send a message to yourself. Follow the directions on the opposite page. It's too easy.

If you have an **EarthLink account,** also see pages 212 and 213 for some special options.

If you have an **America Online account,** just open AOL, sign in (log on), and click the mailbox icon, called "Read," in the upper-left corner of the toolbar. The email will look very similar to what you see on the opposite page.

## Reply to and send new email messages

There are lots of buttons and options in any email program, but don't worry about them all. For now, get used to getting your email, sending email, and replying to email you received. All the rest will start to make more sense after you master these features. Below is what you see when Outlook Express or Netscape Mail is open, with details about what to play with for now.

*Click "New" to get a new message window.*

*The Inbox tells you how many unread messages you have.*

*Click this button to get your email. If you are not connected already, this will connect for you. You will be asked for your password.*

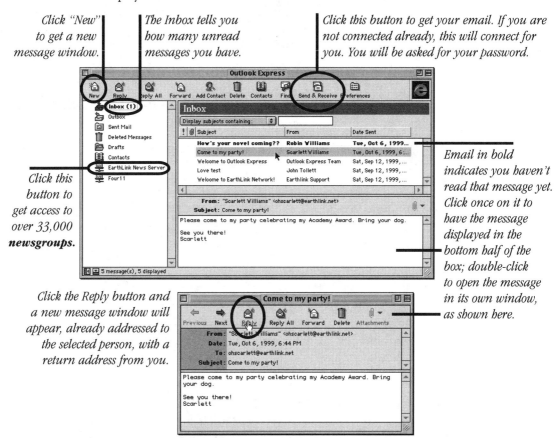

*Click this button to get access to over 33,000 newsgroups.*

*Email in bold indicates you haven't read that message yet. Click once on it to have the message displayed in the bottom half of the box; double-click to open the message in its own window, as shown here.*

*Click the Reply button and a new message window will appear, already addressed to the selected person, with a return address from you.*

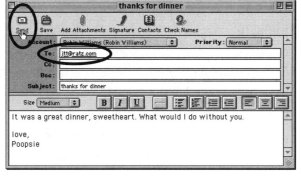

*When your new or reply message is ready to send, click the Send button. If you're not connected, the software will make a connection for you.*

*If this is a new message, make sure you enter an email address to send it to!*

**Tip:** *To send and receive email, you do have to be connected to the Internet. But you can write letters "offline," or when you're not connected to the phone line and so you are not incurring charges. Then when your letters are ready to send, log on and send them.*

### EarthLink email

If you set up your account with EarthLink, you'll get a message on your browser home page, or start page, when you log on to the World Wide Web (shown below), that tells you if you have email or not.

*Your EarthLink home page, or Start Page, tells you if you've received mail at your EarthLink address.*

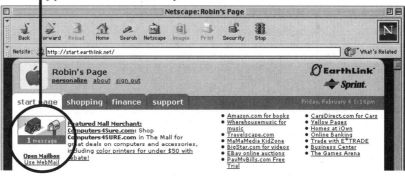

**The first time you click the link "Open Mailbox,"** you will get a message about having to download a file and install it. That might sound a little intimidating, but it really will only take a couple of minutes and this is what it does for you: Once you follow the directions below (or on EarthLink's site), then ever after when you come to this start page, you can click the "Open Mailbox" link and EarthLink will open your preferred email program and put your new mail in it. Now, you don't *have* to do this—you can just ignore the mail link on this start page and go directly to your email program to check your mail. It's up to you; following the directions below will just make it a little more convenient.

1. Click the link "Open Mailbox."

2. In the window that pops up, there's a link that says something like "Download EarthLink Helper." Click it. EarthLink will automatically download the files you need. It only takes a couple of minutes.

3. Quit your browser (press Command Q). You do not have to disconnect from the Internet.

elnhelper10.hqx

Earthlink Helper 1.0.sit

EarthLink Helper Installer

*To "download" means to copy files from another computer to yours. EarthLink copies these files to your hard disk.*

4. On your Desktop, you will see the three files shown to the left. Double-click the one called "EarthLink Helper Installer." It will go do its business, which should take about 30 seconds.

5. You can throw away all three of those files.

6. Open your browser again, and now when you click on the "Open Mailbox" link, your email program will open and you can read your email.

## Read your EarthLink mail anywhere in the world

Do you notice the link below "Open Mailbox," the one that says "Use WebMail"? If you are at someone else's home or office or away on vacation, you can go to any computer, get to the Internet with a browser, and read your EarthLink mail. There are Internet cafes all over the world, so wherever you happen to go you can probably find a computer. Before you leave home, go to **www.netcafeguide.com** and find out where the Internet cafes are. You pay a small fee, log on to their computers, go to EarthLink's web site (www.earthlink.net), and click the "Use WebMail" link. You will get a web page where you can log in with your email address and password, and then you can read and send your email from a tiny cafe in Bangkok or a bustling cafe in Paris. Or from your grandmother's house.

*AOL users: You can also check your AOL mail from any web browser on any computer anywhere in the world. Sign up with AOLNet at* **www.aol.com/netmail***. It's free.*

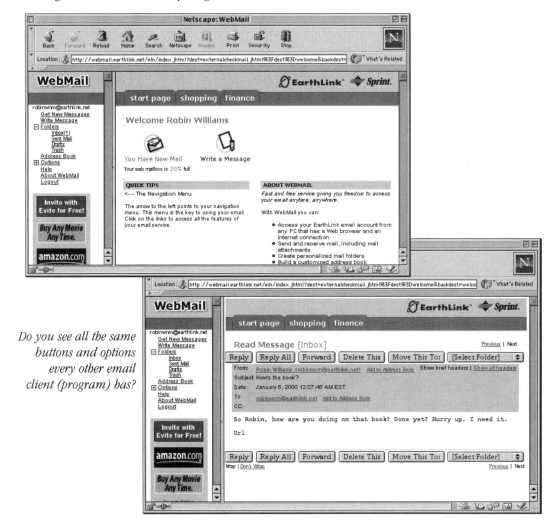

*Do you see all the same buttons and options every other email client (program) has?*

### Step 7: Log off from your ISP (for AOL, see below)

When you are finished surfing the World Wide Web, you need to *log off,* or hang up. There are two steps to this, and it doesn't really matter in which order you do them. You need to **quit** the browser (don't just put the window away!) and **close** the modem connection, or log off. Quitting the browser does not close the connection; if you don't close it, it's the same as having your phone off the hook. (If you have cable or DSL, you don't need to log off!)

If you think you will be logging on again in a short time, like after lunch, you can close the connection, yet leave the browser open and waiting for you to log on again.

### Quit the browser

- From the File menu, choose "Quit."

### Disconnect from the Internet

1. Go to the Apple menu and choose "Remote Access Status."

2. Click the "Disconnect" button.

   *If you want to log on again later,* and your browser is already open because you left it open, use "Remote Access Status" to connect; don't use the "Browse the Internet" icon.

*If you like, you can leave this little dialog box on your Desktop all the time. It will keep you apprised of whether you are online or offline and how much time you've spent there (uh oh). The "Send" and "Receive" bubbles light up when data is coming or going.*

*Click on this little tab. It's probably in the bottom-left corner of your screen. See page 239 for details about the Control Strip.*

**OR close the connection with the Control Strip:** You can also use the Control Strip to connect or disconnect, instead of Remote Access Status. Open the Control Strip (click on the little tab), then click on the connection icon (circled, below). When you click on it, you'll get a little pop-up menu. Choose "Disconnect."

### Log off from AOL

When you "Sign Off" in AOL, the connection is discontinued (you have logged off), but the program is still open; when you "Quit" AOL, the program will quit and you will disconnect. **But** if you log on through your ISP to use AOL, *when you quit AOL you are still connected to the Internet,* so you must disconnect as explained above.

# Make a Web Site 17

When you go to the World Wide Web and poke around, you are jumping from one **web page** to another. A *collection* of web pages for one company, one family, or one topic is called a **web site.** Making a web site is easier than you might think (making a *well-designed* web site is more difficult).

Many iMacs include the software called Adobe PageMill with which you can create web pages. Look in your little packet of CDs that came with your computer; if you find the Adobe PageMill CD, install the software as described on the following page, then follow along in the tutorial in this chapter to build a small, personal web site. I'll also show you how to get to the more sophisticated tutorial provided by Adobe.

Once you finish a web site, it must be uploaded (sent over the Internet) to a *server,* which is a special computer that "serves" web sites up to the Internet so others can use them. Depending on the arrangement with your Internet Service Provider, you might be able to post your web site for free or there might be a small monthly charge. Your service provider will tell you what the address for your web site will be.

In this one chapter, it's not possible to explain everything you need to know to create, upload, and maintain a web site, plus all the information about graphics and web addresses, etc. But if you discover that you really enjoy making your own web pages, get *The Non-Designer's Web Book* by me and John Tollett—it does explain everything you need to know, from start to finish, and it's easy to follow and understand.

## Getting started

*To get the tutorial:*

*Open the PageMill application folder.*

*Find the folder named "PageMill User Manuals" and open it.*

*Inside that window, double-click the file "Getting Started.pdf."*

*This will open a 60-page tutorial. Print it up, and follow the directions. It's great.*

If you want to make a quick little three-page site for yourself just to see how easy it actually is to make a simple site, follow these directions in this chapter. Then if you like working in PageMill, do the Adobe tutorial, which will teach you much more. The "Getting Started.pdf" guide contains, among other things, an introduction to PageMill and a tutorial.

## Install the PageMill software

First, of course, you have to find the Adobe PageMill CD that came with some iMacs. Look in your packet of CDs. If you don't have it, you can always buy the software and follow these same directions. Once you have the CD, do this:

1. Insert the CD into the iMac. It will open to display the window shown below.

2. Double-click the icon labeled "Install PageMill® 3.0." It will walk you through the simple installation process, and you will end up with a folder called "Adobe PageMill 3.0" in your hard disk window.

Don't take the CD out yet—you need it for the next few steps.

*Double-click this icon to install PageMill onto your hard disk.*

Adobe PageMill 3.0

*After installation, this folder will appear on your hard disk. Double-click it to open the window where you will find the application.*

*To make the application easier to get to, make an alias: hold down the Command and Option keys, then drag this icon to your Desktop. You can close the folder. Whenever you want to use PageMill, double-click the alias.*

*You can change the name of the alias. (See page 237 if you're not sure what an alias is.)*

## Make a folder and put some graphics in it

The first step in building a web site is to make a folder in which you will store all of the graphics and pages for your site. When you're done, you'll send this entire folder to a special computer called a server so the world can see it. (If you have a permanent sort of Internet connection, such as DSL, ISDN, cable, or T1 line, you can actually serve the site from your own computer, with security reservations. Check the Help file in the menu bar for directions on using "Personal Web Share," or see *The Little Mac Book*.)

Keeping all of the files you need for the web site stored in one folder ensures that your graphics will actually appear on your page when it gets to the web. So for this first step, you are going to make a folder and put certain graphics inside of it before you begin to make the actual web page.

1. Click on the Desktop (but not in any window) to select it. This will make sure the folder you are going to make will appear right there on the Desktop.

2. Press Command N to make a new folder. The folder will appear as an "untitled folder." It knows you want to change the name, so before you click on anything, just type **MyWebsite**. (If you did click somewhere so the folder name is no longer selected and ready to change, just click once on the folder name again, then type the new name.) Your folder should look like the one shown to the right. Place it over on the right side of your Desktop.

MyWebsite
*This is the folder in which you will store all the files pertaining to your web site.*

3. Now you're going to put some graphics in the folder so you can use them on your web page. The CD should still be in the drive, if you followed the directions on the opposite page; if it isn't, put it back in. Then:

   ■ Double-click the folder "Web Pages and Content."

   ■ Double-click the folder "WebMorsels" to open it. Inside that window is another folder also called "WebMorsels" (why do they do that?); double-click that one also. — *continued*

**4.** Inside the (second) "WebMorsels" folder is a folder called "Bullets." Double-click "Bullets" and you should see the window shown below.

**5.** Click once on the triangle next to "Di" so you can see what's in that folder.

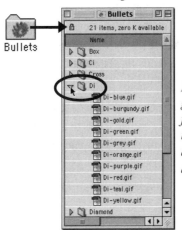

Bullets

*Each of these little items is a web graphic. "Di" apparently stands for "diamond" because each of these graphics is a tiny, colored diamond (◆) that you can use as a bullet on a web page.*

**6.** Drag any of the colored diamond bullets from this window and drop them into your folder called "MyWebsite," which is supposed to be sitting on the right side of your Desktop (if you followed the previous directions).

**7.** Close the "Bullets" window. Close both of the "WebMorsels" windows.

dogWHT.gif

*Put this file, which is a graphic image of a dog wagging its tail, into your folder.*

**8.** Now you should again see the window called "Web Pages and Content." In that window, open the folder "Other Content." In that window, open the folder "Gif_Animations." In that window, open the folder "animals." From that window, drag the file named "dogWHT.gif" and drop it into your web site folder.

**9.** Now here's a trick to close all of those open windows at once: Hold down the Option key, and while that key is held down, click in the close box of the window you see in front of you. **Or** you can press Command Option W, all the windows will close, and you won't even have to pick up the mouse.

*Your folder should look something like this.*

**10.** If you have any other web graphics you want to put on your practice web pages, put them (or copies of them) into your web site folder. Web graphics or photos must be prepared in a special way, but if you received or created any photos that you sent through email, they are probably just fine to put on a web page. If a photo has ".jpeg" or ".jpg" at the end of its name, it's most likely properly prepared to place on a web page.

## Get ready

Now you're ready to open PageMill and start making pages. In this tutorial you'll make three web pages, put text and graphics on each one, link all the pages together, make an email link so people can send you email from your web page, and when you're done I'll show you how you get it onto the World Wide Web. I guarantee it's easier than you think.

### Position your web site folder to the right

- To make it convenient to access the graphics and the web page at the same time while I'm working, I like to open the web site folder, view it "as List" (from the View menu), resize it to a narrow shape, and position it over to the right of the screen, as shown below.

### Open PageMill

- Double-click the PageMill alias you put on your Desktop (per the instructions on page 216). If you didn't put an alias on your Desktop, open the PageMill folder and double-click the PageMill application icon.

  Your monitor should look like this:

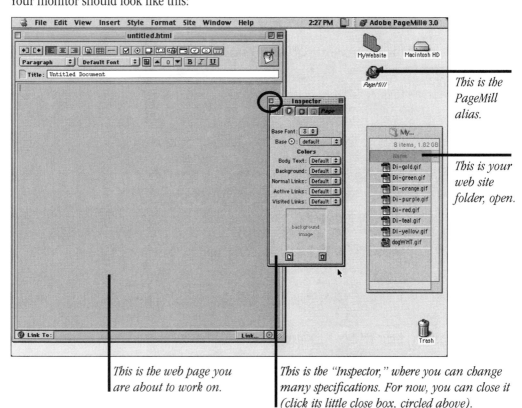

*This is the PageMill alias.*

*This is your web site folder, open.*

*This is the web page you are about to work on.*

*This is the "Inspector," where you can change many specifications. For now, you can close it (click its little close box, circled above).*

## Make the first web page

The first page in a web site is typically called the "home" page. It's like home base, or the table of contents in a book. The visitor should know what this site is about, what other information is available from here, and it should be clear how to get to that other information. In this tutorial, you'll make a small site about yourself, but of course you can change any of the text and graphics to anything you want!

### Name your first web page

*html: This stands for hypertext markup language, which is the code that PageMill writes for you that tells the browser how to display the web page on the screen.*

Before you type onto the page, you should save and name it. The first page of every web site in the world always has the same name: **index.html** (well, there are slight variations, but you don't need to worry about that). So the **file name** of your home page will be index.html. Every web page is considered an "html" page.

1. From the File menu, choose "Save Page As…." You'll get the dialog box shown below, which by now you are surely familiar with.

2. At the Desktop level, find your web site folder. Double-click your folder to open it so you can save this page directly into the folder.

3. Change the name of the file from "untitled.html" to "index.html," then click the "Save" button.

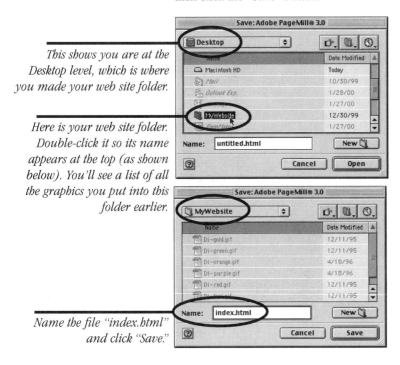

*This shows you are at the Desktop level, which is where you made your web site folder.*

*Here is your web site folder. Double-click it so its name appears at the top (as shown below). You'll see a list of all the graphics you put into this folder earlier.*

*Name the file "index.html" and click "Save."*

### Title your first web page

The **title** of a page is very different from its **html file name.** The html file name is for the computer; the title is for visitors to the site. The title of the page appears in the title bar of the web page when someone else sees it on their screen; when someone saves your page as a bookmark, the bookmark will be the title you have chosen for the page. Even if it isn't quite clear what the title is (don't worry, lots of people don't get the concept right away), just trust me and follow the directions.

1. Just below the toolbar across the top of your new web page it says "Title," and inside that box it says "Untitled Document." Select the text "Untitled Document" and retype it with the title of your page, as shown below.

2. After you type the title, hit Return! This is very important. If you clicked somewhere else without hitting Return, click back in that box at the end of the title and hit the Return key.

*Type the **title** in this box here. Be sure to hit the Return key after you type it!*

*Right now the title bar displays the html file name. But when this page appears on the web, your **title** will be in this spot.*

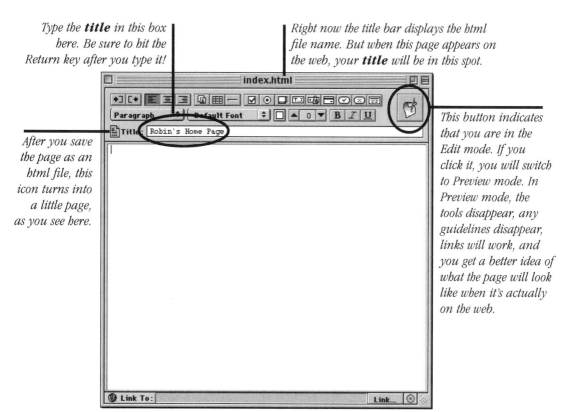

*After you save the page as an html file, this icon turns into a little page, as you see here.*

*This button indicates that you are in the Edit mode. If you click it, you will switch to Preview mode. In Preview mode, the tools disappear, any guidelines disappear, links will work, and you get a better idea of what the page will look like when it's actually on the web.*

### Color the page white

Dark text on a white background is the easiest to read. I'm going to tell you how to change the background to white, but feel free to make it any color you like.

1. From the Window menu, choose "Show Color Panel." You'll get the little panel full of color dots, as shown below. You can drag this panel around by its title bar like any window, and close it by clicking in its close box.

2. Position the pointer directly on one of the color spots, press on the spot, and drag it across the page over to that tiny page icon. Drop the color spot directly on the page icon and voilà, your page is a new color.

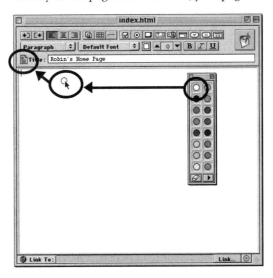

### Type some text on your page

If you've used a word processor, as explained in Chapter 4, you'll feel right at home on this web page. Although I provide you with suggestions of what to type, of course you can type anything you want!

- In the top-left corner of the page you see the insertion point flashing, which is your visual clue that when you type, the text will start here. So start typing. Follow the text shown on the opposite page. Hit a Return at the end of each paragraph (not at the end of each line in the long paragraph!).

When you've typed all that in, I'll tell you how to format it.

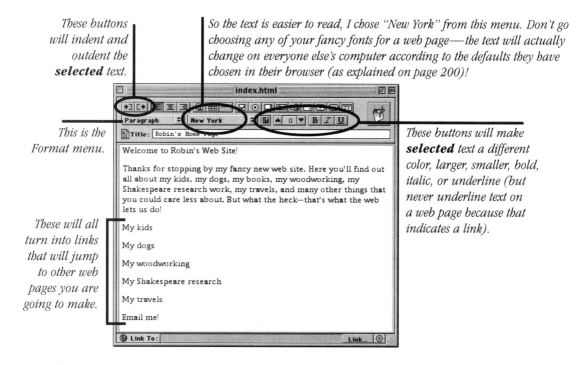

*These buttons will indent and outdent the **selected** text.*

*So the text is easier to read, I chose "New York" from this menu. Don't go choosing any of your fancy fonts for a web page—the text will actually change on everyone else's computer according to the defaults they have chosen in their browser (as explained on page 200)!*

*This is the Format menu.*

*These buttons will make **selected** text a different color, larger, smaller, bold, italic, or underline (but never underline text on a web page because that indicates a link).*

*These will all turn into links that will jump to other web pages you are going to make.*

## Format the text

Make these simple formatting changes. Check the next page (of this book) to see if your web page matches the tutorial.

1. **Indent all of the text** so it doesn't bump into the left edge: From the Edit menu, choose "Select All." Then click the Indent button, circled above. Click anywhere to unselect all the text.

2. **Indent the lines of text that will be links:** Press-and-drag over the lines of text to select them, then click the Indent button. Click anywhere to unselect the text.

3. **Make the heading larger:** Click once anywhere in the heading. From the Format menu right in the toolbar, where it now says "Paragraph," choose "Largest Heading."

4. **Color the heading:** Press-and-drag over the heading to select all of the characters. Either drag a color spot and drop it on the selected text, **or** use the Color menu in the toolbar (circled, above right).

## Add some graphics

Remember those graphics you put in your web site folder? Add them to this page.

- If you followed the directions, you should be able to see your web site folder window on the right, and the web page you are building on the left, as shown on page 219. If not, rearrange things so you can see both windows.

*This is what your bullets
should look like.*

Then simply **drag** one of those tiny diamond graphics from your web site folder and **drop** it right in front of the first link (well, the line of text that *will* be a link as soon as you make it). You'll see the insertion point move around the page as you move the graphic around, and when you let go of the mouse button, that graphic will drop in right where that insertion point is flashing. Try it.

Drag over the other diamond bullet graphics and drop one in front of each link. **Type** one extra space between each bullet and the text.

**If you accidentally put a graphic in the wrong place,** just drag it to where it is supposed to be.

**To get rid of a graphic,** click once on it to select it, then hit the Delete key.

## Make two more web pages

First of all, save the page you just made: press Command S. Then build two more pages in the same way you did the first:

1. **Make a new page:** Press Command N (or go to the File menu, choose "New," then "New Page").

2. **Save the html file:** From the File menu, choose "Save Page As…." *Do not* name this page "index.html." Name it something that gives you a clue as to what the page is about, such as **mykids.html** or **mydogs.html**.

   Notice the format of these file names: use all lowercase letters, no characters except letters or numbers (that is, no apostrophes or colons, etc.), and no spaces. Keep it short.

   *Make sure you save this web page into your web site folder!*

3. **Title the page:** In the title, you *can* use capital letters, spaces, exclamation points, and most other characters. Be sure to hit the Return key after you type the title.

4. **Change the background color of the page:** Drag a color spot from the color panel to the tiny page icon next to the title.

5. **Type the text.**

6. **Format the text.**

7. **Add a graphic:** This time, add the dog graphic you have in your web site folder, the one named **dogWHT.gif**. Just like you did with the bullets, simply drag the graphic file from your web site folder and drop it on the page where you want it to be.

8. **Save the page again:** Press Command S.

*When you view your page in Preview mode, as mentioned below, this dog will animate!*

## Preview the pages

Remember that little Edit/Preview button I pointed out on page 221? You've been working in the Edit mode all this time. But now click that button to pop into Preview mode. If you placed that dog graphic on a page, you'll see it come to life when you view that page in Preview mode.

You cannot make changes to anything while in Preview mode, so make sure you click the button back to Edit mode before you get back to work!

*Edit mode*    *Preview mode*

### Create the links

So now you should have at least three web pages. Let's make links.

#### Make a local link

First, create **local links** to connect your pages to each other. For instance, if you typed "My dogs" on the home page and you made a web page about your dogs, let's link them together.

1.  **On the home page,** select the text that should link to another one of the pages you created (select the text by dragging across it).

2.  **Type the link address:** At the bottom of the web page, click in the "Link To" box. Type the *html file name* of the web page you created that you want this link to jump to, *then hit the Return key.* For instance, if you want that link to go to the web page you named "mydogs.html," then type "mydogs.html" into the "Link To" box. See the example below.

    Be sure to hit the Return key after you type the file name or it won't work! If you did it right, the link will now be underlined and colored blue.

3.  **Test the link:** Click the Edit mode button to switch to Preview mode. Now you can click the link and it will open the other page!

4.  **Make a link back home:** On the second page, you need to make a link to take you back home. First, go back into Edit mode, then simply type the word "Home" on the second page. Select that word and make a link to **index.html**, since that is the *html file name* of your home page. Be sure to hit the Return key after you type the link address.

    You can copy that "Home" link and paste it onto your other pages!

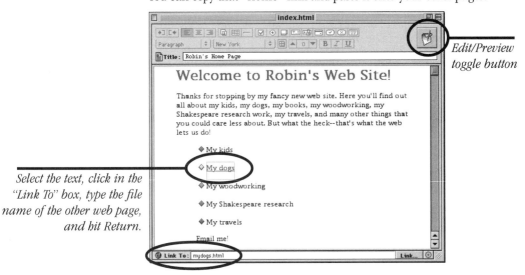

*Edit/Preview toggle button*

*Select the text, click in the "Link To" box, type the file name of the other web page, and hit Return.*

### Make a remote link

Maybe you want to make a **remote link** to some other page on the World Wide Web. For instance, perhaps your Shakespeare research is posted on the university web site. You can link to any other page on the web:

1. **On the web page,** select the text that should link to somewhere else on the web.

2. **Type the entire web address:** At the bottom of the web page, click in the "Link To" box. Type the *entire web address* of the web page you want to link to. You must type the "http://" part of the address as well. If the exact page you want to link to has a long address, you must type the entire long address.

   Hit the Return or Enter key.

If you click this link in Preview mode, PageMill will open your browser and connect to the Internet, so don't click it unless you're ready for that to happen!

### Make an email link

You probably want to have an **email link** so if someone wants to send you email while they're at your web page, an email form will pop up, addressed to you, with a return address from that person.

1. **On the web page,** select the text that should pop up an email form.

2. **Type your email address:** At the bottom of the web page, click in the "Link To" box. Type this simple code: **mailto:**  Yes, include the colon. Immediately after the colon, without inserting a space, type your email address. Be sure to include the @ symbol, and the entire domain name (such as "yahoo.com" or "aol.com"). It should look something like this:

   **mailto:dearrobin@earthlink.net**

   Hit the Enter or Return key.

Even in Preview mode you won't be able to check out your email link, but when you open this in a browser such as Netscape, it will work just fine. In fact, if you click on this email link in Preview mode in PageMill, it will open Netscape and make a connection to the Internet just to prove to you that it works. So don't click it unless you want that to happen.

*Tip:* To create remote links faster, try this:

Select the link text.

Hit the Enter key to select the "Link To" box.

Type the letter "h," then hit the right arrow key; PageMill will type "http://" for you.

Hit the right arrow key again and PageMill will type "www."

Type the middle part of the address, plus the next dot.

If the last part of the address is "com," just hit the right arrow key again and PageMill will type "com" for you.

Hit Enter or Return.

*This is the Inspector.*

## Change the link color

Each of your web pages can have a different link color, which makes it easy to color-coordinate your site.

1. **On the web page,** you don't have to select any text. If the Inspector window isn't showing, go to the Window menu and choose "Show Inspector" (shown to the left).

2. **Choose your colors:** In the Inspector, press on the tiny menu next to "Normal Links," and choose a color from the list.

   "Active Links" is the color the link will change to while someone is holding the mouse button down on the link.

   "Visited Links" is the color they change to after a person has already clicked on those links.

## The finished web site

*This is Url.*

Ah, you're done at last! (Well, at least you're under the temporary delusion that you're done. As Url says, "Web site work is never done.") Your home page might look something like the one shown below. Check every link, and make sure every page has a link back to the home page, and perhaps even links to the other pages in your small site. The next step will be to "upload" the site to the World Wide Web.

*When in Preview mode, you can press on this space and get a list of the other pages you have already created. Choose any one to open that page.*

## Find a host for your web site

To make your web site accessible to anyone surfing the web, you have to upload it to a server. You might also hear this process referred to as "ftp," which stands for file transfer protocol. If you made just a silly practice site, you probably don't want to go through this step, but you should at least read it so you'll know what to do.

Before you can upload your web site, you must arrange for someone to "host" it. If you are a member of America Online, you are allowed two megabytes of free storage space for every screen name and AOL will act as your host (go to keyword "my space"). If you use a local Internet Service Provider, call and ask what they charge to host a web site. Typically you are charged for a certain amount of storage space. If your local provider charges more than $20 a month, check around with your friends and see where they are storing their sites. Check out places like hiway.com and prohosting.com. Your site can be hosted anywhere in the world.

Once you have arranged with a host, they will give you the following pieces of information (write these down and keep them where you can find them again!). This is called your "FTP information."

- Host name    ■ User name    ■ Password
- Remote folder, also known as the *path* or *directory*

*Of course, make sure you have a working Internet connection before you try to upload a site to the web!*

## Upload your web site

So now you are ready to upload your fabulous web site.

1. **Open the site:** From the File menu, choose "Open," then choose "Open Site...." You'll get the Open dialog box, where you need to select your web site folder and click the "Choose" button.

2. **Create the settings:** You'll get a message that you need to create site settings. Click "Yes."

3. In the "New Site" dialog box that you'll get, click "Settings...."

— *continued*

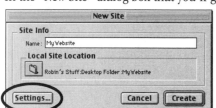

**4.** In the "Add Site Settings" dialog box, enter the FTP information that you got from your web site host. Then click OK (you won't have to do this again). In the "New Site" dialog box that you'll see again, click "Create."

*Once you enter the FTP information for this site, you won't have to do it again—you'll just go straight to the upload menu choice.*

**5.** You'll get something called a "site window" (shown to the left). You really should read the manual to learn about this very important part of the software. For now, go to the Site menu and choose "Upload." PageMill will log on to the Internet and upload your web site to the server. If PageMill has trouble connecting, open the connection your usual way, *then* tell PageMill to upload the site. And now, it's on the web!

**6.** Open your browser and go to the web address that your host told you would be your address. If you see changes that need to be made: Make them in PageMill, and save the page. From the File menu, choose "Upload" and then "Page." In your browser, click the Reload button to see the new page.

*To upload the entire site, along with every graphic, use the Site menu and choose "Upload."*

*To upload individual pages, along with their graphics, use the File menu, choose "Upload," and choose "Page."*

# Other Things You Should Know

This section doesn't contain *everything* else you should know, but just some of the things you will bump up against right away and some things you might find useful.

**Every Macintosh, including the iMac, can read PC disks and documents.** *Every Mac (except very old ones), has software installed on it that allows PC documents to be read. Every Mac can read PC disks, both floppy disks and Zip disks. (A PC, however, cannot read a Mac disk.)*

*Most software applications on the Macintosh can easily open and display PC files such as photos, graphics, layouts, and text documents. Even AppleWorks/ClarisWorks can translate documents from a huge array of other non-Mac applications.*

*Every currently shipping Mac comes with a high-speed Ethernet jack capable of hooking up to standard office networks and using a myriad of laser printers and copiers, even if they're PC based.*

*Mac programs such as VirtualPC and SoftWindows98 allow your Macintosh to run Windows and thousands of PC applications. And there have been public demonstrations of the Mac running such software faster and more stable than PCs themselves.*

**Computer salespeople are paid to sell PCs.**
*Employees at computer equipment chain stores are commonly paid a commission for each PC they sell, but not for Macs. Essentially, they are bribed to sell inferior machines.*

**Apple has happy customers.**
*Apple is "far and away the favorite" in customer loyalty. Mac users are 17 times more likely than Gateway users to be happy, loyal, and to buy another Mac.*
*"Computer Intelligence," quoted in September/October 1998 Mac Today*

**The A.D. Little Report states that Mac users**
*are 50 percent more accurate and 44 percent more productive than Windows/Intel users.*

**Consumer Reports prove it.**
*Apple is rated #1 in Performance & Reliability*
*Apple is rated #1 in Customer Service Satisfaction*
*Apple is rated #1 in Fewest Brand Repairs*

# More about Your iMac

You can live a long time without reading this chapter, but the more you read the more you will feel in control of your computer. This chapter covers some odds and ends that can be quite useful to you, such as creating aliases to make it easy to open files, how to use the Find feature to find documents you thought you misplaced and to search the World Wide Web (on iMacs before Mac OS 9), the important difference between memory and hard disk space, how to backup your software and install new stuff, and a bit more. Skim through this chapter, and when you're ready to absorb it, read just what you need.

## Kilobytes and megabytes—what are they? Who cares?

*There are approximately 1,000 **bytes** in one **kilobyte;** 1,000 kilobytes in one **megabyte;** and 1,000 megabytes in one **gigabyte.***

The terms kilobytes, megabytes, and gigabytes might sound scary, but they're really not. They are just measuring terms, like ounces, pounds, and tons. In the computer, kilobytes are the ounces, megabytes are the pounds, and gigabytes are the tons.

All software, whether it is an application you buy or a document you create, takes up space on your hard disk. How much space it takes up is measured in kilobytes, megabytes, and gigabytes. Your hard disk itself, plus any other kinds of disks you run across, are measured in how much space they have available to hold software. The more gigabytes on your hard disk, the more software you can put on it.

A typical page of word processing might be about 10 **kilobytes,** written as 10 **K,** and pronounced "ten kay." You would say, "This file is 10K."

A typical software program such as AppleWorks might be almost 3 **megabytes,** written as 3 **MB.** You would say, "AppleWorks is 3 megabytes," or "3 megs."

A typical hard disk might be 4 **gigabytes,** written as 4 **GB.** You would say, "I have a 4-gig hard drive."

## Backing up

*One **bit** of information is one electronic pulse in the computer, one off or on signal, a 1 or a 0 (zero). Eight **bits** of information makes one **byte.***

All of your applications and all of your documents are just little "bits" and "bytes" of electronic impulses stored on magnetic disks. As you can imagine, it's a little fragile. Hard disks go bad after three or four years (and sometimes earlier), and other disks can lose their data (their bits and bytes) fairly easily. If you're not careful, you can and will lose important documents and even software you paid for. For this reason, you always want to have a current **backup,** an extra copy, of anything that is important to you.

You already have a current backup of all the software that was originally installed on your iMac—it's on those CDs that came with your computer. If you buy more software, it will probably be on a CD, and once you install the software into your iMac, that CD itself will be your backup of the original software program (CDs are more stable than other disks, such as hard disks, floppy disks, or *Zip* disks).

*Zip disks are the most popular form of "external" storage. They are very small (in physical size) hard disks.*

But you really need to make a backup of everything you *create.* To make a backup all you do is copy the file onto another disk. Now, your iMac did not come with a floppy disk "drive" (a slot in which to insert a floppy disk), nor any other kind of "external" drive in which you can put a disk to copy your software onto. So the first thing you need to do if you want to backup is invest in something like a Zip drive (a drive that "reads" Zip disks, which are small-sized, removable hard disks). Once you have a drive in which you can put another disk, backing up is very easy. This is all you do:

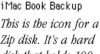

iMac Book Backup

*This is the icon for a Zip disk. It's a hard disk that holds 100 megabytes of data, and it fits in the palm of your hand. You can name the disk whatever you like, just like a folder.*

1. Insert a disk into the external drive. Its icon will appear on your Desktop (as shown to the right).

2. Drag the icon of your document (or whatever file you want to backup) over to the icon of the disk. Drop the icon directly on that disk, just like you drop an icon into a folder. Your iMac will make a *copy* of your original file onto that other disk. The *original file* stays intact on your iMac hard disk, and now you have a *backup copy* on the external disk.

If you have lots of files to backup everyday, you might want to invest in special software that does it for you automatically. Ask around and see what your Mac friends like best, and ask someone to help you install and use it.

## Protecting your software and data

The data on the disks is actually pretty fragile. If you have floppy disks or Zip disks that hold data, here are some rules to adhere to:

- The most important rule is to keep them away from anything with magnets. That includes not only refrigerator magnets, but telephones, cell phones, radios, stereos, cameras, etc. Anything you can put in your purse or glove compartment and that needs to be turned on, you should keep away from disks.

- I don't care what they say at airport security checks, I don't ever put disks through the machine. Even if the x-ray stuff doesn't affect the disks, often the mechanics in the conveyor belt can destroy data.

- Don't keep disks in plastic bags. The static electricity that builds up in the plastic can adversely affect the magnetic data on the disks.

- I've heard that dropping disks can actually shake little magnetic particles off the disks. I can't say that's ever happened to me, but I try not to drop them.

- Don't keep disks in a hot car, and don't let them freeze.

- If you have really important stuff, make more than one backup, and store the various backups in different places so if one place burns down or is burglarized, you still have copies somewhere else.

### Installing new software

Whenever you buy new software, of course you need to **install** it. Your software will typically arrive on a CD, or you might download it from the Internet. Almost all software now has an "installer" utility, as shown below.

*If you see a Read Me file, read it!*

Read Me First!

InstallMDK

Kai's Photo Soap™ SE Installer

Double-click on the installer, and the computer will do the rest. You will be asked where on your hard disk you want it installed; if you know how to "navigate" to another folder on your hard disk, such as your Applications folder, you should do that. If you have no idea how to navigate, go ahead and let the computer put it where it wants for now (which is usually right on your hard disk), and you should read *The Little Mac Book* to really understand navigating.

*navigating: The process of getting around inside of your computer using dialog boxes and digging through folders.*

**Application** software (such as Kai's Photo Soap or Adobe PageMill, packages that might have come with your iMac) will be installed entirely on your hard disk, which means then you can put the CD away in a safe place and save it as your backup in case anything happens to your hard disk. But most **game** and **multimedia** software (such as the MDK game, the multimedia Williams-Sonoma Guide to Good Cooking CD, or the World Book Encyclopedia that might have come with your iMac) installs just *some* of the files onto your hard disk, and you must insert the CD to play the game or use the multimedia package because the program needs those big files on the CD to make itself work.

**Here's an exception:** The application **Quicken** is installed on your hard disk, and you can work directly from your hard disk to create all of your accounts. But if you want to watch the little movies that teach you how to use the application, you will have to insert the Quicken CD.

## Aliases

An alias on the iMac is a tiny little file that goes and gets something else for you. It's like this: Let's say you use Quicken everyday. And everyday you have to open the hard disk window, then open the Applications folder window, then open the Quicken Deluxe window, then double-click on the Quicken Deluxe application icon. That's a pain in the wazoo, yes? And you can't solve the problem by taking the Quicken application icon out of the Quicken folder and putting it on the Desktop where you can get to it more easily because then the program won't even work (the program must stay in its folder to work). So you make an **alias.** An alias, as I said, is a tiny little file that goes and gets something for you. An alias of Quicken can sit right on your Desktop and when you double-click it, it opens Quicken for you. *The alias doesn't do anything except go get the real application.* And aliases are tiny (in file size)—you can put them all over the place. You can make more than one alias of any file, and you can put them on your Desktop, in your Apple menu, in a folder, etc. When you don't want an alias anymore, you can throw it away and it does not affect the real application one bit.

You can always tell if a file is an alias because the name is in italic, as you can see above, to the right.

Quicken Deluxe 2000
*This is the real icon for the application.*

*Quicken Deluxe 2000*
*This is the alias for Quicken. Notice the name is in italic and it has a little arrow on the bottom-left corner (in Mac OS 8.1, you won't see the arrow).*

### Make an alias

1. At the Desktop, click once on the file you want to make an alias of.
2. From the File menu, choose "Make Alias," **or** press Command M.
3. Making an alias this way puts the word "alias" at the end of the name. After you move the alias somewhere else, like to the Desktop, you can remove the word "alias" if you like, or even change its entire name (click once on its *name* and retype).
4. Drag the alias to wherever you want to keep it.

### Find the original of an alias

- To open the folder that contains the original file, click once on the alias, then press Command R (or choose "Show Original" from the File menu).

### Delete an alias

- To get rid of an alias, just throw it in the trash can. It can't possibly hurt anything else, not even the original file.

*Tip: Here's a great shortcut for making aliases. Hold down the Command and Option keys, then press-and-drag the file you want to make an alias of—drag it straight out of its folder, and when you let go, the alias will appear and it won't have the word alias at the end of the name! Try it.*

## Sherlock, also known as Find (pre–Mac OS 9)

*If you are using Mac OS 9 with Sherlock 2, see Chapter 19!*

You may have "lost" files, forgotten where you've put them, or just want quick access to them. Built into your iMac is a great feature that helps you find files. If you are working in any application, choose "Sherlock" from the Apple menu. If you are at the Desktop, choose "Find…" from the File menu. They are the same thing.

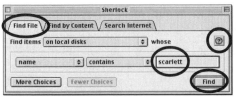

**A basic search** *is very easy. Just type in any portion of the name of a file, then click the "Find" button.*

*The top half of the results lists the files it found. Click once on any file name to see where it is stored, shown in the bottom half. Double-click to open the file.*

*This tells me the selected file named "scarlett/ model" is inside a folder named "models," which is inside a folder named "Virtual Makeover," etc. Instead of digging through those folders to get the file, select the file in the top half and* **press Command E to open the folder** *it is in.*

*For lots more information about Sherlock, click this Help icon.*

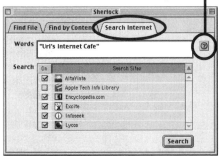

*Click the* **Search Internet** *tab. Type in what you want to find on the Internet. Follow the guidelines for searching on page 206. When you click the "Search" button, the iMac connects to the Internet and searches, but does not open a browser. In the list of results you see on the right, click once on a result in the top portion to get details and a link in the bottom portion; click the link to open your browser and go to that page.*

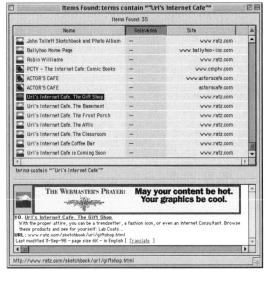

## Control Strip

The Control Strip is that little tab in the lower-left corner of your screen that opens to a strip of icons. You've probably noticed by now that if you click the tab, it either closes up or opens, depending on whether it was open or closed.

*This is the Control Strip when it's closed (left) and when it's open (below).*

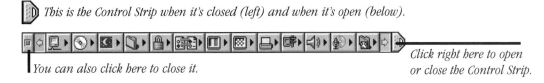

*You can also click here to close it.*

*Click right here to open or close the Control Strip.*

You may also have noticed that if you click on any icon in the strip, you get a little menu of options (as shown below). Each of those icons represents an option that you have elsewhere in your iMac, usually in a control panel (see pages 33–36). The Control Strip lets you access these options without having to open the individual Control Panels. You can change the monitor resolution and colors, adjust the sound volume, open your Internet connection (see page 214), and more.

*Click any icon to get the menu choices.*

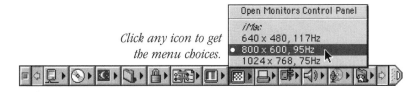

**To move the Control Strip,** hold down the Option key and drag it. You can move the Control Strip to either side of your screen, and you can move it anywhere along the vertical edge, even all the way to the top.

**To rearrange the icons,** hold down the Option key and drag them left or right.

**To delete an icon,** first open the "System Folder," then open the "Control Strip Modules" folder. Drag the icon you want to delete out of the folder; store it in your Utilities folder. It might not disappear from the Control Strip until you restart.

**Hide the Control Strip** if you never use it.

1. From the Apple menu, choose "Control Panels," then "Control Strip."
2. Click the button, "Hide Control Strip."
3. Click the Close Box to put it away.

*This is the Control Strip Control Panel.*

## Memory vs. hard disk

*power user:*
*Someone who knows*
*more about your*
*computer than you do.*

If you know the difference between memory and hard disk, you are way beyond millions of other computer users. If you don't know the difference, read this page and then you, too, can throw around these terms like a *power user.* Knowing the difference will also help you understand and work with your computer. So this is how it works:

*gigabyte: See*
*page 234.*

A **hard disk** in your computer is like a **filing cabinet** in your office: it stores things for you. If you have a four-gigabyte hard disk (like your iMac might), it's like having 400 filing cabinet drawers—you have lots of room to store things like applications, documents, games, etc.

If you're working in your office, you don't climb into your filing cabinet when you want to get things done, do you? What *do* you do? You probably take things out of your filing cabinet and put them on your desk. The iMac does the same thing— when you open an application, the iMac goes into the hard disk (the filing cabinet) and takes a copy of the application and puts it into **memory** (the **desk**). Every-thing the computer works on is temporarily stored in memory, then when you save the file, the permanent item is stored on the hard disk. Memory is also referred to as **RAM,** which stands for *random access memory* (there are other kinds of memory).

As you work on a document, everything you do to it is stored in RAM until you **save** the document. This creates a problem because when that memory gets full of your unsaved work, your computer will check out/crash/go bellyup/bomb. So save often; save every few minutes. Also, as I mentioned, when you open an application a copy of that application gets put into RAM. When you *close* a *document,* the *document* is put away onto the hard disk and taken out of RAM, but the *application* is still there. You must **quit** the application to take that application out of RAM.

If you've ever gotten a message telling you something couldn't be opened because there is **"not enough memory,"** or you crashed and got the message of a **"Type 1 error,"** it's probably because you left an application open, in which case you should read pages 242–243.

Some iMacs have only 32 megabytes of RAM. You can install much more—you can't have too much RAM. The more complex things you do on your computer, such as high-end graphics, music, or multimedia, the more RAM you need. If you hardly understand what RAM is, you probably won't need more than 32 megabytes for a while. When you need more, find a Mac catalog, order it, open your iMac, and insert the memory chip (it's about the size of a stick of chewing gum); have your power user friend help you.

### How big is your hard disk?

Your iMac might have a 4-gigabyte drive or 6, or even 11. To check the size, do this:

Macintosh HD

*Your hard disk icon*
*probably looks like this.*

1.  Click once on the hard disk icon, the one in the upper-right corner of the screen. It's probably named Macintosh HD.

2.  Go to the File menu and choose "Get Info."

3.  In the dialog box that comes up, as shown to the right, you can see how big your hard disk is (the "Capacity"), how much room is left on it ("Available"), and how much space is filled with files ("Used").

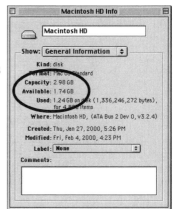

### How much memory do you have?

Invariably someone will ask how much RAM (memory) you have in your computer. If you can tell them with confidence, you will feel empowered. It's easy to find out:

1.  From the Apple menu, choose "About This Computer."

2.  You will get the dialog box shown below. "Built-in Memory" is how much RAM is installed at the moment.

    "Virtual Memory" is how much of the hard disk space is pretending to be RAM. You determine this amount in the Memory Control Panel. For now, don't worry about it. When you are ready to learn more about virtual memory, see *The Little Mac Book*.

    "Largest Unused Block" is how much memory is available at the moment for the computer to work with.

    The bars on the lower-right of the dialog box indicate how much memory the various applications are using. In the example below, PageMaker is taking up a fraction of the 29.4 megabytes allocated to it, and the System itself (the Mac OS) is taking up almost all of its allocated amount.

## The Application menu

If you have problems with running out of memory often, you're probably leaving applications open accidentally. For instance, when you're working in a word processor and you *close* the window of the page you're typing on, essentially you took the *paper* (the page, which is in a window) out of the typewriter (the word processor), but you left the typewriter itself on the desk. The word processor is only put away when you *quit*.

You **close windows;** you **quit applications.** Did you read pages 240–241 about memory and the hard disk? Well, as you open applications and the computer puts them into RAM (into memory), you load up RAM and when RAM gets too full, it either won't let you open anything else or it crashes. To prevent this, **quit** an application when you are finished using it. I know that when you *close* a document, you see the Desktop and it *looks* like the application is gone. It isn't! This is when the Application menu comes in handy—this menu is a list of every application that is still open.

*In this example, one application is open (AppleWorks). The Finder is always open because that's the software that runs the Desktop.*

*In this example, three applications are open. The icon and name in the menu bar, plus the checkmark in the menu, indicate which program you are in at the moment.*

*If you had three applications open and were to check "About This Computer" from the Apple menu, you would see that there wasn't much available memory left.*

## "Out of memory" errors

So if you get a message that the iMac has run out of memory, check the Application menu described on the opposite page. If there is anything at all listed besides "Finder," that item is open and taking up memory.

**To free up the memory,** you must **quit** the applications. Do this:

**1.** *Press* (don't click) on the name or icon in the upper-right corner of the menu bar (the Application menu), and drag down, down, down, off the end of the menu. The entire menu will "tear off." Click anywhere on the screen and the Application menu will "float," like this:

*Note: The Application menu does not tear off and float in **Mac OS 8.1.***

**2.** Click once on any application in the Application list (except Finder) to make that application active.

**3.** *Even if it looks like nothing happened* (that application's name and icon are now in the menu bar), go to the File menu and choose "Quit," **or** press Command Q. That application will disappear from the palette and from RAM.

**4.** Click on any other application in the floating palette, and quit that one. Continue until the ones you don't need right now are all gone.

*Tip: You might want to keep this palette floating around so you always know what is open. And if you are in one application and want to switch to another, **hold the Option key down and click on the name in the palette;** this will automatically hide the application you are leaving (when an application is "hidden," it is still open and available, you just can't see it at the moment).*

## Contextual menus

Contextual menus are menus that pop up with different items in them depending on what you click on, as shown below. There is nothing in the menus that you can't do other ways on the Mac—this feature just makes it easier. (Actually, you can buy or download software from other people that gives you even more options.)

### To use a contextual menu

1. You must be at the Desktop.

2. Hold down the Control key, the one that says "control" on it (not the Command key with the apple symbol).

3. With the Control key down, click on a folder, or inside a window, or on a document icon, the Desktop, or anything else. You'll notice the menu offers different options depending on what you click.

4. Choose your option like you would from any other menu.

*Make an alias of any file.*

*Add an alias to the Favorites menu (see the opposite page).*

*Empty the trash, if there's something in it.*

*Click on a blank spot inside an open window.*

*Click on a blank spot on the Desktop.*

### The Favorites menu (Mac OS 8.5 and higher)

Favorites

*This is the Favorites folder. It's in the System Folder.*

In the Apple menu is an item called "Favorites," which is specifically meant for you to customize. You can put aliases (see page 237) of any file on your hard disk in this menu, then when you want to open that item, you simply use the Favorites menu. **To put an alias of any file in the Favorites menu,** while you're at the Desktop click on the file. Then from the File menu, choose "Add To Favorites," or use the contextual menu as shown on the opposite page. Also see below.

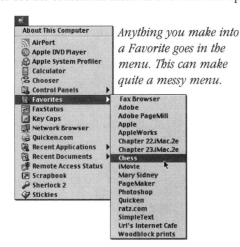

*Anything you make into a Favorite goes in the menu. This can make quite a messy menu.*

*Make folders inside the Favorites folder (shown below), then organize your items.*

*(The alias to the Fax Browser appears at the top of the list because I typed a blank space at the beginning of its name.)*

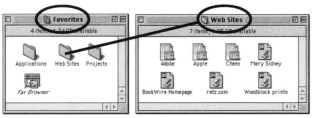

*After you've made a number of favorites, open the Favorites folder (it's inside the System Folder) and organize the files. Every folder you make will become a hierarchical menu, as shown above.*

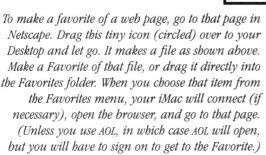

*To make a favorite of a web page, go to that page in Netscape. Drag this tiny icon (circled) over to your Desktop and let go. It makes a file as shown above. Make a Favorite of that file, or drag it directly into the Favorites folder. When you choose that item from the Favorites menu, your iMac will connect (if necessary), open the browser, and go to that page. (Unless you use AOL, in which case AOL will open, but you will have to sign on to get to the Favorite.)*

About This Computer
📶 AirPort
🌐 Apple DVD Player
🎛 Apple System Profiler
🧮 Calculator
🖥 Chooser
📋 Control Panels ▶
📁 Favorites ▶
📠 FaxStatus
⌨ Key Caps
🌐 Network Browser
🔵 Quicken.com
📋 Recent Applications ▶
📋 Recent Documents ▶
📡 Remote Access Status
📖 Scrapbook
🔍 Sherlock 2
🗒 Stickies

*Get the Apple System Profiler from the Apple menu.*

## The Apple System Profiler

Apple provides a central place for keeping track of all kinds of things on your iMac, called the Apple System Profiler (shown below). You might look at this and find it dreadfully dull, but it can be a very important feature for anyone who might work on your machine or anyone who might be providing technical support to you over the telephone.

Each tab across the top holds a page of different specifications. In some of these pages you can click on items and find some fairly intelligible information.

You'll find your serial number, system version, amount of RAM, and more under the first tab, "System Profile," at the bottom left of the screen. You might have to click on that tiny triangle that's pointing toward "Product Information" to display the serial number.

Poke around this profiler if you like, then put it away and remember it on that rainy day when you need to call tech support.

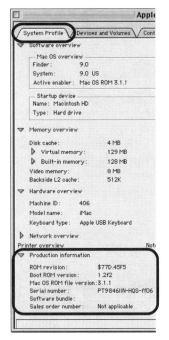

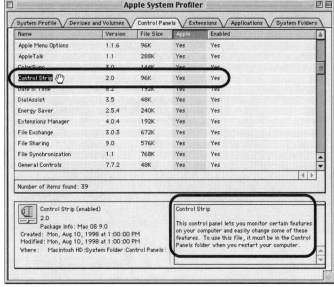

# Sherlock 2

Sherlock 2 is Apple's name for the software program that helps you find all kinds of things—files on your computer, shopping bargains on the Internet, old friends and lovers, the latest news, products and support from Apple, research items, and more. It's called Sherlock 2 to differentiate it from the earlier version that is called just plain Sherlock (both shown below; the first version is explained on page 238). Sherlock 2 is installed automatically with the version of the operating system called Mac OS 9. Look in your Apple menu; you will see either "Sherlock" or "Sherlock 2."

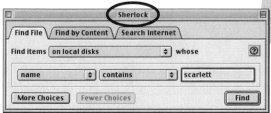

*If Sherlock looks like this, see page 238.*

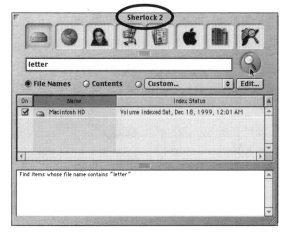

*If Sherlock looks like this, you've got Sherlock 2. Read this chapter.*

## The many faces of Sherlock 2

Sherlock 2 has expanded, along with the Mac, to the Internet; that is, it helps you find items not only on your own hard disk, but out in the global world. It's not a complete replacement for the search tools you find on the web itself, but it can provide a quick and easy way to locate many things. Let's look at a general overview of Sherlock 2.

**Note: If America Online is your only email/Internet service, you must first open and log on to AOL before you can use Sherlock 2 to search the Internet!**

*The buttons across the top of Sherlock 2 represent what Apple calls "channels," or customizable sources of information. Position your mouse over any of the buttons and pause a few seconds—a tag appears that tells you what that channel can help you find. Try it.*

*Across the row, the channels are Files, Internet, People, Shopping, News, Apple, References, and an empty channel called My Channel that you can customize. (All of the channels except Files search for information on the Internet.)*

*Click on a channel to select it; the window will change with each channel. Try it.*

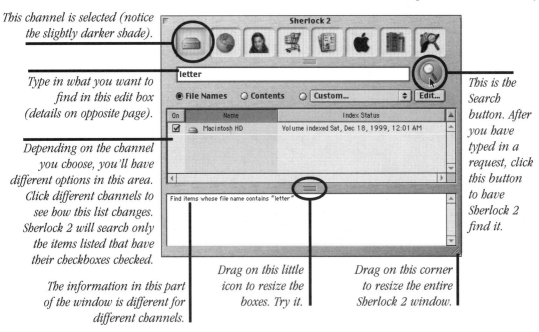

*This channel is selected (notice the slightly darker shade).*

*Type in what you want to find in this edit box (details on opposite page).*

*Depending on the channel you choose, you'll have different options in this area. Click different channels to see how this list changes. Sherlock 2 will search only the items listed that have their checkboxes checked.*

*The information in this part of the window is different for different channels.*

*Drag on this little icon to resize the boxes. Try it.*

*Drag on this corner to resize the entire Sherlock 2 window.*

*This is the Search button. After you have typed in a request, click this button to have Sherlock 2 find it.*

## How to quit Sherlock 2

When you want to put Sherlock 2 away, either press Command Q to quit, **or** click in the little close box in the upper-left corner of the window.

## Do a simple search for a file on your hard disk

First of all, a **file** is anything on your hard disk. Documents, applications, folders, fonts—everything is considered a file. And every file on your Mac is represented by an icon. So let's search for something on your hard disk.

### Search for a file on your hard disk

1. If you are at the Desktop, go to the File menu and choose "Find...," or press Command F.

   If you are in any application (or even if you're at the Desktop), from the Apple menu, choose "Sherlock 2."

2. Click the first channel button, the one with the picture of a hard disk (circled, below; it's probably already selected).

3. In the upper portion of the window you'll see the name of your hard disk (as shown below). Depending on how your computer is set up, you might see other items in that area. Make sure there is a checkbox in any item you want to search.

4. In the edit box (see below), type a word that you think is in some of the files on your computer. For instance, type "letter" or "setup."

5. Make sure the round radio button for "File Names" is checked (shown below).

6. You'll notice in the lower area that Sherlock 2 reiterates what you are looking for.

7. Click the Search button (the round one with the magnifying glass; circled, below).

8. After you do the steps above, turn the page and continue.

**Note:** *It doesn't matter whether you type capital or lowercase letters. If you don't know the exact name of the file, just type any part of it that you think is in the file name.*

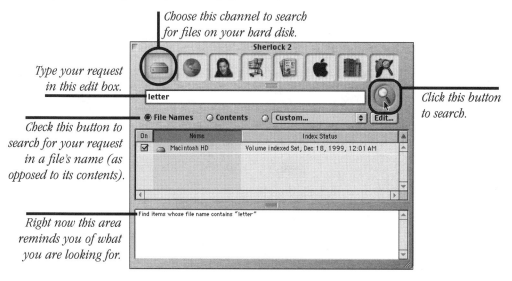

*Choose this channel to search for files on your hard disk.*

*Type your request in this edit box.*

*Click this button to search.*

*Check this button to search for your request in a file's name (as opposed to its contents).*

*Right now this area reminds you of what you are looking for.*

### Opening a found file

Sherlock 2 will take several seconds to search your entire hard disk. The results will look something like those shown below. In the upper portion of the window is a list of all the files that have your request in the file name; click once on any one of those files and in the lower portion, Sherlock 2 will tell you where that file is stored.

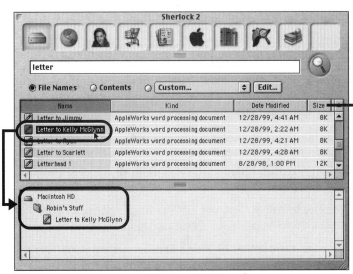

*Click once on the file you were looking for, and in the lower portion of this window you'll see exactly where that file is stored. This example shows that the selected letter is in a folder called "Robin's Stuff," and that folder is on the Macintosh HD (the hard disk window).*

*Click on any of these column headings to organize the content by that heading.*

Once you have located the file you want, there are several things you can do. First, click once on the file name in either the upper or the lower portion of Sherlock 2 to select that file. Then do one of the following:

**Tip:** *Click on a file name to select it, then go to the File menu to see what your options are for that particular type of file.*

- To open the file, double-click the file name, **or** press Command O (for Open).
- To open the enclosing *folder* in which the file is stored, press Command E.
- To print the item (if it's a document), press Command P.
- To delete the file, drag the file from the window to the trash can, **or** select the file and press Command Delete.
- To make an alias of the file, hold down the Command and Option keys and drag the file to the Desktop or into a folder; let go and an alias will appear (see page 237 for information about aliases).

## Narrow your search

If the quick and easy search gave you too many results, you can narrow the search to more specific attributes.

### To narrow a search

1. Open Sherlock 2 and click the "Files" channel button (the hard disk icon).

2. Click the "Edit…" button; you'll see the dialog box shown below.

3. Take a few moments to see what your options are here. Once you click a checkbox, the gray options will become available to you. For instance, you can see below that the "date modified" choice is checked, so the menu next to it is now available. Check the boxes, then click on the menus to see what you can do. Be sure to uncheck any options you don't want to apply before you click the OK button!

4. Once your parameters are set up, click the OK button. You'll go back to the main search window and Sherlock 2 will summarize your search options in the bottom portion of the window. Then click the Search button.

**Tip:** *If you're looking for a file you created or worked on today or yesterday, try the* "Custom…" *menu.*

*Click in the checkbox, then click on the menu to see what your choices are.*

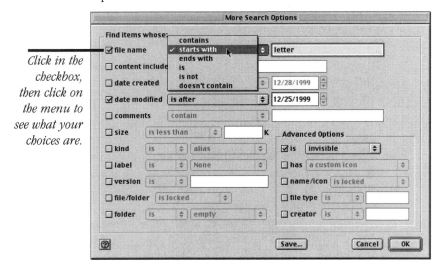

### Search a specific disk or folder

Sometimes you want to search a specific disk, such as a Zip or CD you inserted, or perhaps you want to search only in one particular folder. That's easy to do.

### To search a particular disk or folder

1. Find the icon for that disk or folder on your Desktop.

2. Drag the disk or folder icon and drop it in the top portion of the Sherlock 2 window. Sherlock 2 calls all folders or disks "volumes."

3. Make sure there is a check in the box next to each volume you want to search.

4. Continue with the search as you did on the previous pages.

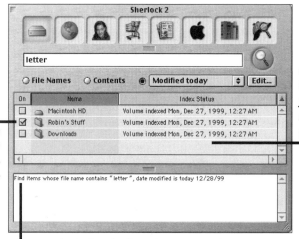

*This shows that of the three "volumes," Sherlock 2 will search only the folder called "Robin's Stuff."*

*Drag the icon of the disk or folder you want to search and drop it in this space.*

*Here Sherlock 2 displays the options I chose when I clicked the "Edit..." button (explained on the previous page).*

## What is the "Contents" button for?

Sherlock 2 lets you search through the **contents** of any file. For instance, maybe you're working on a research project and you've created dozens of files on the topic of chess. You want to find all the papers in your collection that mention "en passant." That's when you click the "Contents" button; instead of searching just the *names* of files, Sherlock 2 will actually read the *contents* of files. For instance, you might have written an article that you named "Special Moves in Chess," and in the article itself you wrote about the en passant move, but you also mention en passant in three other articles with different names—Sherlock will find every file that includes the phrase "en passant" in the text.

**BUT** Sherlock 2 cannot search the contents of your files until it has first **indexed** every file. That is, Sherlock has to read every file on your computer and then organize every word into a database that it can search when you request it.

Logically, if you write more articles after Sherlock has indexed the files on your hard disk, Sherlock has to index things *again* to update and add those new files to its database. To make this easy for you, Apple has set Sherlock 2 to automatically index your hard disk at a certain time every day. You should check to see what the indexing schedule is because it can take an hour or so for Sherlock to index (depending on how many files you have on your hard disk); you might want to change the schedule so it indexes when you are not working on your iMac.

*Depending on how many files you have, indexing can take a while.*

### Check the indexing schedule and change it if necessary

1. Open Sherlock 2 (at the Desktop, press Command F; if you're working in an application, go to the Apple menu and choose "Sherlock 2").

2. From the Find menu, choose "Index Volumes...."

3. There is probably a checkmark in the little box in the "Use Schedule" column. If not, you can click the little box so Sherlock 2 will automatically index the hard drive (it will use the schedule you are about to set).

4. Click the "Schedule…" button in the bottom-left corner. —continued

**Note:** *If you don't want to update the index on a regular schedule, you can open this dialog box, select the disk you want to update (click on its name), and just click the "Update Index..." button. (If you have never indexed the disk, this button says, "Create Index....")*

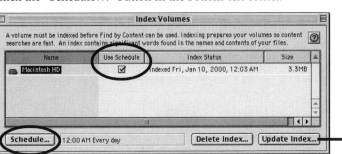

5. The "Schedule" dialog box opens, as shown below. Do you see the time it's scheduled for? The hour in that time slot is selected (it's highlighted).

**To change the hour,** either *type* in a new time or *click* the tiny arrows to the right.

**To change the minutes,** either *tap* the Tab key on your keyboard to select the minutes or *click* on the minutes; then type or use the tiny arrows.

**To change the AM or PM,** either *tap* the Tab key on your keyboard to select the AM or PM or *click* on the letters; then type or use the tiny arrows.

**To change the days,** click in the checkboxes to check or uncheck each day—a check tells Sherlock 2 to index on that day each week.

6. Click the **OK** button when you're finished, then close the "Index Volumes" dialog box by clicking in its little close box in the upper-left corner.

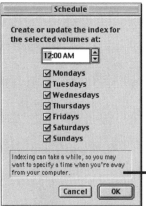

*This is good advice—just remember that your iMac has to be turned on for Sherlock 2 to do its business.*

***Tip:*** *While Sherlock 2 is open, go to the Edit menu and choose "Preferences...." Click the "Languages..." button. You might see many languages in this list that have a checkmark next to them. If you don't have files on your disk in those languages, uncheck each one you don't need. Then click OK in both this dialog box and the "Preferences" box.*

*As the note in the box says, "Selecting fewer languages makes indexing faster and uses less space on your hard disk."*

## Delete the index

In the "Index Volumes" dialog box (shown below), you'll notice a column labeled "Size." This is the size of the database that Sherlock 2 has made. As you create and install more and more files, this database can become huge, which means it uses a large chunk of your hard disk to store the index. You can't throw this file away because it's invisible (which means you can't even find it), but you can use Sherlock 2 to delete it.

1. When Sherlock 2 is open, go to the Find menu and choose "Index Volumes...."

2. Click once on the name of the disk to select it, then click the "Delete Index..." button.

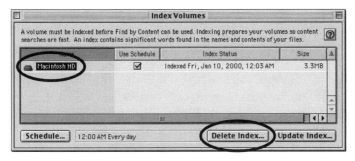

## Find something on the Internet

Besides searching your disk, Sherlock 2 can also search the Internet and the web. Each of the buttons across the top of Sherlock 2 is called a "channel." Each channel is set up to search specific areas of the web (except the very first one that represents your hard disk). When you click on a channel to select it, you'll see the bottom portion of Sherlock 2 change to fit the channel's specifications. Try it.

To search the Internet, Sherlock 2 has to *go* to the Internet, which means you must have your Internet connection already set up and working before you use this feature of Sherlock 2. **If America Online is your only email/Internet/web service, you must first open and log on to AOL before you can use Sherlock 2 to search the Internet!**

### To search the Internet

*Internet*

*People*

*Shopping*

*News*

*Apple*

*Reference*

*My Channel*

1. Open Sherlock 2 (choose "Sherlock 2" from the Apple menu; or if you are at the Desktop, press Command H).

2. Make sure the "Internet" channel button is selected (it should already be selected if you pressed Command H); click once on it to make sure. It will look a little darker than the others after you click it.

   If you are looking for a person, click the "People" channel button instead of the "Internet" channel. If you're looking for news, reference material, or Apple support information, click the appropriate channel. If you want to go shopping, take a look at page 258.

3. Type in the item you wish to look for. If it is a phrase, put quotation marks around the phrase; for instance, if you are looking for a recipe for chocolate pecan pie, type in "chocolate pecan pie" in quotes.

   If you don't use the quotes, Sherlock will find every web page with the word "chocolate" on it, *plus* every page with the word "pecan" on it, *plus* every page with the word "pie" on it. But with the phrase enclosed with quotes, you will only get pages that contain the entire phrase "chocolate pecan pie."

4. Click the Search button (the big one with the magnifying glass). Sherlock 2 will log on to the Internet through your ISP (Internet Service Provider). *Remember, if you use AOL you must first open and log on to AOL before you click the Search button.* Sherlock 2 will go to the World Wide Web and find what you are looking for. Be patient—it might take a minute or two.

5. You will get a list of "results," as shown on the opposite page. Click once on a result and details of that web page will be displayed in the middle panel (also shown). To go to that web page, either double-click the title in the top portion of Sherlock, or single-click the underlined link in the details portion. Read the captions on the illustration on the opposite page.

**1.** *Click the appropriate channel to search.*

**2.** *Type in what you're looking for.*

**3.** *Click the Search button.*

**5.** *Click once on a result to see details below, or double-click to go directly to that web page.*

**4.** *Using the scroll bar, scroll through this list of results.*

**6.** *If you want to see this web page, click once on this link.*

**Tips:** *To resize the results and the details boxes, drag this little symbol.*

*To resize the entire window so you can see the names of pages and the addresses better, drag this corner.*

*To resize the columns, press on the dividing line between the column headings at the top (Name, Relevance, Site) and drag left or right.*

**Tip:** *If you see a link that says "Find similar pages," click it to get a list of more results that match the selected web page.*

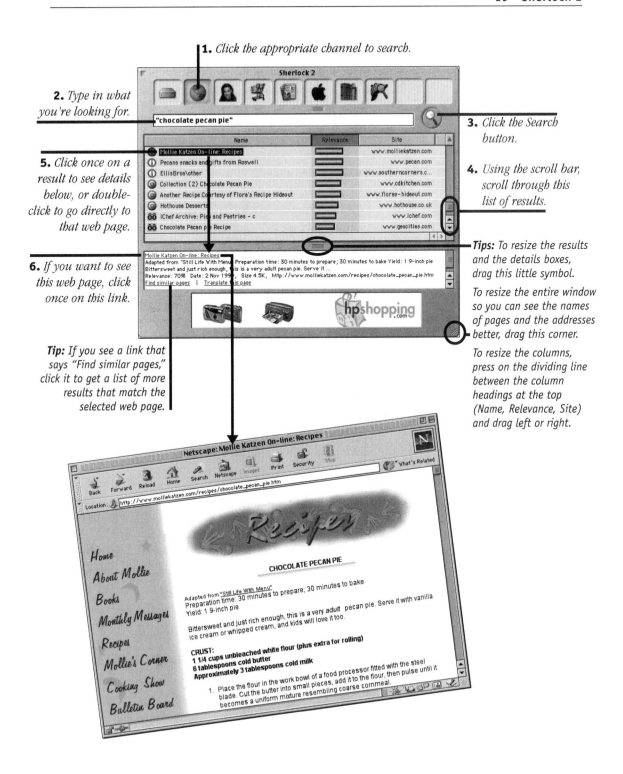

## Shop on the Internet

Sherlock doesn't just *find* you the items you want that are for sale on the Internet—it actually provides you with their prices and availability. Amazing.

Keep in mind that what Sherlock 2 finds is dependent on what is being offered for sale through the selected search sites; in the case of the shopping channel, you can see below that Sherlock 2 is only looking on Amazon, Barnes and Noble, and eBay. That is, if you're looking to compare prices of a down jacket from Lands End, L.L. Bean, and Orvis, Sherlock 2 is not the right tool to use. But considering there are literally millions of items for sale in the search sites listed in Sherlock 2, it's not a bad place to look for many things.

Search using the shopping channel just as explained on the previous two pages: **1)** Click the Shopping channel button, **2)** type in your request (use quotation marks for phrases), **3)** click the Search button, then **4)** double-click the result of your choice *or* **5)** single-click your choice, then click the link in the details box.

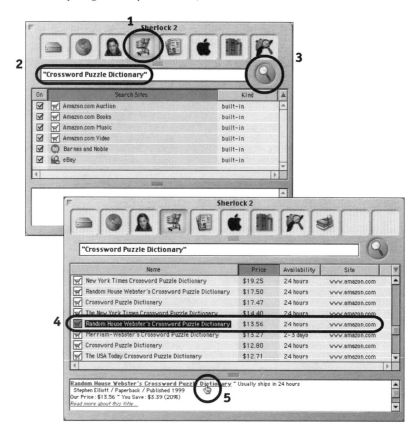

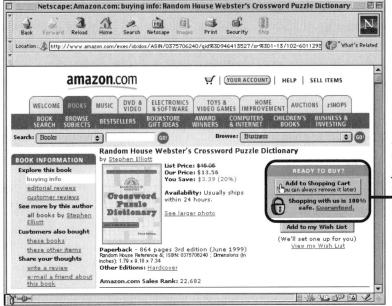

*Depending on which web site you go to, you can choose to buy the selected item.*

*You're not limited to buying just books, of course. Try anything!*

### Customize the channels

You can add search sites to any of the channels, and you can make new channels and customize them. Apple makes it sound real easy—just go to the search site you want to add to a channel and download the plug-in (a small piece of software); drop that plug-in into the top portion of the window in the channel of your choice. That's easy; the problem is that it isn't so easy to find the downloadable plug-ins.

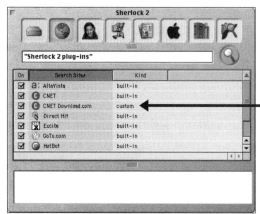

Check the web sites mentioned below. When you find new plug-ins you would like to have, follow the directions on Apple's site for downloading. After it's on your hard disk, drag the icon and drop it into the window of the selected channel. Check these sites: **www.apple.com/sherlock/plugins.html www.apple-donuts.com**

CNET download.src

*Drag the plug-in icon (above) and drop it into the window (left). New plug-ins you add will appear as "custom" instead of "built-in."*

*Sherlock 2 plug-ins will always be named with an extension (three extra letters) of ".src."*

### Extra tip while searching the Internet with Sherlock 2

Chances are that when Sherlock 2 finds some good sites for you, you'll want to bounce back and forth between Sherlock and your browser—clicking on the Sherlock links, checking them out in the browser, going back to Sherlock to click another link, and so on. To make this process easier, drag down the Application menu palette (directions below). Then you can just click the palette button icons to pop back and forth between Sherlock and your browser.

### To make the Application palette

*Zoom box*

*Finder*

*Netscape*

*Sherlock*

*This is the floating Application palette.*

1. Position your pointer directly on the Application menu, which is the one in the far, upper-right corner of your menu bar. It names the current application you are in.

2. Press on that menu and drag your mouse down through the menu and off the bottom, still holding the mouse button down. The menu will "tear off."

3. Resize the floating Application palette: hold down the Command key and click in the tiny little zoom box (circled, left).

4. Let the palette float around on your screen. When you want to go to Sherlock, click the Sherlock icon. When you want to go to Netscape, click the Netscape icon.

5. To put the palette away, just click in its tiny close box in the upper-left.

# AirPort

The AirPort technology is amazingly cool. It lets you connect to the Internet without any wires so you can use your iMac in the kitchen or workshop, or your iBook (the laptop version of an iMac) in your treefort or library, even if there is no phone line around—the computer can be up to 150 feet away from the AirPort Base Station. One of the greatest advantages of having an AirPort setup is that as many as ten computers can all connect to the Internet *on the same line!* No longer do you have to wait for your teenage daughter to stop chatting online so you can get online for that research project. And not only can you get on the Internet, but each iMac with an AirPort card can share files with other computers that are on the same wireless connection, and can even print through the wireless network.

How do you know if your iMac is ready for AirPort? If you still have the box it came in, check the information on the outside. If you don't have the box, check the back of your computer, way at the bottom. Do you see a round button with a slot in it? That button opens a panel so you can install more memory or an AirPort card.

Now, before you get too excited about AirPort, here are a couple of caveats:

- If you have an iMac with an AirPort slot, it came with all the software you need to make AirPort work, **but** you have to **buy** an AirPort Base Station for about $300 and you have to **buy** an AirPort card for each iMac or iBook for about $100. You can buy them at the Apple Store on Apple's web site **(www.apple.com)** or from any Macintosh catalog or online vendor.

  *An AirPort card is about the size of a business card.*

- You cannot connect directly to America Online through the AirPort technology, so if AOL is your *only* connection to the Internet, don't bother thinking about AirPort.

  **If,** however, you also have an ISP connection and you log on to AOL through your ISP, you can certainly use AirPort to get to AOL. If you have not yet set up AOL to connect through your ISP, see page 290 *before* you set up the AirPort.

  If you don't even know what an ISP is (explained on pages 189 and 192) you probably don't have one.

  *The fact that the AirPort does not connect to AOL is not Apple's fault— AOL does not use the industry-standard PPP connection system.*

### Step 1. Before you plug in the AirPort Base Station

There are a couple of things you *must* do and something I *recommend* you do before you plug that little AirPort Base Station in and set it up.

**You must:**

**a.** Make sure your iMac has a working Internet connection through an ISP. If you can get email and browse the World Wide Web, your connection is working. If it isn't, read the section of this book about the Internet and make it work, then come back to this chapter.

**b.** If you use America Online *and* you have another ISP, set up AOL to connect through your ISP, as explained on page 290.

**I recommend:**

**c.** Set up a "location" for your standard modem connection in the Location Manager, as explained below and on the opposite page. This is because the AirPort changes several connectivity settings in your iMac, and if you ever decide you want to get to the Internet *without* using AirPort, you'll have to set up your standard connection all over again. It can be very frustrating.

So set up a location for your standard location, and after you get AirPort working, set up a location for AirPort (see page 266). Then you can switch back and forth between them with the click of a button.

**Is the software installed?**

**d.** Also, check to make sure the AirPort software is installed. Go to the Apple menu. If you see "AirPort" at the top of the list, you've got what you need. Your AirPort Base Station comes with a software CD in case you're installing the card in an iBook (laptop Mac), but since your iMac is ready, you don't need to install anything from that CD.

### Step 2. Make a location for your standard connection

Your iMac has something called the **Location Manager** that makes it easy to switch all sorts of settings. This is particularly useful if you're traveling with your computer (which you're probably not doing with an iMac), but it is also very useful for making it easy to switch between the wireless AirPort connection and your standard modem connection. Don't worry if it doesn't quite make sense yet— just follow the directions and trust me that this will save you frustration later.

**a.** Make sure your standard Internet connection is working properly. If you can connect to get your email and browse the web, it's fine.

**b.** In the Control Strip, click on the Location Manager module and choose "Open Location Manager."

*This is the Location Manager module.*

**c.** When the Location Manager dialog box appears, go to the File menu and choose "New Location..." (shown below).

**d.** In the small dialog box that appears, as shown below, name the new location with the name of your ISP or something that tells you what this location will connect to, like "internal modem." Click the Save button.

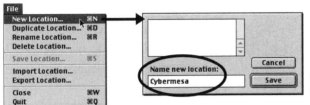

*Cybermesa is the name of my Internet Service Provider.*

**e.** In the Location Manager dialog box (shown below), find the "Edit Location" menu and choose the name of the location you just made.

**f.** Check the boxes "AppleTalk & TCP/IP," "Internet Set," and "Remote Access." If you know what you're doing, check any other boxes whose settings you want to keep in this location; if not, those three will do.

*If you don't see the bottom portion of this dialog box, as shown, click this tiny triangle.*

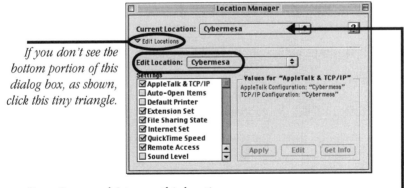

**g.** Press Command S to save this location.

**h.** In the "Current Location" menu at the top of the dialog box (not the menu in the menu bar), choose the location you just made.

**i.** Quit the Location Manager.

*Now* you're ready to set up the AirPort system!

*An AirPort card looks something like this. The one you'll get is probably in a small case called an "adapter."*

### Step 3. Install the AirPort card

Follow the simple directions that came with the AirPort card or the directions in the little "User Guide" that came with your iMac. It's very easy to install and only takes about two minutes.

### Step 4. Connect the AirPort Base Station

Follow the simple directions that came with the AirPort Base Station. Basically, you will plug the AirPort into a power source (like your surge protector), and connect a phone cord from the Base Station to your phone jack. If you use a cable or DSL modem, then you won't use the phone cord—you'll connect an Ethernet cable from the AirPort to the cable or DSL modem.

No cables from the AirPort are connected to your iMac. This means the existing phone cable from your iMac's internal modem (or Ethernet connection to your cable or DSL modem) can stay right where it is in case you need to connect in the standard way through the wires.

*This is the front of the AirPort Base Station. It's about as big as a large tart.*

*This is the back. Notice it has both a standard phone port (called an RJ-11) and an Ethernet port.*

### Step 5. Open the AirPort Setup Assistant

AirPort Setup Assistant

*Open this Assistant.*

In the Assistants folder on your iMac is an icon named "AirPort Setup Assistant." If you don't see the Assistants folder right away because perhaps you reorganized your hard disk, use Sherlock 2 to find it.

Double-click the Setup Assistant icon to open it and start the process. It's very easy—there are no strange numbers you have to enter or strange information you have to get from your ISP—the AirPort takes all of your information from your existing dialog boxes, which is why you have to have a working connection before you set up the AirPort.

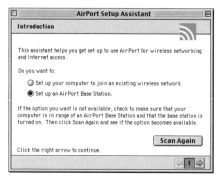

### Step 6. Connect to the Internet

As soon as the AirPort Setup Assistant is finished, you can connect to the Internet.

**a.** In the Control Strip, you have a new module for the AirPort, as shown to the right and below. Click on it and choose "Turn AirPort On."

*This is your new AirPort Control Strip module.*

**b.** Now go right back to that module, click again, and this time you'll see the connection you named in the Setup Assistant. Choose it. You'll be asked to supply the password you created in the Setup Assistant.

*In the AirPort Setup Assistant, I named the wireless connection "roadrat."*

**c.** You are ready to connect to the Internet. If you have a cable or DSL connection, you are accustomed to having your connection on all the time, but if you are used to a standard dial-up modem, you probably use Remote Access to connect. *Don't do that! Don't use Remote Access when you want to connect wirelessly through the AirPort.* **Just double-click your browser or your email application and you're there.**

**Except:** For some reason almost every time you try to go to the first web page you will get an error message like the one shown below (Apple knows this). Click the OK button on the error message, and tell your browser to find that page again. It will.

*Click OK and tell your browser to try again.*

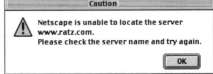

### Step 7. Disconnect from the Internet (if necessary)

If you use a cable or DSL modem: You don't need to turn the AirPort off.

If you use a dial-up connection: You don't really need to turn the AirPort off. Quitting the browser or your email application will disconnect from the Internet and free up your phone line, even with the AirPort on. If you want to free the phone line without quitting the browser, choose "AirPort" from the Apple menu or "Open AirPort" from the Location Manager and click "Hangup AirPort Base Station."

*Before you go anywhere, make sure you complete Step 8 on the next page!*

## Step 8.  Make an AirPort Location

Remember that location you made in Step 2 for your standard connection? Make one now for your AirPort connection so you can easily switch between them when necessary.

**a.** While your AirPort connection is still the active one (that is, you just turned it off and haven't changed any settings anywhere else), go to the Control Strip and open the Location Manager again, as you did in Step 2b.

**b.** The Location Manager has changed the "Current Location" to "AirPort" because that's how you just connected. In the "Edit Location" menu, choose "AirPort," as shown below. Put checks in "AppleTalk & TCP/IP," "Internet Set," and "Remote Access." If you know what you're doing, check any other boxes whose settings you want to keep in this location (see the file sharing note in the sidebar); if not, these three will do.

**Note:** *If you plan to use **file sharing** through AirPort, make sure File Sharing is turned on **before** you open the Location Manager. Then also check the "File Sharing State" box in the Location Manager.*

*For information about sharing files through AirPort, see the Help menu.*

**c.** Save this location: press Command S.

**d.** Make a quick trip to the Preferences from the Edit menu and uncheck the box "Ask me to save any changes upon restart, shut down, etc." Quit.

## Step 9.  Change locations when necessary

After you connect with the AirPort, you will not be able to use your regular, wired connection because all the settings have been changed. To use your standard connection again, go to the Location Manager Control Strip module and choose it, then connect as usual (through Remote Access, for instance). When you want to use the AirPort connection again, go to the Location Manager and choose it.

*If you see this message when you open the AirPort Control Strip module, it means your iMac is using different settings. Click the Location Manager module and change to "AirPort," then you will be able to turn on AirPort.*

# What's a Peripheral, a Hub, and a Port?

## What's a peripheral?

Once you get an iMac or start thinking about one, you'll probably start hearing about "peripherals" as well. A peripheral is any piece of hardware (a physical object) that is not built inside the computer. It is outside, on the periphery, but it connects to the computer.

A printer is a peripheral; a scanner (hardware for getting photographs and drawings inside the computer) is a peripheral; a Zip drive that holds removable hard disks is a peripheral. The modem for my iMac is built-in; the modem for my big Mac is a peripheral—it's a little box that sits outside my computer and connects to it.

## What's a port?

Peripherals connect to the computer through "ports." At first a port might look like a fancy plug socket, like the electrical ones in the wall. The difference between a port and an electrical socket is that a port can send information both ways, both to and from the computer. An electrical socket only sends energy in one direction.

Now, the reason you hear so much about peripherals in relation to the iMac is because the iMac has brand-new port technology. So new, in fact, that you need to be careful about buying peripherals; you need to make sure they can connect to your iMac ports. If you already own peripherals that don't have USB ports, you can get adapters to make the connections.

*Tip: To find out the latest information about iMac peripherals and adapters and everything related, go to **www.macintouch.com/imacusb.html.** Also check the Apple site at **www.apple.com.***

## What is USB?

You'll probably hear the term "USB" often, as well as "peripheral." The acronym USB stands for Universal Serial Bus (which you don't have to remember). A "bus" is the system of wires, ports, and programming that a computer uses to connect peripherals and communicate with them. Until the iMac, Apple used a different sort of bus on Macintoshes, and so this switch to the USB is a big deal; it's the new technology that many (especially older) peripherals can't connect to.

On the side of your computer is a little panel you can open, and inside are the ports (as illustrated below). You'll plug all of your peripherals into this place. The USB ports are the rectangular ones in the middle. Notice you have two of them, and your keyboard is already plugged into one. Your printer, one that either has a USB connector or uses an adapter, will plug into the other port.

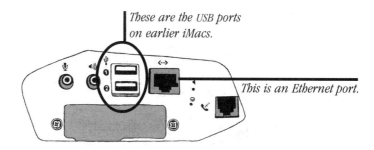

*These are the USB ports on earlier iMacs.*

*This is an Ethernet port.*

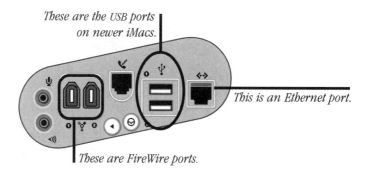

*These are the USB ports on newer iMacs.*

*This is an Ethernet port.*

*These are FireWire ports.*

## Hot swapping

You'll hear that USB devices are "hot swappable." This means that you can swap (connect and disconnect) iMac peripherals without having to turn the computer completely off. On other Macintoshes, you must shut down the computer completely before you change any connections. One recommendation, though, is that even though you *can* swap without turning off the computer, you should at least quit any applications you may have open before you hot swap anything. And never hot-swap while data is going through cables, like when you're copying files to a Zip disk.

## Buy your peripherals carefully!

Make sure any peripheral device you buy either uses an iMac-compatible USB connection or comes with an iMac-compatible adapter so you can plug it into your computer. Because there are many USB devices made specifically for other kinds of computers, you need to make sure you get the correct kind.

### And use the right drivers!

When you connect a new peripheral to a computer, the computer needs certain information to know how to communicate with the new device. This information comes as a piece of software called a **driver.** When you buy a new peripheral, you will get a disk that contains the driver. It's best to install the driver on your iMac *before* you connect the device, and then restart the computer. To install the driver, read the directions in the manual that comes with your peripheral!

EPSON Stylus(EX)

PSPrinter

*These are examples of icons that represent printer drivers.*

### Driver updates

Hardware vendors that make peripherals often update, or improve, their drivers. Sometimes an updated driver can solve certain problems, such as printing problems. You can always go to the vendor's web site and "download" new drivers (which means to copy the driver software from their web site to your own computer). Replace the existing out-of-date driver with the new one.

## You might need a hub

*Note: Actually, you have another open port on the other side of your keyboard. They say you can plug a printer, scanner, or any other peripheral into that keyboard port, although I've noticed that power-hungry peripherals like printers much prefer being connected directly to the computer or into a hub that has a power supply.*

You've noticed that after you plug in your keyboard, you only have one USB port left. But what if you want to add more peripherals to your iMac? What if you get a printer *and* a scanner, a Zip drive, a floppy disk drive, a CD-ROM writer, another kind of printer, and a drawing tablet? Where will you plug them in? Well, to add more peripherals, you need to buy a **hub.** A hub, as illustrated below, is a little box with a USB connector on one end that plugs into that one extra USB port on the side of your iMac. On the other side of the hub are a number of USB ports that you can connect more devices to. In fact, you can connect hubs to hubs to hubs, so in theory you could have up to 127 different peripheral devices attached to your iMac.

Hubs aren't very expensive. At the moment they cost less than $100. Just make sure if you buy one that it is made to work with your iMac.

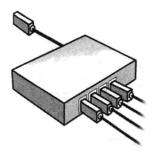

*This is a hub with four USB devices plugged into it. The other end is connected to the iMac USB port.*

*Most hubs also have a power supply, which is good (not shown).*

## Ethernet and Ethernet ports

Ethernet (pronounced *eether net*) is the most common networking system for local area networks, called LANs, which means the computers that are connected together are close enough to be connected with cables (as opposed to a wide area network, a WAN). iMacs have an Ethernet port; it looks like a large phone jack. You can use Ethernet even in your home or small office to connect several computers so you can send files back and forth.

Your printer might have an Ethernet port, in which case you can send data to the printer much faster than through the USB port. If you have a cable connection to the Internet or DSL (digital subscriber line), you'll use the Ethernet port to connect to the special cable or DSL modem, instead of the phone port described below.

### Modem port vs. Ethernet port

You also have a modem port for your internal modem, which looks exactly like a phone jack (because it is), so don't get it confused with the Ethernet port. The Ethernet port is larger than the internal modem port.

*This is what an Ethernet port looks like and the symbol that identifies it.*

*This is the port for an internal modem. Don't get it confused with the larger Ethernet port.*

## Microphone and speaker ports

You'll also see little round ports for a **microphone.** You can attach a microphone for recording new alert sounds, recording sounds for use in iMovie, and even for using with software like ViaVoice Millenium Edition from IBM that lets you talk to your computer instead of having to type.

The port with a **speaker** symbol is for attaching external speakers to your iMac.

On the front of your iMac, right below the screen, are two ports in which you can insert **earphones.** These are great for when your kids want to play a game that has really obnoxious sounds of monsters getting blown up or when you want to listen to opera music extra-loud while you work.

### FireWire ports

*This symbol identifies a FireWire port.*

FireWire is Apple's trademarked version of the standard called IEEE 1394. It's a high-performance "bus" (system of software, hardware, and wires) for connecting up to 63 devices through one port on your Mac. FireWire is only built into the newest iMacs and desktop Macs, like the 1999 blue-and-white G3s and up.

The big deal about FireWire is this: It's extremely fast; you can connect 63 devices in any which way you like, such as in a star or tree pattern, and up to 16 in a single chain; you can swap them in and out without having to turn off the computer; they connect with a simple snap-in cable; and there's no "termination" necessary (which, trust me, is a good thing).

You can (or will be able to) connect a vast array of consumer electronics to FireWire, such as digital cameras, video tapes, and camcorders, as well as DVD (digital video disk) drives, hard disks, optical disks, and printers.

You might hear FireWire ports called IEEE, but IEEE actually stands specifically for the professional society called the Institute of Electrical and Electronics Engineers, and the IEEE is a standard they developed. It has a variety of forms. For instance, the Ethernet standard is IEEE 802.3; the wireless standard is IEEE 802.11; you might hear the FireWire connection on digital cameras called IEEE 1394.

# What's all this Other Stuff on my iMac?

So when you turn on your iMac and open the hard disk window, what do you think of all those folders? All those icons on your Desktop? What are they? Do you need them? It turns out you don't really need a number of these items and others can be neatly stored out of the way. In this chapter I'll explain what all that stuff is, and you can choose what you want to toss.

In this chapter I am assuming you know how to make new folders, move items into folders, take items out of folders, and that you know what an **alias** is. If not, read Chapters 1 and 2 before you begin.

### The Desktop icons in Mac OS 8.x

Below you see the Desktop as it probably appears in any version of Mac OS 8, 8.1, 8.5, or 8.6.

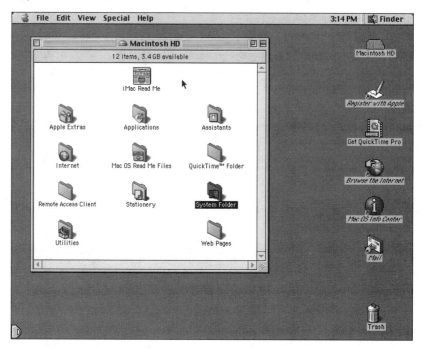

*This is what your Desktop might look like after you clean it up. I moved some folders inside of other ones and deleted a few.*

*If you didn't follow the steps on page 51 to create a Documents folder, you won't see one in your window.*

*Along the bottom are aliases I made of the applications I use often so I don't have to dig through folders to open them.*

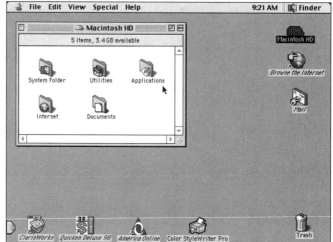

## The Desktop icons in Mac OS 9

Below you see the Desktop as it probably appears in Mac OS 9.

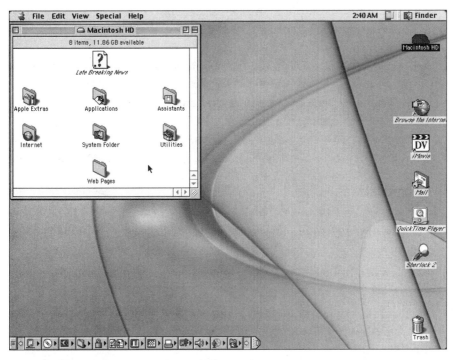

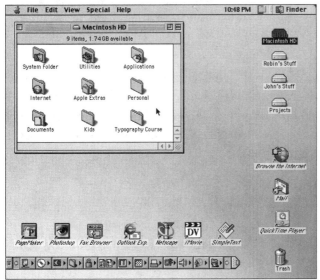

*This is what your Desktop might look like after you clean it up. I moved some folders inside of other ones and deleted a few. This example also shows some new folders I created for organizing my files (like "Kids," "Typography Course," and "Personal").*

*If you didn't follow the steps on page 51 to create a Documents folder, you won't see one in your window.*

*Along the bottom are aliases I made of the applications I use often so I don't have to dig through folders to open them.*

*Notice I have four hard drives! I "partitioned" the large hard drive into four separate ones, as described on pages 295–298.*

iMac Read Me

### iMac Read Me

This is a text file with tidbits of information about your iMac. **Move it to the Mac OS Read Me Files folder.** If you are brand-new to computers, it won't help you much to read it; if you are pretty savvy, read it. You'll find several excellent tips.

Apple Extras

### Apple Extras

This folder stores a lot of the files that you will use a couple of times, then never look at again, such as the tutorial, the Map control panel, registration with Apple, the Mac Info Center, and others. **Put this entire folder into the Utilities folder,** and in a couple of months, after you have surely used these files as much as you ever will, throw away the ones you know you are done with. Don't throw away anything just because you don't know what it is—ask your power user friend first!

Applications

### Applications

This folder stores the applications that came with your iMac, and you should install any new applications you buy into this folder. It's not that there's anything special about the folder; it's just a nice way to keep things organized.

*Some of these items come with one system or the other—you won't have every item in this list.*

| **Definitely Keep** | **Toss if you won't use (you have all this on CD)** |
| --- | --- |
| Adobe Acrobat | Nanosaur (dinosaur shoot-em game) |
| Apple DVD Player | WS Guide to Good Cooking (recipes, food) |
| AppleWorks/ClarisWorks | Quicken Deluxe 98 (personal finance) |
| AppleCD Audio files | FAXstf 5.0 (faxing software) |
| QuickTime | Graphing Calculator |
| SimpleText | iMovie (makes movies from your video camera) |
| Security | Bugdom (cute game) |
| StuffIt Deluxe | Palm Desktop Organizer |

Assistants

### Assistants

The Internet Setup Assistant in this folder is an alias, so if you've already set up your Internet connection, **throw the alias away** (you'll still have the original setup assistant application). You should probably **keep the Mac OS Setup Assistant.** If you have the AirPort Setup Assistant, **keep it. Move the entire Assistants folder into the Utilities folder.**

Browse the Internet

### Browse the Internet

Don't double-click this before you have set up your Internet connection. After it's set up, then anytime you want to go to the World Wide Web, this icon will get you there. It's actually quite handy. I would **keep this and leave it on the Desktop.** Notice it's an alias—you could throw it away and still get to the web.

### iMovie

This is an alias to the application iMovie, which lets you edit your own video movies. If you plan to use iMovie a lot, leave the alias here so you can access the program easily. If you won't be using the application for a while or maybe never, you can throw this alias away—you will still have the iMovie application on your hard disk.

*iMovie*

*You can always make a new alias.*

### Internet

This folder is full of important, good stuff. **Keep everything. Leave the folder right where it is.**

Internet

### Late Breaking News

This alias opens the Mac Help file with links to late-breaking information about Mac OS 9. One link opens a page in the Help file; another link connects to the Internet and takes you to one of Apple's web pages where there is very current information. **Move the alias into the Utilities folder.**

*Late Breaking News*

### Mac OS Info Center

This alias will open your browser and take you to a web site, but the web site pages are on your hard disk so you don't have to connect to the Internet to use the Info Center. You should go there and learn some things; just click around. This icon is an **alias so you could throw it away,** yet still use the Info Center (Mac OS 8.x only, inside the Apple Extras folder).

*Mac OS Info Center*

### Mac OS Read Me Files

This is a whole collection of text files about the Mac and the operating system. You should read them, and you might want to keep them, but I would **move the entire folder into the Utilities folder.**

Mac OS Read Me Files

### Mail

This alias will open the email application that is chosen in the Internet Control Panel (see page 198). It will not connect you to the Internet. If you're already connected and cruising the web, double-click this icon to check your mail while you're online. **If you don't want this alias** on your Desktop, throw it away; then to get to your mail:

*Mail*

In Mac OS 8.x, use the Apple menu: choose "Internet Access," then "Mail."
In Mac OS 9, double-click your email application, or make an alias of that application and put it on the Desktop.

PictureViewer

### Picture Viewer

This alias will open image files of all sorts; just drag a photo or other graphic on top of this alias and the image will usually open right up. (Before the image opens, though, you get an annoying advertisement! Click "Later.") If you don't use this very often, **move the alias into the Utilities folder.**

QuickTime™ Folder

*See page 66 for more information about what is in this folder.*

### QuickTime™ Folder

QuickTime is a thing called an "architecture," meaning it's not really an application that you do anything with—it enables your computer to do special things. QuickTime must be installed in your computer so you can play games, read multimedia files, view certain video clips, etc. **Move the entire folder into the Applications folder.** (If you have another QuickTime folder in your Applications folder, check and see if they both contain the same items and the same versions. If so, you only need one of these folders, the latest one. Toss the other.)

*QuickTime Player*

### QuickTime Player

This alias will open movie files that have been saved in the QuickTime format; you can just drag an icon representing a movie onto this alias and it will open and play. If you don't use this very often, **move the alias into the Utilities folder.**

Get QuickTime Pro

### Get QuickTime Pro

This is an advertisement. If you double-click this, it logs on to your Internet connection (on your dime) and takes you to a web page where you can buy the software. **Throw this away.** If you don't know what QuickTime is, then you definitely do not need to buy the professional version. How rude.

*Register with Apple*

*Register with Apple*

### Register with Apple

Don't double-click this before you have set up your Internet connection. After it's set up, then double-click on this and go through the registration process. **After you have registered, this alias will disappear,** although the original will still be in the Apple Extras folder; you can throw the original away after you register. If you decide to register your iMac by sending in the card through the mail, then you can throw away both this alias and its original right now.

Remote Access Client

### Remote Access Client

This is an important folder because it contains files that connect you to the Internet. But it doesn't have to sit right here in your hard disk window; **move it into the Internet folder.**

### Sherlock 2

This is an alias that opens the application that helps you find files on your computer or stuff on the Internet (see Chapter 19). You can also open Sherlock 2 from the Apple menu, from the File menu (choose "Find…" or "Search Internet…"), or by pressing Command F (to find files on your iMac) or Command H (to find stuff on the Internet). Since there are so many other ways to open Sherlock 2, I chose to delete this alias from my Desktop to avoid the clutter. **Delete it or keep it depending on whether you use it or not.** Remember, deleting an alias does *not* delete the actual application!

*Sherlock 2*

### Stationery

If your Stationery folder contains only two Read Me files like mine does, **throw this whole folder away.** The technology that uses this folder, OpenDoc, has been abandoned.

Stationery

### System Folder

This is the most important folder on your hard disk. Don't go in there. Don't take anything out of it, and don't put anything in it unless you absolutely know it belongs there. **Move this folder to the upper-left of your window.**

System Folder

### Utilities

This folder is like the back closet, the one you store all the odds and ends. Right now it has Disk First Aid, which can solve minor problems on your computer. And it has Drive Setup, which will wipe out your hard disk if you play around with it. Both files are important. Store other utilities in this folder to keep them from cluttering up your hard disk window. **Move this folder to the top row, next to the System Folder.**

Utilities

### Web Pages

This folder contains files for making personal web pages that can be seen on an *intranet* (not the Internet!). If you are in a corporation with a big network that everyone in the corporation uses to communicate with, you are probably on an intranet and you might want to keep this folder. It's also possible to host your own web pages on the Internet if you have a permanent connection such as cable, ISDN, DSL, or similar high-speed line (although there is a security risk). **If you are not on an intranet, or if your modem dials a phone number to get connected to the Internet, you can toss this folder.** If you don't want to toss it yet, at least store it in the Utilities folder.

Web Pages

## What's in the Help menu?

Be sure to poke around in the Help menu, shown below. Just choose items one at a time and see what you get.

**Help Center** brings up the standard Help files.

**Show Balloons** makes little balloons appear that provide (sometimes) useful information about whatever your pointer is pointing at.

*Not all systems have the "Mac Tutorials" option.*

**Mac Tutorials** gives you access to several hands-on tutorials that you should definitely look through (shown below).

**Mac Help** brings up a dialog box where you can search for help on particular topics.

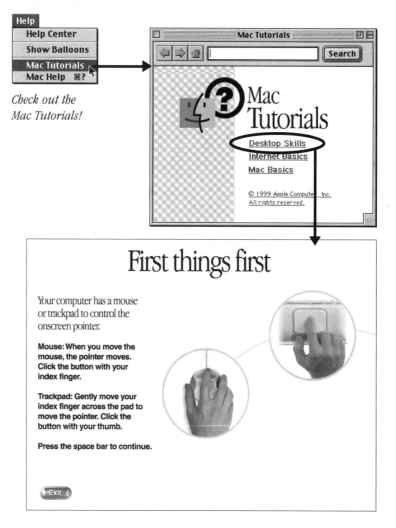

*Check out the Mac Tutorials!*

# Problems and Solutions

This section contains a few questions and answers about the most likely things you might have trouble with. If you're in trouble, also read the booklet that came with your iMac called "Emergency Handbook," which covers more technical stuff than I cover here, or the "iMac Users Guide" that also came with your computer.

**Macintosh is the dominant computer in schools.** Here in New Mexico, the huge Intel facility near Albuquerque gave a very large and very publicized grant to the local school system to buy computers. Intel makes computer chips for PCs. The school system bought Macintoshes. Intel was not happy.

**As of early 2000, there is an installed base of 74,800,000 Macintosh users.** That's hardly a small market. And since Macintosh users are famous for being so devoted to their machines, that's almost 75 million people who have no intention of switching to Windows.

**The overall Apple market share doubled last year.**

**No floppy disks?** NASA purchased over 400 iMacs specifically **because** the iMac does not have a floppy disk drive. Many schools purchase iMacs because they don't have floppy disk drives, which makes it more difficult for people to take software off the machines. Anyway, if you really want a floppy disk drive, you can add one for less than a hundred dollars.

**Difficulty learning your computer?** Half of the families in FamilyPC Magazine's "95 days with Windows 95" gave up. There were "upset over its hardware requirements, frustrated by its slow operation, or just plain fed up with compatibility problems." One of the testers, who dropped out after two months, said, "It has been a time-consuming disaster."

*virus: Software that very mean people write that is **intentionally created to destroy** your work. People who write these are collecting very bad karma. It's interesting that so many more PC users write these than Macintosh users (although it is simply easier to infect a PC than it is a Mac).*

**The PC has over 8,000 viruses that can destroy important data on the machines. The Macintosh has only 47 known viruses.** In over 15 years of working on Macs daily and working with thousands of other Mac users, I have run across 3 of those viruses, and all were fairly benign.

**Microsoft recently dared hackers** to break into their server running the latest edition of Windows 2000 and its corporate security measures. Within an hour a number of hackers had broken in, and the server crashed by itself.

**The United States Army** abandoned Windows NT servers in favor of the Mac OS after a well-publicized break into their web site. The Army's web site administrator stated, "The Mac OS is more secure than its counterparts."

# Do You Have a Problem?

Here are solutions to some of the most common problems you might have on your computer.

## Some problems and some solutions

### Everything I type is underlined! (or bold, italic, etc.)

First of all, select the text that is currently underlined (or bold, italic, etc.) by pressing-and-dragging over the text so it's highlighted. Then go to the menu where you change type styles and choose the one called "Plain Text," or maybe it's called "Normal" or "Regular." (In AppleWorks, go to the Style menu and choose "Plain Text.")

That will remove the formatting you didn't want from the *existing* text, but you might still find that you *continue* to type with that formatting. You see, in every program on the Mac, the insertion point *picks up the formatting of the character to its left* (unless you apply new formatting to the insertion point). So it's easy to fix: click your insertion point directly after the last letter you typed *that does not have* the unwanted formatting. Backspace (delete) one more character to the left, which means you'll delete one good character. Now continue to type. The unwanted formatting should be gone.

### I changed the font from the menu, but my text doesn't change.

You probably did not select the text before you went to the menu to change the font or the style. Remember, always select first, then do it to it.

### Help! Everything I click on in the spreadsheet ends up in the entry bar!!

Don't you hate that? It's because there is a formula in that cell, indicated by the = sign. If you don't want to eliminate the entire formula, backspace in the entry bar until you get rid of all the superfluous junk, *then hit the Enter key*.

To get rid of the whole thing and start over, select all the text in the entry bar, then click that X in the entry bar, to the left of the formula. Or select it all and hit Delete, *and then hit the Enter key!* Even if you delete the = sign, if you don't hit the Enter key the cell still wants to have a formula and will pick up everything else you click on. Hitting the Enter key is the trick.

### I saved a file and now I can't find it! Is it gone forever?

If you really did save it, then it's not gone. Files do not disappear all by themselves—someone has to throw it in the trash can and empty the trash. (I hope your file wasn't inside a folder that you threw away!) Go to Chapter 19 and read about how to use Sherlock 2. It will find your file for you.

### I opened a document that I created yesterday, but it doesn't have my changes. I know I saved them!

This happens all the time until you start becoming totally conscious of *where* you are saving the file. What happened is you saved the document, you worked on it some more, you saved it again, and perhaps you saved it again. At some point, probably after you added graphics or went to look for something else, you accidentally saved the newer copies *into a different folder*. That means you had the old version in one folder, and the newer version in another. Then you quit. When you came back the next day, you opened the older version since it is in the folder where it's supposed to be.

So, to find the newer one, use Sherlock 2 (see Chapter 19). Or if you did put graphics on the page, check the folder where the graphics are stored.

### I was working along in my word processor, and I lost my entire page!

Don't scream. First check the position of the scroll bars, both vertical and horizontal. If the little scroll boxes are anywhere except at the very top of the vertical bar, or at the very left of the bottom horizontal bar, then drag the boxes to the top or to the left.

If you did that and there is really nothing on your page, close the document and when it asks if you want to save the changes, click "No." Open the document again, and everything that was there *the last time you saved* will still be there. Now, of course this means you will only get your document back **if** you saved it recently. If you never saved it at all and you open the document and nothing is there, too bad for you. *SOS: Save often, sweetheart!* It's so sad that we only learn this lesson after we experience a catastrophe. I'm sorry.

**Everything on my page keeps typing centered.**

You have to understand two things so you can control stuff like this:

1) Every *paragraph* can have its own alignment (aligned left, right, centered, or justified) and *you make a new paragraph every time you press the Return key.*

2) The insertion point picks up the formatting (including the alignment) of the character to its left.

So if you centered your headline, then hit a Return, you created a new paragraph and that paragraph is picking up the centered formatting. Since every paragraph can have its own alignment, change the alignment from centered to flush left *while the insertion point is on the next line, not on the same line as the headline!*

If text continues to center itself, select everything, including blank spaces, all the way down the page (except the lines you want to keep centered), then click the flush-left alignment button.

**Everytime I print my one-page document, I get an extra page.**

Click at the end of the very last character on your page. Hold the mouse button down, and drag downward. This will select all the blank space. Hit Delete. That blank space usually gets there by hitting extra Returns. (*You* think that space is empty, but the computer and the printer see Return characters and they think you want to print them; the computer doesn't know that blank space is invisible.)

**When I print a web page from Netscape, it's very tiny.**

In Netscape, go to the File menu and choose "Page Setup." Uncheck the box that says, "Fit in page." Try printing again.

**In Netscape, I can't change some of the defaults, like the home page.**

In the Netscape Preferences (from the Edit menu), find "Identity" in the left panel, which is under the heading "Mail & Newsgroups." Uncheck the box that says, "Use Internet config." Now you can make changes.

**The power flickered while I was working, the computer went down, and now my document is missing the last two hours of work I did on it!**

Yeah, well, that's what happens if you don't save your documents regularly. I'm sorry, but if you did not save and the power went out, that file is really irretrievably gone. Wailing doesn't help. It seems no matter how many times people tell us to save often (save every two or three minutes), we don't do it until we suffer a catastrophe. Also see the tips on the opposite page.

*Remember, all it takes to save is to hold down the Command key (the one with the apple on it), and tap the letter S.*

### All of the icons on my Desktop turned into big ol' dorky buttons and they won't change back, even when I use the View menu.

When you choose a view from the View menu, it applies to the *selected* window, which is the *active* window, the one on top, the one that has the lines in its title bar. If *no* window is selected, then the View applies to the Desktop. The reason it seems difficult to switch the Desktop icons to another view is because it's not really clear at first how to select the Desktop.

So do this: Click **once** on the icon of your hard disk. That will select the Desktop. *Now* go to the View menu and change it back to "by Icon."

### My iMac won't open my application; it tells me there isn't enough memory, but I have a 4 gigabyte hard disk!

*Application menu*

*All the applications listed in this Application menu are currently open. The checkmark is next to the one that is currently "active," or open, in front of you.*

The hard disk has nothing to do with the memory (read pages 240–241 about hard disk and memory). You probably opened several applications already, and then you *closed the documents* but you didn't *quit the applications.* So all of those applications are still hogging the memory.

You need to go to the **Application menu,** which is the little icon on the far right of the menu bar. Press on it and you will see a list of all the applications that are currently open (and using memory), as shown to the right. If you see anything listed besides "Finder," that item is using the memory.

To take it out of memory, you must **quit** the application. Choose an item from the Application menu (anything except Finder). *Now even if you don't see anything different,* go to the File menu and choose "Quit." If there was anything else in the Application menu, go back to that menu, choose another item, and quit that one. Keep doing that until there is nothing left in the Application menu except Finder. Now you can open anything else.

### I double-click on my application icon or I choose my application name from the Application menu, but nothing happens!

I know it *seems* like nothing happened, but something really did. Look at the menu bar, on the far right. The active application's name and icon will be there. Read the page about the Application menu, page 242.

### I can't get an email form on a web site.

You're probably using Netscape Navigator, which is a stripped-down version of Netscape's more powerful browser called Communicator. The stripped-down version does not open email forms, so you need to have a separate email application for it to use. On your iMac you have Microsoft Outlook Express, so go to the Internet Control Panel, click the "E-mail" tab, and at the bottom of that window, choose your "Default E-mail Application." You have to restart your browser for this to take effect.

**I'm stuck in a game or a Setup Assistant and can't get out!**

Hold down the Command key (the one with the apple on it) and tap the letter Q. That's the Quit shortcut and it works everywhere.

**I opened a Control Panel (or something like), and now I want to close it but there's no close box or OK button or anything.**

Hold down the Command key and tap the letter Q. That's the Quit shortcut and it works everywhere.

**I want to be a registered owner of my AppleWorks/ClarisWorks program, but I didn't get a registration card.**

When you register your iMac, it will automatically register the software.

**I was going through the web tutorial in this book, but had to leave the computer. When I came back, I was disconnected.**

If your browser is still open, go to the Apple menu and choose "Remote Access Status." Click the "Connect" button that appears.

If you quit your browser, double-click on the "Browse the Internet" icon again to start over. If you don't have that icon anymore, go to the Apple menu and choose "Remote Access Status." Click the "Connect" button that appears. Then reopen your browser.

**The Williams-Sonoma cooking guide doesn't work or is having problems.**

You must turn File Sharing off. The cooking guide hates file sharing. Go to the Apple menu, to Automated Tasks, and choose "Stop File Sharing." Or use the File Sharing control panel, or the File Sharing button in the Control Strip (). You might have to reinstall the guide if it still doesn't work right.

**That lady who reads every message out loud is making me crazy! How can I get rid of her?**

From the Apple menu, slide down to Control Panels, and choose "Speech." Press on the little menu for "Options" and choose "Talking Alerts." Uncheck both boxes. Close the Control Panel. She's silenced.

**My CD won't come out.**

Drag the icon of the CD to the trash can; that makes the tray pop open or the disk pop out. If you get a message that the CD cannot be ejected because something is still in use, perhaps you read a ReadMe file and SimpleText is still open: Check the Application menu and make sure no applications are still open (see page 242), then drag the CD to the trash again.

If that didn't work: **iMacs with CD trays:** Restart the computer and immediately push the CD tray button. If it's really stuck, straighten a paper clip and gently push it in that tiny hole on the tray door. **iMacs without CD trays:** Restart the computer and hold the mouse button down. The CD should pop out.

### I type in a web address and hit Return, but I get a page telling me it found 3,000 sites for that address.

You are entering the web address in the wrong place—you're entering it into the search field on a search engine page.

*The web address goes in here.*

*Not here.*

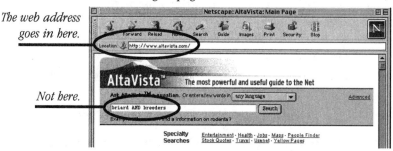

### I double-clicked several of those icons on the Desktop, but all they do is ask me if my computer is set up for Internet access.

Those icons are meant to get you to the Internet to do things like browse the web or get your email (see Chapter 22 for explanations of each icon). Once you have established an Internet connection, those icons will do what they are supposed to do without bugging you. If you're not going to get yourself connected, you can throw away most of those icons you see on the right side of your Desktop (again, see Chapter 22).

### My application quits regularly because it says I don't have enough memory, but it is the only thing I have open.

Every application has its own "allocation" of memory, which is a certain portion of the computer's RAM (random access memory) it takes for itself. You can increase or decrease this allocation. If you use large files, like huge spreadsheets, you might want to increase the allocation. (If you want to use Netscape at the same time as AOL, you might want to decrease the allocation, depending on how much memory (RAM) you have to spread around.)

To allocate more or less memory, the application must not be open. You must find the *original* of the application; you can't do this on an alias or on a document. (If you have an alias, select the alias and press Command R to find and select the original.)

1. Once you've found the original, click once on it to select it.
2. Press Command I to get the Get Info box (shown to the left).
3. In the "Show" menu, choose "Memory." (If you don't have that option, you did not actually select the original *application icon;* perhaps you selected a *document icon?*)
4. In the "Preferred Size" box, enter the amount you want to allocate, generally at least 20 percent more than what is already there. Do not enter less than the suggested size or minimum size. Close the Get Info box.

## America Online

America Online is a great tool. If you're not already a member, you'll find the software inside the Internet folder. Open the America Online folder, double-click the icon (shown to the right) and follow the directions.

America Online

To browse the web through AOL, there are a couple of small adjustments you should make. After you are a member, open AOL; you don't have to sign on yet to make these changes (you can if you want to).

### Change the graphics default so all the graphics don't look so ugly

1. Click on the item in the toolbar called "My AOL," which gives you a menu, shown to the left. Choose "Preferences" (**A**).

2. In the Preferences dialog box, click on the little icon on the left called "WWW" (**B**).

3. Uncheck the box for "Use compressed images" (**C**).

4. Click the button "Advanced Settings…" (**D**) and change the font default for web pages (see the next task, below).

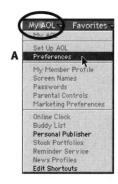

### Change the default font for web pages

5. Follow the steps above to get to the "Advanced Settings" dialog box.

6. On the left, click on "Language/Fonts" (**E**).

7. In the "Fonts" section (**F**), choose New York for the "Proportional font." If Monaco is not already selected for the "Fixed-width font," choose it now.

8. Click OK. If you want to make your toolbar smaller, go to the next task, below. If you like the big buttons across the top, then skip the rest and click the OK button to close the Preferences now.

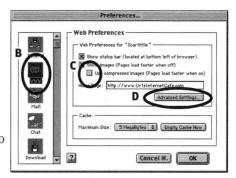

### Make the AOL toolbar smaller so you have more room for the browser window

9. In the Preferences dialog box, scroll down to the Toolbar icon.

10. Click the button, "Text Only." Click OK to close the Preferences dialog box.

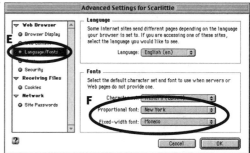

## If you have both an ISP connection and AOL . . .

You might have problems switching from one to the other because of something called the AOL Link. But you can sign on to America Online through your ISP connection. This means you are paying for your ISP time plus your AOL time, but AOL gives you a cheaper rate if you use an ISP. It saves so much hassle, and often your ISP connection is more stable anyway (you'll crash less) than the AOL connection. Make sure you have an ISP connection established and have set up your iMac with it before you follow these steps.

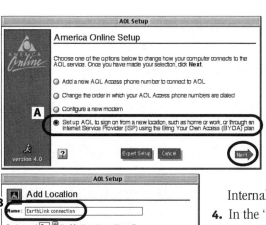

1. Open AOL, but don't sign on. At the Welcome screen, click the "Setup" button.

2. In the AOL Setup dialog box that appears, click the button for signing on with an ISP, what AOL calls their "Bring Your Own Access" plan (**A**). Click the "Next" arrow.

3. In the "Add Location" section, type the name of your ISP (**B**) so you will know which location to choose when signing on. Make sure the iMac Internal 56K modem is selected (**C**). Click the "Next" arrow.

4. In the "Add Connections" section, click the button to "Add a TCP connection" (**D**). Click "Next."

5. You will see your Welcome screen again, and in the "Select Location" menu is your new option (**E**).

6. Sign on with your new location, and change your billing plan:
   - From the Help menu, choose "Accounts and Billing."
   - Select "Change Your Billing Method or Price Plan."
   - Click "Update Pricing Plan."
   - Choose "$9.95/BYOA." Click "Display Plan" to see if that's what you want. If so, just continue following the directions.

**Important Note!** If you use your ISP connection to log on to AOL, then when you quit AOL, your connection is still open—it does not disconnect automatically. Use "Remote Access Status" from the Apple menu to disconnect.

## Browsing the web in AOL

AOL has its own browser, which is a version of Microsoft Internet Explorer. If you've used other browsers before, the AOL arrangement might be a little confusing at first but it will only take a minute to get used to it. Below are the key features that correspond to other browsers.

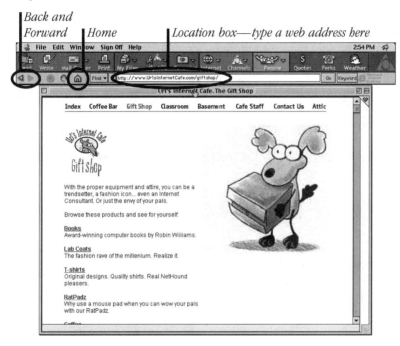

*If you haven't been to the web on AOL before, either click the "Go to the Web" button on the first screen that shows up, or use the Internet menu in the toolbar and choose "Go to the Web." Or just type a web address in the Location box (circled, above left).*

### Browse with Netscape in AOL

If your only connection to the Internet is with AOL (you don't use an ISP), you might think you're stuck with AOL's browser. You're not. If you prefer Netscape, you can use Netscape, if you have enough memory in your iMac. If all you have is the original 32 megabytes on an older iMac, then you won't be able to use the two applications together (unless you allocate less memory to Netscape, which is very easy to do; see page 288). Either way, just do this:

*memory: See page 240 if you're not even sure what memory is, and see page 241 if you're not sure how much memory you have.*

1. Make an alias of Netscape (see page 237 if you don't know what an alias is or how to make one) and put it on your Desktop, down near the trash can.

2. Sign on to AOL.

3. While you're connected to AOL, double-click the Netscape icon on your Desktop. AOL will drop into the background and you can browse the web on Netscape, using your AOL account. When you're ready to quit, get AOL from the Application menu (page 242) and quit.

## The most important prevention and solution tips

You will find yourself doing one or all of these three techniques regularly.

### 1. Restart

If you run into trouble like a frozen screen or even a bomb icon, you will usually have to restart. The process is different on older iMacs than it is on newer iMacs. How do you know if your iMac is "older"? Just try the keyboard shortcut and see.

### Try the restart keyboard shortcut

- Hold down the Control and Command keys and hit the Power key at the top of the keyboard. But this doesn't work on all iMacs.

### If the keyboard shortcut doesn't work

#### Newer iMacs, including DV models

- Go to the side panel and find the tiny little button with a triangle on it, as illustrated below. Push it once.

   (Do not push the other button—it's a programmer's button. If you accidentally push it and get a blank box, push the restart button.)

*This is the Restart button on* **newer iMacs.**

### Older iMacs

- To restart after a crash, get a paperclip. Unbend it. Go to the right side of your iMac and open that little door. See the tiny hole with the triangle label above it? Poke that paperclip into that round hole, push gently, and the Mac will restart.

   (Do not push the paperclip into the other hole—it's a programmer's reset button. If you accidentally push it and get a blank box, do the restart again.)

*This is the Restart paperclip hole on* **older iMacs.**

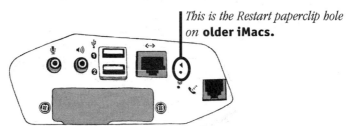

### 2. Rebuild the Desktop

Whenever things are acting a little screwy, rebuild your Desktop. It solves an amazing variety of unexplained problems. Whether things are acting screwy or not, you should rebuild at least once a week. The technique below restarts with the extensions off (as described in #3, below), and rebuilds the Desktop. This is how to do it (read all the directions first, then try it):

a. If your computer is **on,** quit all the applications.
From the Special menu, choose Restart.

If your computer is **off,** turn it on.

b. Instantly hold down the Shift, Option, and Command keys. Keep holding them down. You will get a message telling you extensions are off. When you see that, you can let go of the Shift key (but you don't have to). Keep the Option and Command keys down until you get a message telling you that your Desktop is going to be rebuilt, and is that okay with you? Click the OK button.

c. After it boots all the way up, **restart again** without holding any keys down to load your extensions.

### 3. Restart with extensions off

If you're not quite sure what extensions are or how to use the Extensions Manager, see the following page. Don't be turning things on and off indiscriminately, though, because you can cause yourself a lot of grief! Ask your power user friend.

If you need to restart with extensions off for some reason, like you are trying to find out which extension might be causing you problems, or perhaps you need to install some software and it told you to restart with extensions off, just hold down the Shift key and choose Restart from the Special menu; keep the Shift key held down. After you see a message telling you extensions are off, you can let go of the Shift key.

If you know which extension(s) you want to turn off or on, hold down the Spacebar instead of the Shift key as you restart. Keep the Spacebar down and the Extensions Manager will appear; you can turn items on or off, then continue booting up. (The Spacebar trick doesn't work on all iMacs.)

*power user:* Someone who knows more than you about the Mac.

## Turn off a conflicting extension

Extensions are small pieces of software that your operating system uses. Many programs, when you install them, add more extensions. These extensions can conflict with each other. If someone tells you to "turn off an extension" or "turn off a control panel," follow the directions below to do it.

**If you experience trouble with your brand-new iMac while trying to register your fax software or while trying to connect to the Internet through Apple's setup program,** you probably need to turn off the "Serial Port Monitor," as specifically shown below.

### Turn off an extension or control panel (or turn one on)

1. From the Apple menu, slide down to "Control Panels," then out to the side and choose "Extensions Manager." You'll get the large window shown below.

2. In the long list of control panels, extensions, shutdown items, startup items, and System Folder items, find the name of the item you want to turn off. If you are looking for the "Serial Port Monitor," go all the way to the bottom of the list, under "Startup Items" (shown below, circled.)

*Click the tiny arrow to hide or display the contents under each heading.*

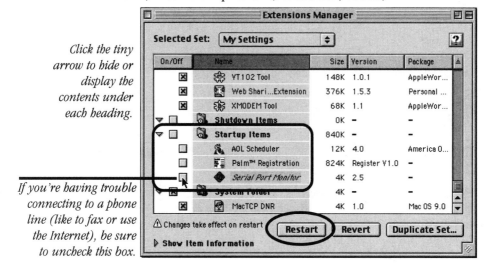

*If you're having trouble connecting to a phone line (like to fax or use the Internet), be sure to uncheck this box.*

3. An "x" in the box indicates that item is loaded into the system and running. Click in the box to remove the "x" (turn that item off); click again to put the "x" back in the box (turn it on).

4. You have to restart for any changes to take effect. Click the "Restart" button (circled, above). If you had documents open on your screen that were unsaved, you will be asked if you want to save them before the iMac restarts.

## Reformat your entire hard disk

Sometimes things get so screwy on your computer that, as a last resort, you need to totally reformat the hard disk. For instance, on my new iMac DV, all sorts of little things were going wrong—I couldn't receive faxes, eventually I couldn't even send faxes, my Zip drive wouldn't always work, sometimes I couldn't shut down, etc. So I backed up everything I had installed (as explained below) and reformatted the entire hard disk, taking it down to "zeros" (flatline). Now everything works beautifully, as it should. Before you attempt reformatting your hard disk, read all the way through this page and the next.

*If things are screwy even after you totally reformat, have your memory chips checked. Bad memory can make all sorts of weird things happen.*

### Think about partitioning the drive

If you have a large hard disk, like over 4 gigabytes, you should think about partitioning it (separating it) into several smaller volumes (individual hard disks). This makes it easier for your computer to find what it needs, it helps prevent files from becoming too fragmented, and can help your computer work faster. If you ever need to recover the data from a bad disk, it can be much less expensive to recover an individual partition than to recover the entire hard disk. Also, partitions can separate your work from someone else's who uses the computer—you can each have your own hard disk space. Or perhaps you need to install a different operating system such as Virtual PC so you can run Windows applications on your iMac—make a partition specifically for Windows stuff.

### Back up everything you installed or created!!!

**Very important:** Reformatting your hard disk in this manner (down to zeros) will absolutely positively destroy every single thing on your entire hard disk and it will be impossible to recover any of it!!! If you have installed any new software or fonts at all or if you have created any new documents, you must back them up (make copies of) onto something like Zip or Jaz disks before you reformat. If you don't know how to do that, have your power user friend help you. Do not proceed without first backing everything up. **Except:** All of the software that came on your iMac will be restored at the end of this process, so don't worry about FAXstf, Palm Organizer, AppleWorks, etc. But even though the software applications themselves will be restored, any address lists you created in your fax or email programs, bookmarks in your browser, dates made in your organizer, etc., *will be gone.* If you're not perfectly clear on how to back up your necessary files, please have a friend over who knows what they are doing to help you!

If you've only had your computer a couple of days and haven't created anything of your own, go ahead and do this process.

### So back everything up before you begin

I cannot be held responsible for any files you lose if you insist on not backing up everything you need! Proceed at your own risk.

You cannot reformat the drive that is running the computer, so you have to put in a CD and let the system on the CD run the computer. So what you are about to do is this: You're going to insert a CD and boot (start up) from that CD, reformat the drive down to zeros (destroying every tiny iota of data on the entire hard disk), then reinstall everything like it was when it came from the factory, but it will work even better. (Don't ask me why. It just does.)

*The CD called "Software Install" is for reinstalling software programs individually.* **It is your backup CD for most of your applications.**

iMac Restore CD

*The CD icon is probably gray because its window is open.*

1. You'll find a CD in your packet called "Software Restore." Insert it into your iMac.

2. After you see the CD mount (its icon appears on your Desktop and its window opens), you need to restart and you need to hold the C key down. This will force the iMac to boot from the CD, which is what you want. So go to the Special menu, choose "Restart," and then immediately hold the letter C on the keyboard down and keep it down until the iMac boots.

3. After it starts back up, you'll notice that the CD icon is now the one in the top-right corner of your Desktop. The "volume" or disk that is running the computer is always the one in the top position on the right. You'll also see your Macintosh HD icon, *below* the CD icon. And the background probably looks different. That's good; that's what you want.

4. In the CD's open window (shown below), double-click the folder "Utilities."

5. In the "Utilities" window, double-click the icon named "Drive Setup."

*Open this folder. Inside that folder, open the "Drive Setup" application.*

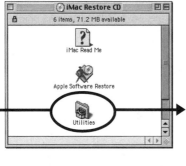

*Double-click the Drive Setup icon to open the application.*

6. In the "Drive Setup" window, click the name of your hard disk.

7. With "Drive Setup" open, you have new menu items, just like in any application. From the Functions menu, choose "Initialization Options."

8. Check the box "Zero all data." Click OK. (You could always choose to do a "low level format," but it doesn't clear up as many problems.)

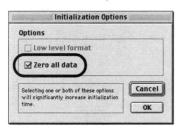

9. Back in the "Drive Setup" window, click "Initialize…." You'll get the dialog box shown below.

*I hoped you backed up everything you need!*

*Remember, the ellipsis (three dots) indicates you will get a dialog box. Do you see the difference between the "Initialize" buttons in the "Drive Setup" window and the "Initialize" window? Which one will actually start the initialization process?*

10. Click "Custom Setup…." You'll get the dialog box shown below. You need to:

   a. Choose how many partitions you want to divide your large hard disk into, if at all. See the information about partitions on page 295. If you plan to do digital video, you should make one partition with at least 5 or 6 gigabytes. You can rename these partitions later, as you'll see on the following page.

   b. Choose "Mac OS Extended" as the "Type." Apple recommends you choose this "Extended" format for large drives. It makes smaller little cubbyholes on the disk, called "sectors," in which the computer stores data.

   c. Resize your partitions (volumes) by dragging the dividers between them.

   d. Click OK.

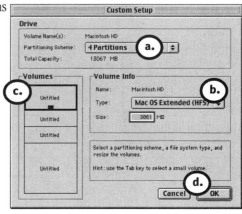

—continued

**11.** Now you're back at the "Initialize" dialog box. This is your last chance to back out. If you really want to destroy every single piece of data on your iMac and start all over again with a perfectly clean slate, click "Initialize." You'll get a little dialog box that tells you how far along the process is. This can take an hour or two, so go take a break.

**12.** When that initializing process is complete, you must restore all the software, including the operating system. The CD window is probably still open (if not, open it). This time, double-click on the icon labeled "Apple Software Restore."

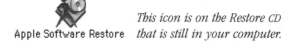

*This icon is on the Restore CD*
*that is still in your computer.*

**13.** In the "Apple Software Restore" dialog box, do this:
   **a.** Click the "Erase" button (there's nothing to erase anymore!).
   **b.** Choose the disk (also called "volume" or "partition") on which to restore/install the software. This will be your *boot disk,* the one that will contain the operating system and run the computer.
   **c.** Click the "Restore" button.

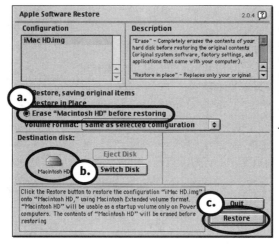

*It is possible to use this application to "restore" your original software without reformatting your disk first. Keep that in mind for future need.*

*Tip: If for some reason your CD insists on starting up your iMac after you reboot (restart), restart again and hold the mouse button down; keep holding it down and your CD should eventually pop out and your iMac will boot from your hard disk.*

**14.** After the process is complete, restart your computer. If necessary, reinstall any other software you had added, and replace any of your files you had created.

# The Stuff at the End

# Index!

graphic links, 203
home page, 182
how to make one, 215
links, 184, 201
 colors of, 228
 email link, 227
 local links, 226
 remote links, 227
navigation bar, 184,
 202, 203
Netscape prints tiny
 pages, 285
pages are in windows,
 201
table of contents to, 182
titles of web pages, 221
underlined text on
 pages, 184
URLs, 184
where to type it, 184
**WebTV box, 173**
**wide area network, 271**
**Williams, Cliff, 103**
**Williams, Jeffrey, 103**
**Williams, Kelly, 250**
**Williams, Patricia, 103**
**Williams, Reilly, 206**
**Williams, Ryan, 250**
**Williams, Shannon, 103**
**Williams-Sonoma Guide**
 **to Good Cooking**
 how to use it, 69
 if you have errors, 287
 must turn off File
  Sharing, 287
**windows**
 active, 44
 Button view, 32
 clues in, 27
 expand folders in;
  use triangles, 30
 from folders, 42
 gray, 44
 how many items in, 27
 how to use them, 24
 List view, 30
  expand folders in;
   use triangles, 30
  triangle in column
   headings, 30
 move multiple items, 49

move them, 25
parts of, 24
put something inside, 47
quiz on, 27
rearrange the columns, 31
remove items from, 48,
 49
resize columns, 31
resize windows, 25
select multiple items in,
 49
sort button, 31, 93
switch order of listed
 items, 31
top level window, 44
triangle in column
 headings, 30
**Windows applications**
 **on your iMac, 295**
**word processor**
 what is it? 62
 clear vs. delete, 86
 closing documents, 91
 color text, 83
 create another docu-
  ment, 91
 cut, copy, paste, 85
 formatting text, 81, 83
  example of, 84
 help! formatting won't
  come off, 283
 more than one document
  open, 91
 open a new document, 77
 page disappeared! 284
 professional guidelines
  for text, 94
 ruler in, 81
 undo, 86
**World Book Encyclopedia,**
 **73**
**World Wide Web**
 what is it? 182
 browser to see pages, 183
 examples of web pages,
  184
 web address, where to
  type it, 184
**wrap, word wrap, 79**
**WS Guide icon, 69**

**Yahoo**
 @ symbol in, 205
 drill down, 205
 how to use it, 205
 web address for, 208
 word search, 206, 207

**Zip disks**
 as backups, 234
 drive for, 235
 external storage, 234
 icon for, 235
**zoom box**
 illustration of, 24
 resize window with, 25

## Robin Williams

I live on several acres just south of Santa Fe, New Mexico, where I can see every sunrise and sunset, every moonrise and moonset. I have three kids, several dogs, and lots of books.

## Other books by Robin

*The Little Mac Book*

*The Little iBook Book*
   (and John Tollett)

*The Mac is not a typewriter*

*The Non-Designer's Design Book*

*The Non-Designer's Type Book*

*The Non-Designer's Web Book*
   (and John Tollett)

*The Non-Designer's Scan and Print Book*
   (and Sandee Cohen)

*Windows for Mac Users*
   (and Cynthia Baron)

*A Blip in the continuum*
   (and John Tollett)

*How to Boss Your Fonts Around*

   and several other books

## Colophon

I created this book on an iMac DV using Adobe PageMaker 6.5, which I love, and Extensis PageTools, which makes my life so much easier. The fonts used are the Tree family from [T-26], Garamond Condensed from Adobe Systems, and ITC Officina Sans from ITC.